RUNNER'S WORLD®

RUN LESS RUN FASTER

RUNNER'S WORLD®

RUN LESS RUN FASTER

BECOME A FASTER, STRONGER RUNNER WITH THE REVOLUTIONARY **FIRST** TRAINING PROGRAM

BILL PIERCE, SCOTT MURR, AND RAY MOSS

Notice

This book is intended as a reference volume only, not as a medical manual. The information given here is designed to help you make informed decisions about your health, diet, fitness, and exercise program. It is not intended as a substitute for professional fitness and medical advice. If you suspect that you have a medical problem, we urge you to seek competent medical help. As with all exercise programs, you should seek your doctor's approval before you begin.

Mention of specific companies, organizations, or authorities in this book does not imply endorsement by the publisher, nor does mention of specific companies, organizations, or authorities imply that they endorse this book.

Internet addresses and telephone numbers given in this book were accurate at the time it went to press.

Rodale books may be purchased for business or promotional use or for special sales. For information, please write to: Special Markets Department, Rodale Inc., 733 Third Avenue, New York, NY 10017.

Printed in the United States of America
Rodale Inc. makes every effort to use acid-free ♾, recycled paper ♻.

TABLES 2.2, 2.3, 2.4, and 2.5, on pages 30–37, were compiled by Alan Jones, 3717 Wildwood Drive, Endwell, NY 13760; AlanLJones@stny.rr.com; http://home.stny.rr.com/alanjones/AgeGrade.html. Done in conjunction with Rex Harvey, World Masters Athletics, June 24, 2004. Used by permission.

ILLUSTRATIONS BY KATIE BLAKER
BOOK DESIGN BY SUSAN EUGSTER

Library of Congress Cataloging-in-Publication Data
Pierce, William James, date
Runner's world, run less, run faster : become a faster, stronger runner with the revolutionary first training program / Bill Pierce, Scott Murr, and Ray Moss.
p. cm.
Includes index.
ISBN-13 978–1–59486–649–4 paperback
ISBN-10 1–59486–649–X paperback
1. Running—Training. 2. Running—Physiological aspects. I. Murr, Scott, date II. Moss, Ray, date III. Title.
GV1061.5.P54 2007
796.42—dc22 2007008696

Distributed to the trade by Holtzbrinck Publishers

8 10 9 paperback

We inspire and enable people to improve their lives and the world around them

For more of our products visit **rodalestore.com** or call 800-848-4735

Contents

Foreword

Given the time-stressed lives that we lead, all runners have the same goal: to run the best we can with the limited amount of time at our disposal. After work, family, daily errands, and keeping up with piles of laundry, how ya gonna fit in enough good workouts to reach your goals? It's the biggest running challenge we face. And Bill Pierce, Scott Murr, and Ray Moss have the answer with their training program. I know no other running book that comes close to providing the proven, efficient training system you'll discover within these pages.

But I don't want you to think that their training program is easy. It's not. I learned this the hard way a couple of Aprils ago, when I visited Bill and his colleagues at Furman University in Greenville, South Carolina, and spent several days training with them. In particular, I ran with Bill and his brother Don. Both are about the same age as I and have the same ability level, which we learned over a low-fat Italian dinner on my first night in town. The next day, we ran one of Bill's favorite interval workouts, 5 × 1000 meters on a gorgeous curving path along a tree-lined lake on the Furman campus. We warmed up with a relaxed mile or two, and then began the 1000-meter repeats. I felt that I was in good shape at the time, but it took all my resolve to match strides with Bill. While I wouldn't say I was running 100 percent as hard as I could, I certainly wasn't lollygagging. Call it a 98 percent effort. I was pooped.

Fortunately, the training method conceived by the team of professors and coaches at the Furman Institute of Running and Scientific Training (FIRST) provides plenty of recovery between hard efforts. I was happy to take the next day off and simply stroll around campus for 30 minutes. Bill played tennis.

That brought us to Day 3, a tempo training day. After another several-mile warmup, Bill and Scott took off on a steady 4-mile run that was supposed to be hard but controlled. For them, I think it was. For me, however, it was too much. I lagged about 30 seconds behind Bill, wondering how he could run hard again just 48 hours after our 1000-meter repeats. The obvious answer: He's been training this way for nearly 20 years. His body has adapted to the FIRST program and gotten stronger and faster with it. I hadn't been following the FIRST program—though it didn't take me long to decide that I should. Who doesn't want the most fuel-efficient car or the lowest-interest mortgage or the runners' training program that provides the best results in the least amount of time?

The thing I most appreciate about the FIRST approach is that it's scientifically based and meticulously measured. Many coaches and personal trainers develop their plans according to their "proven successes." Unfortunately, they have no scientific or statistical analysis to back up their claims. They might be good enough coaches, but they've never actually studied how well their plans work.

Bill, Ray, and Scott have—extensively.

The FIRST team, being college professors before they became coaches, have always approached the FIRST system as a scientific experiment. They've measured all their runners before and after beginning the training program, and the results could very well have proven the system an absolute bust. But that's not what happened. Instead, the experiments have produced consistently spectacular outcomes. The runners train less than they used to, and 16 weeks later, they're running faster.

It sounds like snake oil, but it's not. Just ask Bill for a peek into his bulging folder of thank-you letters and e-mails. A runner's success can never be guaranteed. Life happens to us all—we have to change jobs, we get injured, we're waylaid by a family health crisis . . . the list goes on and on. But the FIRST program is more closely studied and more guaranteed than any other running program I have ever seen. What's more, you'll spend less time training than you are right now. You have nothing to lose. It's a win-win program that has worked for hundreds of other runners, and there's no reason it can't work for you.

Amby Burfoot
EXECUTIVE EDITOR,
RUNNER'S WORLD MAGAZINE

Preface

For many years, Scott Murr—my running partner—and I had the same pretraining routine. We would meet in the locker room, lace up our running shoes, and then bemoan the training run that awaited us just beyond the gymnasium doors. It's not that we were lazy or disliked running—just the opposite. In fact, that was the problem. We enjoyed running so much that every training run became a training *race*. We ran 6 days a week, and every day, our "training" run resulted in a competition. No matter how much we both insisted that "Today, we'll take it easy," at some point, one of us would push the pace and then the race would be on! No rest days. No speed days. Nothing but race days. I'm sure that many training partners could offer the same testimony.

Scott and I began running together when he was a senior at Furman University in Greenville, South Carolina, and I was a first-year professor there. Over the next 20 years, we spent countless hours running, swimming, biking, rowing, and experimenting with different training regimens. Because we were (or in Scott's case, were about to be) health or exercise scientists, our conversations about training were always heavily laced with exercise science principles, and we began exploring how our training experiences and education could help us develop a smarter way to train.

The catalyst for our change in thinking was, perhaps, the aging of the senior member of our duo: me. While I was still running well in my age group, it was no longer a mystery who would finish first in those training run/races. Recognizing that we were no longer competitive with each other, we began coaching each other. We also began entering triathlons.

The triathlon experience led us to a discovery that we hadn't expected. Initially, as we began training for triathlons, we struggled to maintain 6 days of running each week as we simultaneously added swimming and biking. Not surprisingly, that led to total exhaustion. Reluctantly, we gave up some of our running days in order to add more biking and swimming, having quickly realized that that was the only way we could be competitive in triathlons. Common sense, plus the perceived wisdom of the exercise science community, told us that because we were running less, our running performance would inevitably suffer. So you can imagine what a shock it was when our running—in every kind of race, from 5-Ks to marathons—*did not falter.* It was with this realization that the seeds of what would become the FIRST training program were sown.

Our diversified training was more fun, more interesting, less stressful, and, somehow, just as effective. And because of the limited number of running days per week, we were forced to take a more scientific approach to our run workouts in order to maximize the benefits. We experimented with other types of aerobic training, searching for those that would effectively complement our running. Finally, after years of personal testing, on the road and in scientific study, the Furman Institute of Running and Scientific Training (FIRST)—and its unique training approach—was launched.

The idea for a running institute was the culmination of our shared running experiences and on-the-run conversations spanning 2 decades. Our discussions were enhanced when Ray Moss, PhD, joined the Furman University faculty. Ray had studied under Jack Daniels, PhD, the renowned exercise physiologist and world-famous running coach, at the University of Texas. Ray brought to Furman extraordinary laboratory experience and skills. He built a Human Performance Laboratory that enabled us to add the scientific testing component necessary for a research institute.

As the running institute moved from concept closer to reality, we were fortunate to have Mickey McCauley, a licensed USA Track and Field coach and former collegiate half-miler, join the Furman fitness center staff as a fitness specialist. Mickey provides important coaching experience and expertise in training sprinters and middle distance runners, as well as distance runners.

Since offering its initial program in 2003, FIRST has presented more than 100 free-to-the-public lectures, completed three in-depth training studies, coached scores of runners to personal best race times, and conducted hundreds of lab assessments. FIRST training programs are being used by runners on six continents. We are gratified that runners are achieving personal goals with our training programs. The most satisfying aspect of our work has been that many runners report that the 3-days-a-week running schedule has enabled them to return to running and racing even after they had resigned themselves to believing that they could no longer do so. That service to runners supports our primary mission of promoting lifelong participation in running and physical activity while helping runners of all ages and abilities realize their potential through individually tailored training programs.

I will represent my coauthors, Scott Murr and Ray Moss, as the voice of this book. As narrator, I will share with you our personal and professional experiences in exploring how to train efficiently.

Bill Pierce
AUGUST 2006

REAL RUNNER REPORT

My name is Melissa Kennedy, and I am a 57-year-old female runner who just completed the Boston Marathon using your program. I first heard about your program in Runner's World *magazine and decided, even though I was using another program to train for the Chicago Marathon, that this program was the one I would use to train for Boston in the middle of the winter. I felt that running only 3 days a week would work for me when the weather was so unpredictable in January and February. I could also see that not running every day would keep me injury-free. So I started right after Christmas, using swimming and Spinning class as my usual cross-training choices. The 3 running days were hard, but I tried to follow the pacing that you suggested. My results in a couple of key races before Boston were amazing, and I knew this program was really working for me. The icing on the cake was running 3:27:25 in Boston, 3 full minutes better than Chicago on a tougher course! This was my second fastest marathon time ever. Though tired near the end, I was able to stay close to my goal pace the whole way. This program really works!*

As I come off of training for the marathon, I'm wondering whether running 3 days a week and cross-training 2 or 3 other days is something I should do all the time. As I get older, I worry about getting injured or overdoing when I run every day. Is there a way I can alter your marathon program to use the same idea for regular training? I would appreciate any suggestions you can give me.

Thanks again for a great program. When I train for the New York Marathon in the fall, I'll definitely be using your program again.

Melissa Kennedy

TEACHER

AMITYVILLE, NEW YORK

SECTION I

The FIRST Approach

1

The FIRST "3plus2" Program

Scott Infanger was sitting in his Nashville, Tennessee, apartment when the mail carrier delivered his August 2005 issue of *Runner's World*. Scott, a 29-year-old doctoral student at Vanderbilt University, had run five marathons with a personal best of 3:25, 15 minutes slower than the time he needed to qualify for Boston. The fact is that after running steadily faster times in his first three marathons, he had plateaued. One of the magazine's cover stories, about a 3-day-per-week running program that claimed it could help you run faster, seemed written with him in mind. Though he suspected it was nothing more than marketing hype, he decided to give the article a read.

Despite his initial cynicism, Infanger soon found himself genuinely intrigued. The article's author, former Boston Marathon winner Amby Burfoot, was extolling the program as the real deal. The article detailed how the program had been developed by exercise scientists and tested with real runners, who had improved their marathon times by an average of 19 minutes during a 16-week training program. And not just 4:00 or 5:00 marathoners, but sub-3:00 marathoners, as well.

At the same time, a Washington, D.C., attorney, Aaron Colangelo, was flipping through his mail when the same cover article caught his eye: "Train Less, Run Faster." Aaron had run multiple marathons with the same best time and, just like Scott, needed to knock off 15 minutes for Boston.

However, unlike Scott, he had decided that with his busy professional life, marathon training was too demanding to allow another attempt. Nonetheless, his curiosity took him directly to the article. *This might be exactly what I'm looking for,* he thought. Running 3 days a week would not be overwhelming, and he did enjoy biking and swimming, which could satisfy the program's cross-training component.

Both Scott and Aaron read the entire six-page feature. Interested readers were pointed to the Furman Institute of Running and Scientific Training (FIRST) Web site for more information. Soon, both were on their computers and found that the institute was advertising for volunteers for a 16-week fall marathon training study. Applications were due in 10 days. Applications from the two Boston hopefuls were soon on their way to FIRST.

Scott and Aaron were two of the 27 participants selected from applicants across the country, from California to Massachusetts. Their next step would be to travel to Furman University in Greenville, South Carolina, and complete a laboratory testing battery that required being weighed underwater to determine body composition, and running on a treadmill to exhaustion in order to gauge maximal oxygen consumption and lactate threshold. Both Scott and Aaron wondered what all of this meant and how it would help their running. They found out when they received a packet with their test results and a 16-week detailed training program. The training programs specified for every workout how far each was to run, how fast, and with what recovery time.

Scott and Aaron were to perform the three weekly running workouts and two cross-training workouts exactly as specified and report their results via e-mail. They would then receive immediate feedback from the FIRST faculty, which would include any necessary modifications for the next week's workouts based on how they were performing.

After 15 weeks of faithfully following the program, Aaron and Scott traveled back to South Carolina for their post–training program laboratory assessments. What would the lab numbers show? Had the targeted workouts resulted in an improvement? Would 3:10 be attainable?

After completing their exhaustive treadmill tests, each sat down with me to review the results. The physiological test data confirmed what they had reported in their weekly training reports—they were fitter and faster. Now it was time to develop a race strategy and determine a race pace. Because the faster times that they had seen in their training were consistent with their physiological test improvements, we told them that with smart pacing, a Boston qualification was not out of reach, but it would be tough. It would take a focused effort.

Ten days after their post-test in the Furman University Human Performance Laboratory, Aaron and Scott gave determined efforts at the Kiawah Island Marathon and quickly reaped the benefits of their disciplined 16 weeks of training. Both ran smart races with good pacing, with more than enough left over for a strong finish. Aaron was 30 seconds under 3:10, and Scott made his Boston qualifying time with a whole 9 seconds to spare.

Aaron's and Scott's performances, while impressive, are not exceptional. Rather, they are consistent with the advances that others have accomplished using the FIRST training method.

Can all runners benefit using the FIRST **"3plus2"** training program? Our research studies say, *yes*. Most of the runners in our training studies have improved both their race performances and their physiological profiles. Why? Simply put, the training programs are designed with the purpose of improving speed and endurance. The underlying concept of the FIRST training approach is quality over quantity. Most runners measure their training by the number of miles run, rather than how those miles were run. Our ***Training with Purpose*** programs provide structure and specific workouts tailored to your current fitness level.

As a result of the many letters from readers with questions about the training program and requests for advice, we developed this training book to provide runners with a complete guide for using the FIRST training method. This book is not a comprehensive compendium of running research, knowledge, and training information. Those books have been written. Here, we have compressed our collective knowledge, experience, and research into a training method that provides specific workouts laid out in 16-week training schedules for races from 5-Ks to marathons. These concise and easy-to-follow training programs have been tested with runners of wide-ranging abilities. Along with the training schedules, we include answers to many of the most frequently asked questions that we have received from runners around the world.

WHAT IS THE FIRST PHILOSOPHY?

At the heart of the FIRST philosophy is the belief that most runners do not train with purpose. When runners are asked to share their typical training week and the objective of each run, they are at a loss as to explain why they do what they do. Not having a training plan that incorporates different distances, paces, and recoveries means that runners won't reach their potential. Nor will they garner maximum benefits from their investment in training time. The FIRST program makes running easier and more accessible, limits overtraining and burnout, and substantially cuts the risk of injury while producing faster race times. By focusing on efficient, purposeful training, FIRST enables runners to meet their goal of running faster without sacrificing job, health, family, and friends.

THE FIRST "3PLUS2" TRAINING PROGRAM AND ITS COMPONENTS

Three quality runs each week plus two cross-training workouts are the foundation of the breakthrough FIRST approach. The three runs—track repeats, tempo run, and the long run—are designed to work together to improve endurance, lactate-threshold running pace, and leg speed. For each run, FIRST prescribes specific paces and distances that are based on a runner's current level of running fitness. The three quality runs, including prescribed paces and distances, are described in detail in Chapter 4. Having a specific goal for each training run is another of the program's innovations.

FIRST's prescribed paces are usually reported by runners as being faster than their normal running speed. Generally, this is because our ***Training with Purpose*** philosophy favors quality over quantity, intensity over frequency, fast running over the accumulation of miles. If you want to run faster, you need to train faster. In fitness terms, you need to employ the principle of specificity. In addition to running less, what sets the FIRST program apart from other training programs is that it emphasizes a faster pace for the long runs than what other training programs typically recommend. In our studies, we've discovered that focusing on a designated, demanding pace for the long runs prepares runners physiologically and mentally for racing, particularly for the marathon.

The physiological value of this faster running is that it increases the muscles' ability to metabolize lactate. Why is this important? The accumulation of excess lactate inhibits aerobic energy availability for muscular action. By training at a higher intensity, the muscle adapts to this increased energy demand by developing the ability to use lactate as an energy source, rather than have it accumulate in the muscles and blood.

The FIRST training program differs from the typical running program not only by its emphasis on intensity but also by building in more recovery time between running workouts. Without sufficient recovery, it is difficult to have quality workouts. Muscles need time to recover from the stress of hard workouts. Stressing specific muscle fibers repeatedly, day after day, in the same pattern causes accumulated fatigue. In other words, running 6 miles, 5 days a week results in muscular fatigue, not muscular adaptation. However, using those same muscle fibers for different types of activities will permit recovery and recharging of the muscle's energy stores (glycogen). So you can engage in another aerobic activity and reap the cardiorespiratory benefits while the muscle fibers used in running are recharging for the next hard running workout. Chapter 7 explains further the importance of rest and recovery.

Many running programs ignore the benefits of cross-training in favor of running additional miles. FIRST's cross-training workouts not only enhance fitness but also add variety, which ultimately reduces vulnerability to overuse injuries. Plus, your training will be more interesting. Cross-training workouts at prescribed intensities increase bloodflow around muscles, which in turn increases the muscle's ability to utilize oxygen and fat as energy sources for exercise. Using fat as an energy source spares the limited stores of carbohydrates (glycogen). Therefore, cross-training provides the same benefit as the additional running miles of other typical running programs. In Chapter 5, the cross-training workouts that are an essential part of the "**3plus2**" training program are described in detail.

WHERE'S THE PROOF?

Although we were convinced from our own experiences that these three running workouts, coupled with vigorous cross-training, would help runners improve both their race times and overall health, we were eager to conduct training studies with a variety of runners. We had designed the training programs to help runners train effectively and efficiently while helping them avoid overtraining and injury. But could we prove that the programs were, in fact, doing all these things?

Exercise science studies testing the effectiveness of training regimens are typically conducted in laboratories, where potentially confounding variables can be controlled. We stewed over how to design our studies. Our goal was to test a program that would enable us to generalize the results to the typical runner, not just male college freshmen. Many research studies involve male college freshmen as subjects because they are easily accessible to professors. We wanted to test our programs on "real" runners—fast, slow, male, female, young, old, novices, race veterans—performing their training without direct supervision. That required giving up control. We also wanted to find out whether our program worked under the conditions that real runners would face—finding an accessible running track, having a measured running course for tempo and long runs, and being able to maintain a specific pace for a workout.

We posted announcements on our Web site and at local running stores, fitness centers, and running clubs, hoping to attract a wide array of runners. All three of our studies attracted more than twice as many applicants as the 25 spaces that were available in the study. We promised runners free laboratory fitness assessments, individually designed training programs, and weekly feedback on their training reports in exchange for a promise to adhere to the training program and file a weekly report.

We began the fall 2003 study by having all of the selected applicants come to Furman University's Human Performance Laboratory for a battery of fitness tests. After completion of the tests, subjects received an analysis of their fitness level and a 4-week training schedule. Adjustments were made to their weekly training regimens after their weekly training logs were evaluated by the FIRST coaches. After 4 weeks, they received another revised training schedule to match the changes in their fitness levels based on their reported training workouts. After 16 weeks of following the individualized training programs that were given to them, the runners were brought back to our laboratory for a replication of the laboratory fitness assessment. The results confirmed that the runners had improved their maximal oxygen consumption by an average of 4.8 percent, their running speed at lactate threshold by 4.4 percent, and their running speed at maximal oxygen consumption by 7.9 percent. These three critical running performance variables had been enhanced by following a three-quality-runs-per-week training program. We now had data to support our personal experiences.

IMPROVEMENT IN KEY PERFORMANCE MEASURES 2003 MARATHON STUDY

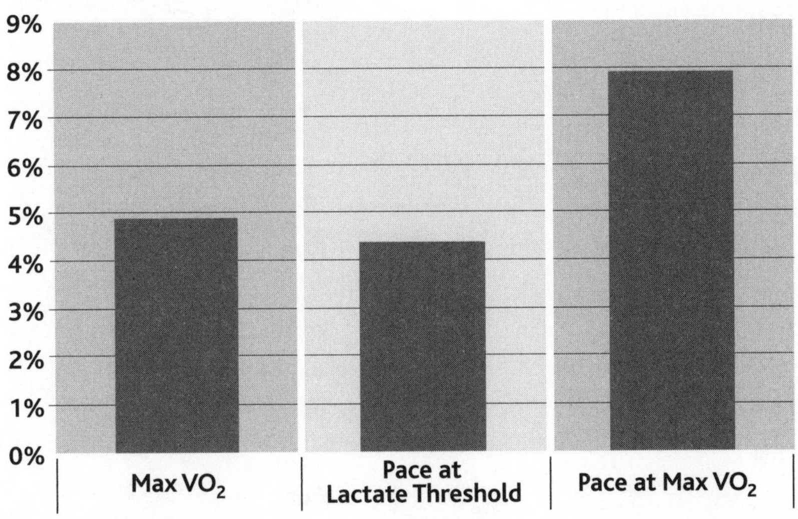

In 2003, we had been worried that if we insisted that runners complete a marathon at the end of our 16-week study, we might not attract enough subjects. However, the study participants enthusiastically endorsed the program, with many asking if they could continue training with us and wanting to know if they could be in the next study. We decided that requiring participation in a marathon would not deter participation in a replicated study. Plans began immediately for a fall 2004 study to further test the effectiveness of our training program. We had shown that this program would improve a runner's fitness. Would it improve what really matters to them—their marathon finish time?

In 2004, as we had done for the previous study, we tried to select a wide array of runners from the large pool of applicants for the marathon training study. The 25 selected runners began by visiting our Human Performance Laboratory for the same battery of fitness tests that we had utilized in the 2003 study. After we collected and analyzed the data, we developed individualized training programs for each participant. After completing 15 weeks of training, 23 runners—one had dropped out due to injury and another due to a personal problem—returned to the laboratory to repeat the fitness tests. The results showed that they had improved

IMPROVEMENT IN KEY PERFORMANCE MEASURES 2004 MARATHON STUDY

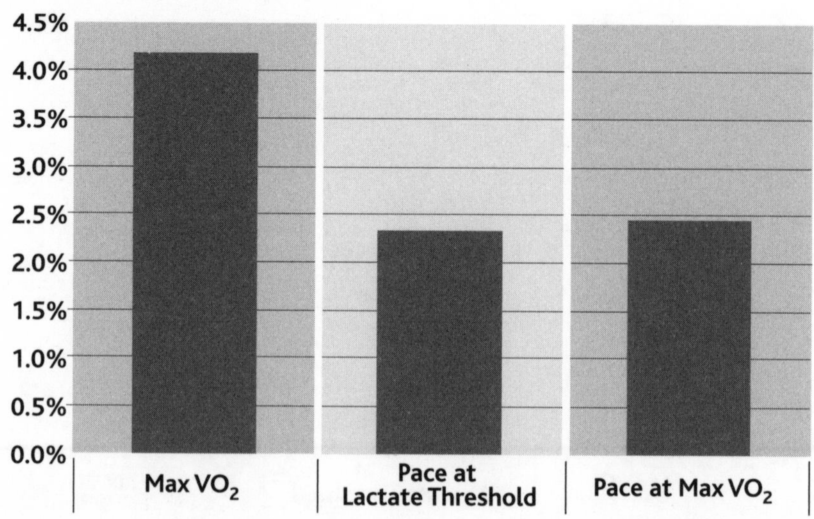

their maximum oxygen consumption by an average of 4.2 percent, their lactate threshold running speed by 2.3 percent, and their running speed at peak oxygen consumption by 2.4 percent.

A week later, we met the 23 runners at the Kiawah Island (South Carolina) Marathon. We were nervous and preoccupied about how they would perform. Would the eight who had never run a marathon be able to finish? Would the veteran marathoners who were accustomed to running 5 and 6 days a week be able to perform as well when only having run 3 days a week for the past 16 weeks? Twenty-one of the 23 attempted the marathon, while the other two participants decided to run the half-marathon because of setbacks that had prevented them from doing all of the workouts. We met the runners at the halfway mark, recording their times and providing encouragement. Although they were on their assigned paces at that point, we knew from our own marathoning experience that feeling good and running well after 13.1 miles provides little insight as to what your ultimate marathon performance will be.

Our first finisher was under 3 hours, ninth place overall, and more than 24 minutes faster than his previous best marathon. We were thrilled that his success was mirrored by the other participants in our study. The eight first-time marathoners finished with very respectable times. For those who had previously run a marathon, the average finish time improvement was 19:48. By all measures, our training study was a resounding success.

Amby Burfoot, executive editor of *Runner's World*, had taken an interest in our institute and our training program. He knew about our study and was eager to see the results. Once he reviewed the data and read the participants' evaluations of the study, he traveled to Greenville to interview us about the study and to talk to the participants about their experiences. He published the feature article on the program that Scott Infanger and Aaron Colangelo would read and eventually follow. In that article, he reported on how the runners had significantly improved their marathon times with our training program.

What followed that August 2005 article was a flood of requests to participate in our fall 2005 marathon training study. We were shocked by the applications from all across the country. It became clear after phone conversations with inquiring applicants that runners were excited about a program that improved marathon times by nearly 20 minutes. After reviewing the applications for our study, we chose runners from 11 states. Applicants were eager to participate in the study, even though it would entail travel to Greenville from all over the eastern half of the United States.

As with the previous two studies, the runners completed a battery of fitness tests in our Human Performance Laboratory in August and again just after Thanksgiving to measure any changes. They followed a 16-week training program tailored to their running fitness as determined by their laboratory test results and a running performance test. To measure their fitness level and to determine the paces for their training workouts, we required each to complete a workout that consisted of running 1600 meters three times with a 1-minute recovery between each of the 1600-meter runs.

Even though we had 2 years of proof that our training program enabled runners to improve their fitness and race times, we were concerned about the expectations of the runners in our latest study. Soon after their arrival in Greenville for their initial testing, they began commenting that they were hoping for the same improvement as the participants in the study reported in the *Runner's World* article. Once again, we were anxious about the outcome of our study. Perhaps these runners would be different from the previous group. Because of their willingness to invest their resources and trust in our program, we were feeling a little more pressure to deliver the results they'd read about in the *Runner's World* article. It's one thing for runners within the county to visit our campus for testing and training. It's quite another for runners to fly to Greenville, South Carolina, get a taxi to bring them to the Furman University campus to be tested in the Human Performance Laboratory, get a taxi back to the airport, and fly back to Boston, New York, or Washington, D.C. But that's what these runners did. We realized that these folks were serious about getting faster. Did they have as much room for improvement as the previous two running study cohorts? Would restricting these veteran marathoners to 3 days a week of running improve their marathon times?

Because these veterans had more extensive running histories and more of them were accustomed to running 5 to 7 days each week, we were convinced that the cross-training was an essential component for this group. For that reason, we made the cross-training mandatory for participation in the study.

We began testing the study participants after completion of 15 weeks of training. In test after test, we saw improvements similar to those we had experienced in the two previous studies. We followed those tests with counseling sessions on race strategies and the all-important decision of what pace to run: Try running too fast and you'll fall apart at the end; choose a pace that's too slow and you'll fail to run to your potential. We used the results of the laboratory tests and the 15 weeks of training data to counsel the runners on challenging, but realistic, goal finish times.

For a variety of reasons—injuries, and personal and professional conflicts—we ended up with 17 runners who had completed the training program at Kiawah on the morning of the marathon. Of those 17 runners, 14 had run marathons before. As with the previous year, we checked their time at the halfway point and again with 2 miles to go. Our first runner finished under 3 hours, with a personal best time. Personal best times became common for our runners. Of the 14 who had previously

IMPROVEMENT IN KEY PERFORMANCE MEASURES 2005 MARATHON STUDY

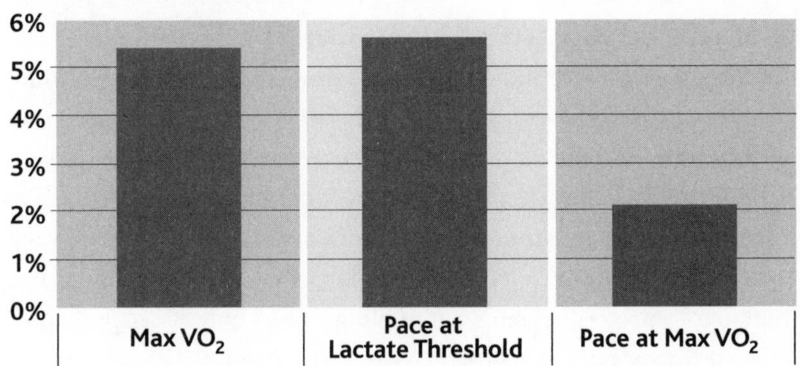

run a marathon, 12 had personal best times. One runner, who had achieved his personal best marathon time 27 years before, in 1978, did not achieve a personal best time but did improve upon his times from the past 10 years. All three of the first-time marathoners ran well and were pleased with their finish times.

In all three studies, the runners showed significant improvement over the 16 weeks of training. All three running performance variables showed statistically significant improvements. And, most important to the runners themselves, each improved on at least one of the running performance variables. You can read more about these studies' results in Chapter 6.

The three-quality-runs-per-week training program enabled all of the first-time marathoners to finish, very much satisfied with their performance times. More impressive were the personal best times recorded by more than 70 percent of the veteran marathoners. Running only 3 days a week, coupled with 2 cross-training workouts, enabled even veteran marathoners who were accustomed to running 5 or 6 days a week to improve their physiological profiles in the laboratory assessment, as well as to improve their marathon performances.

Training with Purpose means having workouts designed to specifically target the determinants of running performance. These studies indicate that our "**3plus2**" training program is an efficient and effective way to get fitter and faster.

WHY DOES FIRST APPEAL TO RUNNERS?

Runners tend to have more confidence in methods that their training friends have used successfully, and not those of Olympic champions. The programs in this book have been used successfully by runners of vastly varying abilities. Runners also like structure and accountability. The FIRST training programs specify both distance and pace for each workout, so there is a clear measure of performance for each training run. Running 7 miles is one thing, but running 7 miles only 30 seconds slower than 10-K pace is quite another.

FIRST Success

I have been meaning to get in touch to send you massive thanks!

I followed your program for this year's London Marathon, my 10th marathon, after it was issued in *Runner's World UK*. I have tried lots of different approaches to mileage and training, all resulting in similar times. The past 2 years my times at London were 2:45 and 2:44. This year, following the birth of our first child, training time was seriously reduced, so your plan seemed to be the only option.

I followed your plan and chose swimming for cross-training. I went into race day hoping to go below 2:45 to guarantee the championship entry for the following year. I started to push from about 16 miles (where I normally start to fatigue majorly) and still felt strong. I crossed the line in 2:40:38, which was a personal best by over 3 minutes.

Compared to the previous year, I had run less than half the [training] mileage, but ran 4 minutes faster [during the race] with a much stronger second half. Your training kept it all interesting, and I never felt that tired on the training.

Many thanks,

Robert Hall
INSURANCE BROKER
OXTED, SURREY, ENGLAND

CAN ALL RUNNERS BENEFIT USING THE FIRST TRAINING PROGRAM?

Our research says *yes*, for age-group runners. This training program was designed for regular runners aspiring to improve their running. The FIRST training programs have been used to improve running performances by 5:00 marathoners and sub-3:00 marathoners, by runners preparing for their first 5-K or marathon, and by runners in their early twenties as well as veterans in their sixties and seventies. In addition, the **"3plus2"** training program is extremely flexible and can be adjusted to fit all types of runners, from those who have limited time to train to those who make training a major focus in their lives.

2

Realistic Goals

Why is it that runners are disappointed with race finish times? Often, it is not because of a poor performance but the result of an unrealistic goal. For example, a runner who just finished a 10-K in 40:30 might be despondent because she had hoped to run under 40:00. It very well may be that she just ran a superb race. That is, based on her 5-K and half-marathon times, her predicted 10-K time may have been 41:00, which means that she ran 5 seconds per mile faster than what was predicted. She just had a remarkable performance from what had to be a great effort, but her expectations prevented her from enjoying and taking pride in it.

The question to ask is, why and how did she establish 40:00 as her target finish time for the 10-K? Most likely, her disappointment is a result of wanting to be a "thirtysomething" 10-K runner, just as runners want to be "threesomething" or "twosomething" marathoners. If I had been coaching her, I would have told her that, based on her recent performances at these other race distances and on her training paces, running 10 seconds per mile faster than what was predicted was unlikely; trying to do so would likely cause her to fade over the last couple of miles. I would have said, "Let's set three goals for your 10-K: (1) 41:15, an acceptable run

(continued on page 20)

The Runner Writes:

Dear FIRST:

My friend Beth and I read about your program in *Runner's World* and have since downloaded the half-marathon training program and have been following the schedule religiously in preparation for the Big Sur Half. We have some questions about the program and wanted to ask for your response.

Both my friend and I trained and completed our first marathon in October of 2004, and we have completed several halfs. We became interested in this program to improve our time and perceived effort for the half distance. We both cross-train doing yoga and weights on non-running days and have done so for several years, so our fitness level is pretty good.

How should we decide what our goal pace should be for the half distance?

Also, why does the program ask you to run greater than the half distance up to 15 miles? What's the benefit of running more than the race distance?

Thanks again,

Tara Sporer
Director, Customer Operations
Solana Beach, California

FIRST Replies:

We can give you several ways to predict your half-marathon pace if you can supply some finish times for races of any distance.

Running 15 miles will improve your endurance, which is an important component of the half-marathon.

Dear FIRST:

Thank you so much for your quick response. Recent Finish Times:

5-K: 23:40

Half-Marathon: 1:52:00; 1:50:30; 2:03:00

Marathon: 4:15:00

Tara

FIRST Replies:

Your 5-K time of 23:40 predicts a 49:30 10-K, which is approximately a 7:58-per-mile pace. Typically, you can expect to run the half-marathon at about 20 seconds slower per mile than 10-K pace. That means that you need to work on your endurance. That's why the 15-mile training runs will serve you well.

Dear FIRST:

Thanks for the information—race day is on Sunday at the Big Sur Half. The training program has been intense, but I think my friend and I will both see results! That said, how many seconds per mile do you think we will shave from our training run pace on race day—just due to race day adrenaline? I have been doing long training runs at about at 8:20 to 8:40 pace. Thanks again. We'll give you a report of our results next week.

Tara

FIRST Replies:

Typically, the taper and race day arousal will result in a half-marathon race pace that is 15 to 20 seconds per mile faster than your long run pace. So, I'd predict 8:05 to 8:20 per mile on race day.

Dear FIRST:

I wanted to let you know the results of the Big Sur Half that I ran. I ran a 1:46:23, 8:09 pace. Your predictions on my performance were right on. My friend Beth also had her best time ever. We really enjoyed the program and are now wondering, what's next for us to do—start back on it again, turn it up a notch, add hills?

Tara

representing a good effort; (2) under 41:00, faster than predicted, representing a very good performance; and (3) better than 40:45, an outstanding effort and performance."

As it was, our 10-K runner had an outstanding effort and performance, but she was disappointed because she did not have a realistic goal. She could have benefited from good coaching advice. That's why we wanted to address this important topic so early in this book.

Of course, we want to encourage runners to challenge themselves and identify ambitious goals. However, running too fast early in the race because you chose an overly ambitious, unrealistic goal almost always leads to dire consequences in the second half of the race. You'll be disheartened when an outstanding performance is unsatisfying, not because you haven't reached your goal, but because you chose an arbitrary and unrealistic goal in the first place.

I find that many of the runners applying to FIRST for coaching have unrealistic goals. At least, they are unrealistic in the short term. They may be able to reach their goals with steady and wise training over a period of 2 years. But many expect miracles in 16 weeks. These unrealistic goal times result when runners select goals arbitrarily—usually, round numbers or, in many cases, a qualifying time such as that for the Boston Marathon. Our mission at FIRST of helping runners set realistic goals is just as valuable as our individually tailored training programs.

How do runners undermine their own performance? Consider this example. A runner with a 5-K race finish time of 22:00 has a predicted marathon time of 3:34:05 (using Table 2.1 on page 28). If he sets 3:30 as a goal, he will need to run slightly more than 9 seconds faster per mile than the pace required to run a 3:34:05. Attempting to run 9 seconds per mile faster than what your current fitness level indicates for 26.2 miles will most likely result in a disappointing finish. You may question what element was missing in your training program when, really, the only thing missing was a realistic goal.

On pages 18 and 19 is a series of messages that I exchanged with a runner. You'll see that choosing the right goal helped her have a realistic finish time and helped to identify her need for more endurance.

This exchange of messages shows how we used race finish times and long training run times to help Tara choose a realistic goal finish time. By analyzing her performance times from different race distances, we were able to help her focus her training on endurance, her weakness. The 15-mile runs that she was reluctant to do certainly helped her improve her half-marathon time to a level consistent with the finish time predicted by her 5-K race time.

REALISTIC GOALS: THE ESSENTIALS

How to Select Your Goal Finish Time

Use the time from your most recent race (5-K, 10-K, half-marathon, or marathon) to estimate a target time for one of the other distances (see Table 2.1). If you don't have a recent time, go to a track and do an all-out 5-K time trial.

Commonly Asked Questions about Goal Selection

Q. ***How does the selection of the goal finish time affect your performance?***

> **A.** Selecting a goal finish time that's too ambitious will cause you to run too fast at the start. That fast start will likely result in a slower pace in the latter part of the race and a disappointing finish time.

Q. ***If my 10-K time predicts a 3:13 marathon, is it okay to set 3:10 as my goal?***

> **A.** Running 3 minutes faster than your predicted marathon finish time means running 7 seconds faster per mile than the pace that is presumably representative of your current fitness level. For most marathoners, running 7 seconds per mile faster for the entire distance would be challenging and, most likely, not realistic. Trying to do so could lead to a disappointing finish time.

Q. ***Would it be reasonable to expect an improvement over a 16- to 18-week training period that would make the 3:10 in the previous question possible?***

A. Absolutely. That's why we train. While there are no guarantees due to numerous variables (weather, course, personal health, etc.), a good marathon training program can produce that result. We have had runners in our training programs make much bigger improvements. For the purpose of setting a revised goal, though, don't *assume* that improvement without confirmation from a shorter race or improved training times. In particular, we rely on long run training times to judge a runner's improvement and his or her potential marathon performance; we use tempo training times to determine a runner's improvement and his or her potential 5-K and 10-K goal times.

Q. ***What distance is the best predictor? What if the 5-K and 10-K predict different marathon finish times?***

A. The distance closest to the predicted race distance is going to be the better predictor, assuming that the races were run under similar conditions. That is, a 10-K is a better predictor of your marathon finish time than a 5-K race finish time, and a half-marathon finish time will be a better marathon predictor than the 10-K time.

If your 5-K predicts a faster marathon time than what you are able to run, it is an indicator that you have more speed than endurance and you need to concentrate on improving your longer runs. Conversely, if your marathon finish time predicts a faster 5-K time than you are able to run, you need to work on speed and leg turnover.

Q. *Are the prediction tables accurate for everyone?*

A. Individuals differ in their abilities. Some runners have more speed than endurance, and vice versa. For some runners, their 5-K finish times will predict a faster marathon than what they can run, while for others, their marathon times are faster than what their 5-K times predict.

Q. *Are there differences in the tables for men and women?*

A. We have observed in our FIRST studies that if you have a male and a female with the same 5-K time, the female will likely run a faster marathon than the male. Conversely, if you have a male and a female with the same marathon time, the male will likely run a faster 5-K than the female.

Q. ***How does the course profile affect the goal finish time?***

A. The fastest road racing times in the world at all distances have been set on flat courses with few turns. Hills, turns, and rough or uneven surfaces all tend to slow the pace. While many runners will say that a flat course is boring and that they welcome a change in repetitive, concentrated muscular contractions, there is a time cost for those changes.

Goal Selection and Your Age

Q. ***Does age make a difference in the prediction tables?***

A. Aging runners usually have more endurance than speed. If a 55-year-old runner and 20-year-old runner have the same 5-K time, it is likely that the 55-year-old would run the faster half- or full marathon. Conversely, if the 55-year-old and the 20-year-old had the same marathon time, the 20-year-old would likely have a faster 5-K time.

Q. ***As I get older, my race times are slower. Is there a way to determine comparable times at my present age to those that I ran when I was younger?***

A. Yes. World Masters Athletics has developed tables that adjust performances for aging. The age-graded standards permit runners to compare their performances, or percentages, to other runners' or to their own performances at a younger age. It is a method that aging runners can use to set realistic goals.

For example, a 50-year-old female with a marathon time of 3:55 can go to Table 2.2 on page 30 ("Female Road Running Age Factors") and convert that 3:55 to an equivalent time for a marathon run at prime marathon age (21 to 29) for females by multiplying her 3:55 (235 minutes) by the 0.8469 factor for 50-year-old female marathoners. That produces a 3:19:01 age-adjusted performance time.

Q. *How do I determine my age-graded performance level percentage?*

A. Use Table 2.4 on page 34 if you are a female or Table 2.5 on page 36 if you are a male to find your age-graded standard, and then divide the standard by your race time. For example, a 60-year-old male with a 5-K time of 20:00 would divide the standard of 16:02 for a 60-year-old male by 20:00. The result (962 seconds/1200 seconds) would be 80.2 percent. That percentage could be compared with the age-graded percentages of performances run at earlier ages or with other runners of different ages.

Using age-graded standards is a way for coauthor Scott Murr, my brother Don, and me to compare our performances. The three of us have trained and raced against each other for decades. None of us is still in his prime. In our prime, our personal best times were nearly identical. Now that aging has separated us at the finish line, we can use age-graded standards to continue our competition. At the time this was written, we all ran the same 5-K race. The results were: Scott, age 44, 18:04; Don, age 59, 20:14; and me, age 56, 19:57. Who had the best performance? The answer lies in Table 2.5. Scott's age-graded Performance Level Percentage was 77.8 percent, Don's was 78.6 percent, and mine 77.7 percent. Don, who was the slowest to reach the finish line, had the highest quality performance based on age.

Q. *How do I convert my current race time to an equivalent race time at an earlier age?*

A. Use Table 2.2 on page 30 if you are a female or Table 2.3 on page 32 if you are a male to find your age factor. Multiply that age factor by your current race time to determine your equivalent race time at your prime-age time. For example, that 60-year-old male whose time is 20:00 for the 5-K would multiply that 20:00 by the age factor of 0.8043 and see that his 20:00 5-K at age 60 is equivalent to a 16:05 at prime 5-K performance age for males, which is the 22- to 28-year age group.

Using the same 5-K race to compare Scott's, Don's, and my race times converted to prime-time equivalent performances also produces interesting results. By using the conversion factors in Table 2.3, we find that Scott's 18:04 5-K race time at age 44 is equivalent to running a 16:34 at prime race age. Don's 20:14 at age 59 is equivalent to a 16:25 at prime race age. My 19:57 at age 56 is equivalent to a 16:36 at prime race age. For me, that's encouraging, since my 5-K PR (personal record) 20 years ago was 16:39. The fountain of youth can be found in age-graded tables.

REALISTIC GOALS: THE SCIENCE

In the seminal book *The Lore of Running,* Tim Noakes, MD, claims that the best predictor of running performance at any distance is a running time test, rather than a laboratory assessment of physiological measures. Marathoners can utilize various prediction formulas based on their race times at shorter distances. Numerous prediction tables exist, for distances from 800 meters to ultramarathons. All of these tables assume appropriate race-specific training on the part of the runner. Table 2.1 provides comparable race times for four popular race distances. This table was developed by calculating race finish times as percentages of the world records.

Selecting a target finish time based on recent performances will likely give a marathoner a realistic goal, rather than selecting arbitrary threshold goals such as "finishing under 3 hours," or "qualifying for the Boston Marathon," which may be overly ambitious and insufficiently specific for designing the proper pace. Finish goal times should be based on a recent race and training times.

An Early Fast Pace Has Consequences

Running authors Bob Glover and Pete Schuder caution that if runners are more than 2 minutes faster than their target half-marathon split, they have blown their marathon and will suffer for it over the last few miles. Marathoners commonly refer to a dramatic slowing of pace in the marathon as "hitting the wall." Speculations about the causes of hitting the wall include a variety of physiological explanations.

However, David Costill, a noted exercise physiologist and running researcher, states that hitting the wall is simply a matter of poor pacing. As Stephen Seiler, an exercise scientist at the Institute of Sport at Agder College in Norway, explains, "An early misuse of pace results in a lactic acid accumulation that cannot be eliminated without a subsequent decrease in speed." Furthermore, he reports that for each second gained by going under optimal pace in the first half of a race, 2 seconds are lost in the second half due to premature fatigue. That means that a marathoner with a goal of 3 hours who runs the first half in 1:28, who has presumably run 2 minutes faster than an even, or optimal, pace, would stand to lose 4 minutes in the second half and finish in 3:02, 2 minutes slower than goal finish time.

No matter how strongly we advocate not running the first half of the race too fast, most runners fail to follow that advice. There are good reasons for their failure. The excitement of race day causes the adrenaline to flow, and the exuberance from that excitation causes the runner to lose the ability to judge pacing. Certainly, having runners surround you at the start of the race distorts pacing. Since you are running with the crowd, it doesn't feel too fast. When you are rested from your prerace taper, your target pace feels easier in the early part of the race than in training. For all these reasons, you get the sense that *This is my day!* and you begin revising your goal finish time downward. However, during the second half, you begin to feel fatigued because you have withdrawn your stored energy in the muscle cells too rapidly, and as the miles go by, you are forced to revise your goal finish time upward. Your marathoning experience will be much more satisfying and pleasant if you have a strong finish than if you fade over the last few miles—even if you run the same race time.

We have analyzed thousands of race finish times and find that only about 2 percent of runners run the second half of the race in the same time as the first half. Run the first half too fast, and you slow down at a much faster rate in the second half. Run the first half too slow, and you can't make up the time in the second half. We strongly believe that running even splits is a desirable goal and a realistic one for 5-Ks, 10-Ks, and half-marathons. It is far more difficult to maintain a constant pace over 26.2 miles. For the marathon, you should strive to keep the disparity between the two halves less than 5 minutes—for example, 1:32 for the first half and around 1:35 to 1:37 for the second half.

Getting Older Means Getting Slower

Aging runners need to be aware that their performances will decline. Exceptions are those runners who don't begin racing until they are older. Runners slow with age, generally beginning around 35 years of age. The declining performance appears first with shorter races, as speed is affected more than endurance. Runners who continue to train seriously will typically experience racing decrements less than 1 percent per year from their late thirties to mid-forties. The slower performance times will most likely occur sooner in the shorter races—5-K to 10-K—than in the longer races. Marathoners can still run their best times in their late thirties and early forties. For runners who sustain their training, performance losses in the 0.5 percent to 1 percent range can be expected from the mid-forties to mid-fifties. The slowing of performance times accelerates after age 55, with annual performance decrements ranging from 1 percent to 2.5 percent.

REALISTIC GOALS: FINAL THOUGHTS

Train Wisely, Race Smart, and Savor Those Best Performances

When good, consistent training has produced a high level of fitness and race conditions are ideal, a PR is more likely. What often follows a personal best performance is that the runner then considers that PR to be the standard by which to measure subsequent performances. Those performances that produce PRs need to be appreciated and enjoyed with an understanding that a confluence of many factors contributed to that achievement. It is not fair or reasonable to expect subsequent performances to equal or exceed that PR under less-than-ideal conditions. We

(continued on page 38)

Table 2.1 Race Prediction

EQUIVALENT PERFORMANCES AT DIFFERENT DISTANCES

5-K	10-K	HALF-MARATHON	MARATHON
0:15:00	0:31:23	1:09:32	2:25:58
0:15:10	0:31:44	1:10:18	2:27:35
0:15:20	0:32:05	1:11:04	2:29:13
0:15:30	0:32:26	1:11:51	2:30:50
0:15:40	0:32:47	1:12:37	2:32:27
0:15:50	0:33:08	1:13:23	2:34:05
0:16:00	0:33:29	1:14:10	2:35:42
0:16:10	0:33:49	1:14:56	2:37:19
0:16:20	0:34:10	1:15:42	2:38:57
0:16:30	0:34:31	1:16:29	2:40:34
0:16:40	0:34:52	1:17:15	2:42:11
0:16:50	0:35:13	1:18:01	2:43:48
0:17:00	0:35:34	1:18:48	2:45:26
0:17:10	0:35:55	1:19:34	2:47:03
0:17:20	0:36:16	1:20:20	2:48:40
0:17:30	0:36:37	1:21:07	2:50:18
0:17:40	0:36:58	1:21:53	2:51:55
0:17:50	0:37:19	1:22:40	2:53:32
0:18:00	0:37:40	1:23:26	2:55:10
0:18:10	0:38:01	1:24:12	2:56:47
0:18:20	0:38:21	1:24:59	2:58:24
0:18:30	0:38:42	1:25:45	3:00:02
0:18:40	0:39:03	1:26:31	3:01:39
0:18:50	0:39:24	1:27:18	3:03:16
0:19:00	0:39:45	1:28:04	3:04:54
0:19:10	0:40:06	1:28:50	3:06:31
0:19:20	0:40:27	1:29:37	3:08:08
0:19:30	0:40:48	1:30:23	3:09:45
0:19:40	0:41:09	1:31:09	3:11:23
0:19:50	0:41:30	1:31:56	3:13:00
0:20:00	0:41:51	1:32:42	3:14:37
0:20:10	0:42:12	1:33:28	3:16:15
0:20:20	0:42:32	1:34:15	3:17:52
0:20:30	0:42:53	1:35:01	3:19:29
0:20:40	0:43:14	1:35:47	3:21:07
0:20:50	0:43:35	1:36:34	3:22:44
0:21:00	0:43:56	1:37:20	3:24:21
0:21:10	0:44:17	1:38:07	3:25:59
0:21:20	0:44:38	1:38:53	3:27:36
0:21:30	0:44:59	1:39:39	3:29:13
0:21:40	0:45:20	1:40:26	3:30:51
0:21:50	0:45:41	1:41:12	3:32:28
0:22:00	0:46:02	1:41:58	3:34:05
0:22:10	0:46:23	1:42:45	3:35:42
0:22:20	0:46:44	1:43:31	3:37:20

5-K	10-K	HALF-MARATHON	MARATHON
0:22:30	0:47:04	1:44:17	3:38:57
0:22:40	0:47:25	1:45:04	3:40:34
0:22:50	0:47:46	1:45:50	3:42:12
0:23:00	0:48:07	1:46:36	3:43:49
0:23:10	0:48:28	1:47:23	3:45:26
0:23:20	0:48:49	1:48:09	3:47:04
0:23:30	0:49:10	1:48:55	3:48:41
0:23:40	0:49:31	1:49:42	3:50:18
0:23:50	0:49:52	1:50:28	3:51:56
0:24:00	0:50:13	1:51:14	3:53:33
0:24:10	0:50:34	1:52:01	3:55:10
0:24:20	0:50:55	1:52:47	3:56:48
0:24:30	0:51:16	1:53:34	3:58:25
0:24:40	0:51:36	1:54:20	4:00:02
0:24:50	0:51:57	1:55:06	4:01:39
0:25:00	0:52:18	1:55:53	4:03:17
0:25:10	0:52:39	1:56:39	4:04:54
0:25:20	0:53:00	1:57:25	4:06:31
0:25:30	0:53:21	1:58:12	4:08:09
0:25:40	0:53:42	1:58:58	4:09:46
0:25:50	0:54:03	1:59:44	4:11:23
0:26:00	0:54:24	2:00:31	4:13:01
0:26:10	0:54:45	2:01:17	4:14:38
0:26:20	0:55:06	2:02:03	4:16:15
0:26:30	0:55:27	2:02:50	4:17:53
0:26:40	0:55:48	2:03:36	4:19:30
0:26:50	0:56:08	2:04:22	4:21:07
0:27:00	0:56:29	2:05:09	4:22:44
0:27:10	0:56:50	2:05:55	4:24:22
0:27:20	0:57:11	2:06:42	4:25:59
0:27:30	0:57:32	2:07:28	4:27:36
0:27:40	0:57:53	2:08:14	4:29:14
0:27:50	0:58:14	2:09:01	4:30:51
0:28:00	0:58:35	2:09:47	4:32:28
0:28:10	0:58:56	2:10:33	4:34:06
0:28:20	0:59:17	2:11:20	4:35:43
0:28:30	0:59:38	2:12:06	4:37:20
0:28:40	0:59:59	2:12:52	4:38:58
0:28:50	1:00:20	2:13:39	4:40:35
0:29:00	1:00:40	2:14:25	4:42:12
0:29:10	1:01:01	2:15:11	4:43:50
0:29:20	1:01:22	2:15:58	4:45:27
0:29:30	1:01:43	2:16:44	4:47:04
0:29:40	1:02:04	2:17:30	4:48:41
0:29:50	1:02:25	2:18:17	4:50:19
0:30:00	1:02:46	2:19:03	4:51:56

Note: If your race time falls between two listed times, use the slower time.

Table 2.2 Female Road Running Age Factors
WORLD MASTERS ATHLETICS

AGE	5-K	10-K	HALF-MARATHON	MARATHON
15	0.9550	0.9546	0.9363	0.9250
16	0.9670	0.9667	0.9533	0.9450
17	0.9790	0.9788	0.9703	0.9650
18	0.9893	0.9892	0.9848	0.9821
19	0.9961	0.9961	0.9945	0.9936
20	0.9996	0.9996	0.9994	0.9993
21	1.0000	1.0000	1.0000	1.0000
22	1.0000	1.0000	1.0000	1.0000
23	1.0000	1.0000	1.0000	1.0000
24	1.0000	1.0000	1.0000	1.0000
25	1.0000	1.0000	1.0000	1.0000
26	1.0000	1.0000	1.0000	1.0000
27	1.0000	1.0000	1.0000	1.0000
28	1.0000	1.0000	1.0000	1.0000
29	1.0000	1.0000	1.0000	1.0000
30	0.9997	0.9997	0.9997	0.9996
31	0.9989	0.9989	0.9986	0.9984
32	0.9974	0.9974	0.9970	0.9965
33	0.9954	0.9954	0.9946	0.9937
34	0.9928	0.9928	0.9915	0.9902
35	0.9897	0.9897	0.9878	0.9859
36	0.9859	0.9859	0.9834	0.9808
37	0.9816	0.9816	0.9783	0.9749
38	0.9768	0.9768	0.9726	0.9682
39	0.9713	0.9713	0.9661	0.9608
40	0.9653	0.9653	0.9590	0.9526
41	0.9587	0.9587	0.9513	0.9435
42	0.9515	0.9515	0.9428	0.9337
43	0.9438	0.9438	0.9337	0.9232
44	0.9355	0.9355	0.9238	0.9123
45	0.9266	0.9266	0.9133	0.9014
46	0.9171	0.9171	0.9024	0.8905
47	0.9071	0.9071	0.8915	0.8796
48	0.8965	0.8965	0.8806	0.8687
49	0.8856	0.8856	0.8697	0.8578
50	0.8747	0.8747	0.8588	0.8469
51	0.8638	0.8638	0.8479	0.8360
52	0.8529	0.8529	0.8370	0.8251
53	0.8420	0.8420	0.8261	0.8142
54	0.8311	0.8311	0.8152	0.8033

AGE	5-K	10-K	HALF-MARATHON	MARATHON
55	0.8202	0.8202	0.8043	0.7924
56	0.8093	0.8093	0.7934	0.7815
57	0.7984	0.7984	0.7825	0.7706
58	0.7875	0.7875	0.7716	0.7597
59	0.7766	0.7766	0.7607	0.7488
60	0.7657	0.7657	0.7498	0.7377
61	0.7548	0.7548	0.7389	0.7265
62	0.7439	0.7439	0.7280	0.7151
63	0.7330	0.7330	0.7171	0.7034
64	0.7221	0.7221	0.7062	0.6915
65	0.7112	0.7112	0.6953	0.6794
66	0.7003	0.7003	0.6844	0.6671
67	0.6894	0.6894	0.6735	0.6545
68	0.6785	0.6785	0.6626	0.6417
69	0.6676	0.6676	0.6517	0.6288
70	0.6567	0.6567	0.6408	0.6155
71	0.6458	0.6458	0.6299	0.6021
72	0.6349	0.6349	0.6190	0.5885
73	0.6240	0.6240	0.6081	0.5746
74	0.6131	0.6131	0.5971	0.5605
75	0.6022	0.6022	0.5855	0.5462
76	0.5913	0.5913	0.5731	0.5317
77	0.5804	0.5804	0.5601	0.5169
78	0.5695	0.5695	0.5464	0.5019
79	0.5586	0.5586	0.5320	0.4868
80	0.5471	0.5471	0.5169	0.4713
81	0.5344	0.5344	0.5012	0.4557
82	0.5205	0.5205	0.4848	0.4399
83	0.5054	0.5054	0.4677	0.4238
84	0.4891	0.4891	0.4499	0.4075
85	0.4716	0.4716	0.4314	0.3910
86	0.4529	0.4529	0.4123	0.3743
87	0.4330	0.4330	0.3925	0.3573
88	0.4119	0.4119	0.3720	0.3401
89	0.3896	0.3896	0.3508	0.3228
90	0.3661	0.3661	0.3289	0.3051

Compiled by Alan Jones in conjunction with Rex Harvey.

A 50-year-old female with a 5-K time of 26:00 can determine her adjusted time by multiplying her time by the age factor of 0.8747, which produces a time of 22.74 minutes, or 22:45. Her 26:00 5-K at age 50 is considered equal to a 22:45 achieved from age 21 to 29. She can compare her performance time with what she ran in her twenties or compare with her 24-year-old daughter's time.

Table 2.3 Male Road Running Age Factors
WORLD MASTERS ATHLETICS

AGE	5-K	10-K	HALF-MARATHON	MARATHON
15	0.9266	0.9266	0.9209	0.9151
16	0.9419	0.9419	0.9372	0.9324
17	0.9550	0.9550	0.9513	0.9475
18	0.9670	0.9670	0.9643	0.9615
19	0.9790	0.9790	0.9773	0.9755
20	0.9893	0.9893	0.9884	0.9875
21	0.9961	0.9961	0.9958	0.9955
22	0.9996	0.9996	0.9995	0.9995
23	1.0000	1.0000	1.0000	1.0000
24	1.0000	1.0000	1.0000	1.0000
25	1.0000	1.0000	1.0000	1.0000
26	1.0000	1.0000	1.0000	1.0000
27	1.0000	1.0000	1.0000	1.0000
28	0.9999	0.9999	1.0000	1.0000
29	0.9991	0.9991	1.0000	1.0000
30	0.9975	0.9975	1.0000	1.0000
31	0.9952	0.9952	1.0000	1.0000
32	0.9922	0.9922	0.9998	1.0000
33	0.9885	0.9885	0.9984	1.0000
34	0.9840	0.9840	0.9960	1.0000
35	0.9788	0.9788	0.9925	1.0000
36	0.9729	0.9729	0.9878	0.9990
37	0.9662	0.9662	0.9820	0.9960
38	0.9592	0.9592	0.9750	0.9910
39	0.9521	0.9521	0.9675	0.9840
40	0.9451	0.9451	0.9599	0.9759
41	0.9380	0.9380	0.9524	0.9679
42	0.9310	0.9310	0.9448	0.9599
43	0.9240	0.9240	0.9373	0.9519
44	0.9169	0.9169	0.9297	0.9439
45	0.9099	0.9099	0.9222	0.9358
46	0.9028	0.9028	0.9146	0.9278
47	0.8958	0.8958	0.9071	0.9198
48	0.8888	0.8888	0.8995	0.9118
49	0.8817	0.8817	0.8920	0.9038
50	0.8747	0.8747	0.8844	0.8957
51	0.8676	0.8676	0.8769	0.8877
52	0.8606	0.8606	0.8693	0.8797
53	0.8536	0.8536	0.8618	0.8717
54	0.8465	0.8465	0.8542	0.8637

AGE	5-K	10-K	HALF-MARATHON	MARATHON
55	0.8395	0.8395	0.8467	0.8556
56	0.8324	0.8324	0.8392	0.8476
57	0.8254	0.8254	0.8316	0.8396
58	0.8184	0.8184	0.8241	0.8316
59	0.8113	0.8113	0.8165	0.8236
60	0.8043	0.8043	0.8090	0.8155
61	0.7972	0.7972	0.8014	0.8075
62	0.7902	0.7902	0.7939	0.7995
63	0.7832	0.7832	0.7863	0.7915
64	0.7761	0.7761	0.7788	0.7835
65	0.7691	0.7691	0.7712	0.7754
66	0.7620	0.7620	0.7637	0.7674
67	0.7550	0.7550	0.7561	0.7594
68	0.7479	0.7479	0.7486	0.7514
69	0.7402	0.7402	0.7410	0.7434
70	0.7319	0.7319	0.7334	0.7353
71	0.7230	0.7230	0.7253	0.7272
72	0.7134	0.7134	0.7166	0.7185
73	0.7031	0.7031	0.7071	0.7091
74	0.6923	0.6923	0.6969	0.6990
75	0.6808	0.6808	0.6860	0.6882
76	0.6687	0.6687	0.6744	0.6766
77	0.6559	0.6559	0.6622	0.6644
78	0.6425	0.6425	0.6492	0.6515
79	0.6285	0.6285	0.6356	0.6379
80	0.6138	0.6138	0.6212	0.6236
81	0.5985	0.5985	0.6062	0.6085
82	0.5825	0.5825	0.5905	0.5928
83	0.5660	0.5660	0.5740	0.5764
84	0.5488	0.5488	0.5569	0.5593
85	0.5309	0.5309	0.5391	0.5415
86	0.5124	0.5124	0.5206	0.5229
87	0.4933	0.4933	0.5014	0.5037
88	0.4735	0.4735	0.4815	0.4838
89	0.4531	0.4531	0.4609	0.4632
90	0.4321	0.4321	0.4396	0.4419

Compiled by Alan Jones in conjunction with Rex Harvey.

A 43-year-old male with a marathon time of 2:55:30 can determine his age-adjusted time by multiplying his time by the age factor of 0.9519, which produces a time of 167.06 minutes, or 2:47:04. He can compare his age-adjusted time with what he ran between prime male marathon ages of 23 to 35 years.

Table 2.4 Female Road Running Age Standards
WORLD MASTERS ATHLETICS

AGE	5-K	10-K	HALF-MARATHON	MARATHON
15	0:15:30	0:31:47	1:10:19	2:26:24
16	0:15:18	0:31:23	1:09:04	2:23:18
17	0:15:07	0:30:59	1:07:51	2:20:20
18	0:14:58	0:30:40	1:06:51	2:17:53
19	0:14:51	0:30:27	1:06:12	2:16:17
20	0:14:48	0:30:21	1:05:52	2:15:31
21	0:14:48	0:30:20	1:05:50	2:15:25
22	0:14:48	0:30:20	1:05:50	2:15:25
23	0:14:48	0:30:20	1:05:50	2:15:25
24	0:14:48	0:30:20	1:05:50	2:15:25
25	0:14:48	0:30:20	1:05:50	2:15:25
26	0:14:48	0:30:20	1:05:50	2:15:25
27	0:14:48	0:30:20	1:05:50	2:15:25
28	0:14:48	0:30:20	1:05:50	2:15:25
29	0:14:48	0:30:20	1:05:50	2:15:25
30	0:14:48	0:30:21	1:05:51	2:15:28
31	0:14:49	0:30:22	1:05:56	2:15:38
32	0:14:50	0:30:25	1:06:02	2:15:54
33	0:14:52	0:30:28	1:06:11	2:16:17
34	0:14:54	0:30:33	1:06:24	2:16:45
35	0:14:57	0:30:39	1:06:39	2:17:21
36	0:15:01	0:30:46	1:06:57	2:18:04
37	0:15:05	0:30:54	1:07:18	2:18:54
38	0:15:09	0:31:03	1:07:41	2:19:52
39	0:15:14	0:31:14	1:08:09	2:20:56
40	0:15:20	0:31:25	1:08:39	2:22:09
41	0:15:26	0:31:38	1:09:12	2:23:32
42	0:15:33	0:31:53	1:09:50	2:25:02
43	0:15:41	0:32:08	1:10:30	2:26:41
44	0:15:49	0:32:25	1:11:16	2:28:26
45	0:15:58	0:32:44	1:12:05	2:30:14
46	0:16:08	0:33:05	1:12:57	2:32:04
47	0:16:19	0:33:26	1:13:51	2:33:57
48	0:16:31	0:33:50	1:14:46	2:35:53
49	0:16:43	0:34:15	1:15:42	2:37:52
50	0:16:55	0:34:41	1:16:39	2:39:54
51	0:17:08	0:35:07	1:17:39	2:41:59
52	0:17:21	0:35:34	1:18:39	2:44:07
53	0:17:35	0:36:02	1:19:42	2:46:19
54	0:17:48	0:36:30	1:20:45	2:48:35
55	0:18:03	0:36:59	1:21:51	2:50:54

AGE	5-K	10-K	HALF-MARATHON	MARATHON
56	0:18:17	0:37:29	1:22:59	2:53:17
57	0:18:32	0:38:00	1:24:08	2:55:44
58	0:18:48	0:38:31	1:25:19	2:58:15
59	0:19:03	0:39:04	1:26:33	3:00:51
60	0:19:20	0:39:37	1:27:48	3:03:34
61	0:19:36	0:40:11	1:29:06	3:06:24
62	0:19:54	0:40:47	1:30:26	3:09:22
63	0:20:11	0:41:23	1:31:48	3:12:31
64	0:20:30	0:42:00	1:33:13	3:15:50
65	0:20:49	0:42:39	1:34:41	3:19:19
66	0:21:08	0:43:19	1:36:11	3:23:00
67	0:21:28	0:44:00	1:37:45	3:26:54
68	0:21:49	0:44:42	1:39:21	3:31:02
69	0:22:10	0:45:26	1:41:01	3:35:21
70	0:22:32	0:46:11	1:42:44	3:40:01
71	0:22:55	0:46:58	1:44:31	3:44:54
72	0:23:19	0:47:47	1:46:21	3:50:06
73	0:23:43	0:48:37	1:48:16	3:55:40
74	0:24:08	0:49:29	1:50:15	4:01:36
75	0:24:35	0:50:22	1:52:26	4:07:56
76	0:25:02	0:51:18	1:54:52	4:14:41
77	0:25:30	0:52:16	1:57:32	4:21:59
78	0:25:59	0:53:16	2:00:29	4:29:48
79	0:26:30	0:54:18	2:03:45	4:38:11
80	0:27:03	0:55:27	2:07:22	4:47:20
81	0:27:42	0:56:46	2:11:21	4:57:10
82	0:28:26	0:58:17	2:15:48	5:07:50
83	0:29:17	1:00:01	2:20:46	5:19:32
84	0:30:16	1:02:01	2:26:20	5:32:19
85	0:31:23	1:04:19	2:32:36	5:46:20
86	0:32:41	1:06:59	2:39:40	6:01:47
87	0:34:11	1:10:03	2:47:44	6:19:00
88	0:35:56	1:13:39	2:56:58	6:38:10
89	0:37:59	1:17:51	3:07:40	6:59:30
90	0:40:26	1:22:51	3:20:10	7:23:51

Compiled by Alan Jones in conjunction with Rex Harvey.

A 50-year-old female with a marathon time of 4:00 can determine her performance level percentage (PLP) by dividing 2:39:54 by 4:00 (159.9 minutes/240 minutes), which produces a PLP of 67%. That same woman could compare her 5-K performance of 26:00 with her marathon performance by dividing 16:55 by 26:00 (16.9 minutes/26 minutes), which is a 5-K performance level percentage of 65%. Her marathon PLP of 67% is superior to her 5-K PLP of 65%. She can conclude from these two performances that her marathon performance was better than her 5-K.

Table 2.5 Male Road Running Age Standards
WORLD MASTERS ATHLETICS

AGE	5-K	10-K	HALF-MARATHON	MARATHON
15	0:13:55	0:28:59	1:04:18	2:16:30
16	0:13:42	0:28:30	1:03:11	2:13:58
17	0:13:30	0:28:07	1:02:15	2:11:50
18	0:13:20	0:27:46	1:01:25	2:09:55
19	0:13:11	0:27:26	1:00:36	2:08:03
20	0:13:02	0:27:08	0:59:55	2:06:30
21	0:12:57	0:26:57	0:59:28	2:05:29
22	0:12:54	0:26:52	0:59:15	2:04:59
23	0:12:54	0:26:51	0:59:13	2:04:55
24	0:12:54	0:26:51	0:59:13	2:04:55
25	0:12:54	0:26:51	0:59:13	2:04:55
26	0:12:54	0:26:51	0:59:13	2:04:55
27	0:12:54	0:26:51	0:59:13	2:04:55
28	0:12:54	0:26:51	0:59:13	2:04:55
29	0:12:55	0:26:53	0:59:13	2:04:55
30	0:12:56	0:26:55	0:59:13	2:04:55
31	0:12:58	0:26:59	0:59:13	2:04:55
32	0:13:00	0:27:04	0:59:14	2:04:55
33	0:13:03	0:27:10	0:59:19	2:04:55
34	0:13:07	0:27:17	0:59:27	2:04:55
35	0:13:11	0:27:26	0:59:40	2:04:55
36	0:13:16	0:27:36	0:59:57	2:05:03
37	0:13:21	0:27:47	1:00:18	2:05:25
38	0:13:27	0:28:00	1:00:44	2:06:03
39	0:13:33	0:28:12	1:01:12	2:06:57
40	0:13:39	0:28:25	1:01:41	2:08:00
41	0:13:45	0:28:37	1:02:11	2:09:03
42	0:13:51	0:28:50	1:02:40	2:10:08
43	0:13:58	0:29:04	1:03:11	2:11:14
44	0:14:04	0:29:17	1:03:42	2:12:21
45	0:14:11	0:29:31	1:04:13	2:13:29
46	0:14:17	0:29:44	1:04:45	2:14:38
47	0:14:24	0:29:58	1:05:17	2:15:49
48	0:14:31	0:30:13	1:05:50	2:17:00
49	0:14:38	0:30:27	1:06:23	2:18:13
50	0:14:45	0:30:42	1:06:57	2:19:27
51	0:14:52	0:30:57	1:07:32	2:20:43
52	0:14:59	0:31:12	1:08:07	2:22:00
53	0:15:07	0:31:27	1:08:43	2:23:18
54	0:15:14	0:31:43	1:09:19	2:24:38
55	0:15:22	0:31:59	1:09:56	2:26:00

AGE	5-K	10-K	HALF-MARATHON	MARATHON
56	0:15:30	0:32:15	1:10:34	2:27:22
57	0:15:38	0:32:32	1:11:12	2:28:47
58	0:15:46	0:32:49	1:11:52	2:30:13
59	0:15:54	0:33:06	1:12:31	2:31:41
60	0:16:02	0:33:23	1:13:12	2:33:10
61	0:16:11	0:33:41	1:13:53	2:34:42
62	0:16:19	0:33:59	1:14:36	2:36:15
63	0:16:28	0:34:17	1:15:19	2:37:50
64	0:16:37	0:34:36	1:16:02	2:39:27
65	0:16:46	0:34:55	1:16:47	2:41:05
66	0:16:56	0:35:14	1:17:33	2:42:46
67	0:17:05	0:35:34	1:18:19	2:44:30
68	0:17:15	0:35:54	1:19:06	2:46:15
69	0:17:26	0:36:16	1:19:55	2:48:03
70	0:17:38	0:36:41	1:20:44	2:49:53
71	0:17:51	0:37:08	1:21:38	2:51:46
72	0:18:05	0:37:38	1:22:38	2:53:51
73	0:18:21	0:38:11	1:23:45	2:56:10
74	0:18:38	0:38:47	1:24:58	2:58:43
75	0:18:57	0:39:26	1:26:19	3:01:31
76	0:19:18	0:40:09	1:27:48	3:04:37
77	0:19:40	0:40:56	1:29:26	3:08:01
78	0:20:05	0:41:47	1:31:13	3:11:44
79	0:20:32	0:42:43	1:33:10	3:15:50
80	0:21:01	0:43:45	1:35:19	3:20:20
81	0:21:33	0:44:52	1:37:41	3:25:17
82	0:22:09	0:46:05	1:40:17	3:30:43
83	0:22:48	0:47:26	1:43:10	3:36:43
84	0:23:30	0:48:56	1:46:20	3:43:21
85	0:24:18	0:50:34	1:49:51	3:50:42
86	0:25:11	0:52:24	1:53:45	3:58:53
87	0:26:09	0:54:26	1:58:06	4:08:00
88	0:27:15	0:56:42	2:02:59	4:18:12
89	0:28:28	0:59:15	2:08:28	4:29:42
90	0:29:51	1:02:08	2:14:41	4:42:43

Compiled by Alan Jones in conjunction with Rex Harvey.

A 43-year-old male with a marathon time of 2:55:30 can determine his performance level percentage (PLP) by dividing 2:11:14 by 2:55:30 (131.2 minutes/175.5 minutes), which produces a PLP of 75%. That same man could compare his 5-K performance of 18:00 with his marathon performance by dividing 13:58 by 18:00 (13.97 minutes/18 minutes), which is a 5-K performance level percentage of 78%. His marathon PLP of 75% is inferior to his 5-K PLP of 78%. He can conclude from these two performances that his 5-K performance was better than his marathon performance.

suggest that runners train wisely and be prepared for those times when conditions are ideal.

Hooray for Age-Adjusted Times!

These days, I set my personal running goals based on my age-adjusted times. I calculate my race times from 5-Ks to marathons to see how they compare with what I ran 10, 20, or 30 years ago. Remarkably, while my times are slower today, the age-adjusted times are nearly identical to those of yesteryear. For example, my recent 3:11:47 marathon time, or age-adjusted 2:44:06, is nearly the same as my best time of 2:44:50.

The same age adjustment exercise gives me my time goal for my next race. No need to fret about another birthday; an age-adjusted, realistic, slower goal finish time will also come inexorably. Believe me, physiology proves that a slower goal time is needed.

Scan the race results from any race, and you will find that the finish times get slower for the 5-year age groups starting around 45 years old. Some shorter races have slower times starting around age 35. So far, we have not discovered how to stop the aging process. By continuing to train seriously, you can at least slow the deterioration. Occasionally, remarkable race times are posted by runners in their fifties, sixties, seventies, and even eighties. Recent sub-3:00 marathons run by a septuagenarian should inspire us all.

Don't let slowing performances make you think about retiring to the couch or the golf course. This chapter emphasizes the importance of setting realistic goals. Just as important, it shows you how to develop reasonable expectations for your performances. Use the age-adjusted tables to compare your past performances with today's. Age-adjusted goals provide incentive, motivation, and realistic measures of our running accomplishments for the decades after our personal best times are set.

3

FIRST Steps for the New Runner

Can new runners use the FIRST programs? Absolutely. As long as you don't try to run too often, too long, or too fast, too soon. We want new runners to enjoy their activity and keep enjoying it for a long time. That requires progressing slowly and not becoming a running dropout because of burnout, overtraining, or injury.

Injury, in particular, is common among novices because they are motivated and excited to go farther and faster. That zeal is reinforced because the gains as you begin an exercise program are very large. Those big gains encourage you to do more and more. We point out to beginners that small gains that seem subtle from day to day become dramatic over several months and years. We encourage all new runners to develop a solid base before tackling lofty goals such as marathons. Use this book to help pace yourself.

We regularly hear from new runners who have never run a race of any distance, and they often ask whether we have a marathon schedule for the new runner. Frequently, the person who contacts us is hoping to run a marathon in the next 6 months. While it is possible to survive the distance walking and running, we advise against attempting such a challenge without adequate preparation. Think 5-K or 10-K. It is much more enjoyable and healthier to train properly while still satisfying some reasonable intermediate goals prior to attempting the challenge of 26.2 miles.

In this chapter, you will find beginning runner training programs that progress conservatively, starting with a combination of walking and running. Follow the programs as designed, even if it feels too easy at first.

The Runner Writes:

Dear FIRST:

I have a few questions regarding running. First, how many days a week do you think I should run? I am a 35-year-old mother of three. Is there a certain program I should follow to reduce my risk of injury? These and any other tips you could give me would be helpful. I am on the path to making running a priority, but I wanted some general info to get started again. Also, is it realistic for me as a new runner to think about running a half-marathon?

Thanks,

Jennifer Arends
Mother
Travelers Rest, South Carolina

FIRST Replies:

Establish a running base of 15 miles per week with a long run of 5 miles before beginning the half-marathon training program. Begin walking and jogging so that you can establish a regular habit of exercise while beginning to condition your body. Increase your walking/jogging time gradually.

You must walk before you run. Gradual progression is the key. We designed a program for the complete beginner that provides a progressive increase in overload on the muscles, heart, and lungs. As your body adapts to the stress of walking and running, increase the total number of exercise minutes and the percentage of those minutes you spend running. At first, do not worry about pace, but focus on increasing endurance.

Your body needs to adapt to the new stresses associated with running. Even if your cardiorespiratory system is not being stressed, your anatomical structures may be overtaxed and weakened due to your newfound activity. Gradually building a solid base from which to progress will ensure safe training and positive movement toward your goals.

At some point, your progress may become interrupted by fatigue. Pay attention to your body, and recognize the signs of prolonged fatigue. Individuals vary considerably in how much training they can tolerate. Know your threshold of training. Insert a rest and recovery day regularly to

Set an initial goal of finishing a 5-K race. If you follow our program, you will be able to do that in 12 weeks. After completing the 5-K Novice Training Program (Table 3.1 on page 46), you will then be ready for the 12-week 5-K Intermediate Training program (Table 3.2 on page 48). Then you can focus on running faster. The 12-week 5-K training program in Chapter 4 (Table 4.4 on page 82) will enable you to increase your endurance and speed for an even better performance.

We are aware that it has become popular for new runners to enter a half-marathon or marathon with less than 6 months to prepare for it. Many charitable institutions have organized training groups to participate in races as part of their fundraising activities. We applaud these fundraising successes and the incentive to be physically active that they provide. However, we wish that some of the organized training groups focused on shorter races initially. We believe it makes sense to progress from shorter race distances to longer ones so that you are properly prepared to meet the challenges you'll face, to avoid injury, and to see your participation as a lifelong activity instead of a one-time event. By adhering to our training programs, you can progress from novice to runner and see your fitness, health, and performance improve.

FIRST training programs are designed to help you ***run***, not just ***survive***, the distance. Completing a race is more enjoyable when you are prepared for the challenge. Our goal of promoting running as a lifelong physical activity is more likely to be achieved if runners have a positive experience.

prevent that overtrained condition. Sometimes, it takes more than a day—it might take a very easy training week.

Many runners who decide to start running do so for weight loss. Be careful if you are overweight, because running is a weight-bearing activity and extra pounds add stress to your joints, muscles, bones, and connective tissue. Non-weight-bearing cross-training is especially valuable for losing weight without elevating your risk of injury.

The letter on pages 40 and 41 from a new runner and our reply provide advice for anyone just starting a running program.

BECOMING A RUNNER: THE FIRST STEPS

- Select a 5-K race 3 to 4 months in advance.
- Schedule your workouts in advance.
- Get proper shoes.
- Find a training partner.
- Make a commitment: Complete an entry form and pay the entry fee!
- Make training a habit.
- Choose a safe place to walk and run.
- Progress gradually.
- Cross-train (see Chapter 5).
- Do the FIRST stretches, drills, and strength training (see Chapters 12 and 13).

Frequently Asked Questions on Becoming a Runner

Q. *How do I get started?*

A. First, make sure that you don't have any health problems that would prevent your starting an exercise program. If you have any existing medical problems or if you are over 40 years of age, we recommend that you get clearance to begin an exercise program from your physician.

Q. *What about shoes?*

A. Get proper shoes and clothing for exercise. There are many good running shoes available, each with different features. Find someone who is knowledgeable about running shoes to assist you in choosing a shoe that fits you properly. You can usually find knowledgeable sales assistance at running specialty stores. Try visiting several running stores. It will take only two or three visits before you see trends in recommendations.

Q. *When and where should I run?*

A. Whether you run in the morning, at noon, or in the evening is largely a personal preference. Be realistic in deciding what schedule you are most likely to follow consistently. You don't have to work out at the same time each day. Plan ahead and consider your other obligations. Schedule a time for your run, and consider that an important personal priority. Consistency is essential in establishing a habit.

Choose a place that is safe to run. A running track is a good place to start. Preferably, run in daylight. If you must run in the dark, choose a place that is well-lit. You must be mindful of safety and security. Many runners have sprained an ankle stepping off the curb in the dark. It may also be a good idea to invest in some reflective gear while you're at the running specialty store.

Q. *How much should I do at first?*

A. FIRST has developed three 12-week programs that progress very gradually. Follow these programs carefully, and you will enjoy the benefits of improved fitness and health, along with the exhilaration of completing a 5-K race. It's important that you don't try to do too much too soon. It's equally as important that you are faithful to the program and establish consistency in your training.

If you have done some running in your past or if you regularly play other sports—basketball, tennis, cycling, etc.—and are not overweight, you may be able to begin with the Intermediate

(continued on page 48)

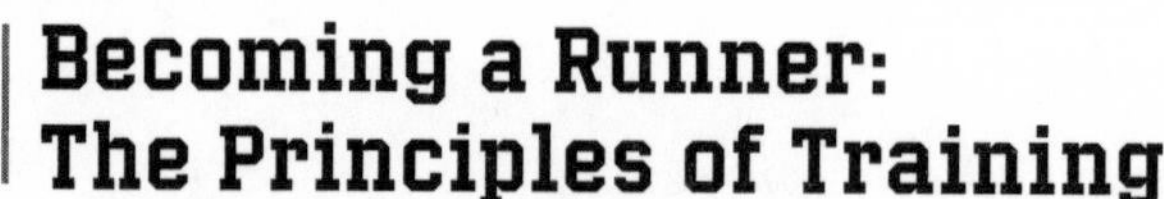

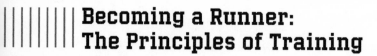

Becoming a Runner: The Principles of Training

There are five key principles of training that apply to becoming a runner. These five principles should be incorporated into any training program. FIRST training programs adhere to these five basic training principles.

PRINCIPLE #1

Progressive Overload: The gradual increase of training stress will cause the body to adapt in response to that overload. These adaptations occur at the cellular level, and this adaptation process will continue as long as the overload doesn't overwhelm the system. That is why the additional stress—increased exercise time and intensity—must increase gradually.

PRINCIPLE #2

Specificity: The improvement from training will be specific to the type of training. Specificity applies to the mode (type) of exercise, intensity (speed or pace), and duration (distance or total time run). Obviously, to become a good runner, you need to run. The question is how much of your training needs to be mode-specific. The FIRST program requires a smaller percentage of your total training to be running than other running programs. As we explain throughout the book, our experience and research show that a high level of fitness and running success can be achieved with running three times a week.

The FIRST training approach adheres to the principle of specificity for intensity. We advocate that to run faster, you must incorporate faster running in your training. Runners report that the FIRST training paces are challenging. Runners report that running hard in training helps them run faster in races more than running more frequently in training. Pace-specific training is the primary basis of FIRST training.

A question that arises concerning duration specificity is, "Why don't you include a 26-mile run in your marathon training?" FIRST training relies on relatively fast paces for its long runs. Rather than have runners plod along for 26 miles in training runs, we recommend running close to marathon pace for 15- and 20-mile runs, an approach that runners report prepares them for their race-day target pace. Again, pace specificity prepares the body physiologically, neuromuscularly, and biomechanically.

PRINCIPLE #3

Individual Differences: Beginning runners will soon find that they may improve more than their training partners and that others improve faster than they do. Individuals are different in their anatomies and physiologies. Individuals respond differently to the same training regimen. It is important that you realize that the most important factor you consider is your own progress—where you are now, as opposed to where you were or where you will be 3 months from now.

There will always be others who are fitter and faster and others who are less fit and slower. The principle of individual differences also applies to rest and recovery.

PRINCIPLE #4

Law of Diminishing Returns: One of the benefits of being a novice is that your early progress is substantial. As you progress through the training programs and you get fitter and faster, you are approaching your optimal performance. As you near that point, small improvements come from lots of hard training, as opposed to the large improvements that came from moderate training when you were first beginning.

PRINCIPLE #5

Reversibility: Use it or lose it! The gains that you make can be lost if you stop training. Consistency is the key to fitness.

FIRST encourages regular year-round training. That is one of the attractive features of running three times per week. Runners do not feel overwhelmed and overstressed with the rigors of daily running, which causes some runners to stop running for long periods. Interruptions in regular physical activity cause a loss of fitness that leads us to try to make up for those losses too fast once we return to training. The training does not have to be at full intensity year-round; low to moderate intensity can help you maintain fitness and avoid the stress and injuries that come from sudden increases in physical activity.

Table 3.1
5-K NOVICE TRAINING PROGRAM

This program is designed to gradually move the inactive individual from walker to runner. It begins primarily with walking, interspersed with short intervals of running during a half-hour workout. The first workout in Week #1 includes walking for 10 minutes. Following that 10 minutes of walking, you will run for 1 minute and then walk for 2 minutes, which will be repeated four times. After completing the fourth repetition of 1-minute running, walk for 10 minutes to complete the workout. Run at a comfortable pace. (Note: W = Walk; R = Run)

WEEK	WORKOUT #1	WORKOUT #2	WORKOUT #3
1	32 min total: W 10 min (R 1 min, W 2 min) × 4 W 10 min	32 min total: W 10 min (R 1 min, W 2 min) × 4 W 10 min	32 min total: W 10 min (R 1 min, W 2 min) × 4 W 10 min
2	32 min total: W 10 min (R 2 min, W 2 min) × 3 W 10 min	32 min total: W 10 min (R 2 min, W 2 min) × 3 W 10 min	32 min total: W 10 min (R 2 min, W 2 min) × 3 W 10 min
3	32 min total: W 10 min (R 2 min, W 1 min) × 4 W 10 min	32 min total: W 10 min (R 2 min, W 1 min) × 4 W 10 min	35 min total: W 10 min (R 3 min, W 2 min) × 3 W 10 min
4	36 min total: W 10 min (R 3 min, W 1 min) × 4 W 10 min	36 min total: W 10 min (R 3 min, W 1 min) × 4 W 10 min	40 min total: W 10 min (R 3 min, W 1 min) × 5 W 10 min
5	44 min total: W 10 min (R 4 min, W 2 min) × 4 W 10 min	44 min total: W 10 min (R 4 min, W 2 min) × 4 W 10 min	45 min total: W 10 min (R 4 min, W 1 min) × 5 W 10 min
6	50 min total: W 10 min (R 4 min, W 1 min) × 6 W 10 min	50 min total: W 10 min (R 4 min, W 1 min) × 6 W 10 min	50 min total: W 10 min (R 5 min, W 1 min) × 5 W 10 min

WEEK	WORKOUT #1	WORKOUT #2	WORKOUT #3
7	56 min total: W 10 min (R 5 min, W 1 min) × 6 W 10 min	56 min total: W 10 min (R 5 min, W 1 min) × 6 W 10 min	55 min total: W 10 min (R 6 min, W 1 min) × 5 W 10 min
8	About 50 min total: W 10 min R 1 mile W 5 min (R 6 min, W 1 min) × 3 W 10 min	About 50 min total: W 10 min R 1 mile W 5 min (R 6 min, W 1 min) × 3 W 10 min	About 45 min total: W 10 min R 1 mile W 5 min R 1 mile W 10 min
9	About 35 min total: W 10 min R 1.5 miles W 10 min	About 40 min total: W 10 min R 1.5 miles W 5 min R 0.5 mile W 5 min	About 35 min total: W 10 min R 2 miles W 5 min
10	About 35 min total: W 10 min R 2 miles W 5 min	About 35 min total: W 10 min R 2 miles W 5 min	About 40 min total: W 10 min R 2.5 miles W 5 min
11	About 40 min total: W 10 min R 2 miles W 10 min	About 40 min total: W 10 min R 2 miles W 10 min	About 45 min total: W 10 min R 3 miles W 5 min
12	About 40 min total: W 10 min R 2 miles W 10 min	About 49 min total: W 10 min R 2 miles W 10 min	About 45 min total: W 10 min R 3.1 miles (5-K) race W 5 min

Table 3.2
5-K INTERMEDIATE TRAINING PROGRAM

This training schedule is for the runner who has completed the Novice Training Program or who can run 5 kilometers. The workouts include the basic FIRST Key Runs described in Chapter 4. The paces for the Intermediate program can be found in Chapter 4 (Tables 4.1 to 4.3).

WEEK	KEY RUN WORKOUT#1	KEY RUN WORKOUT#2	KEY RUN WORKOUT#3
1	10 min warmup run 2 × 400 10 min cooldown run	1 mile warmup run 1 mile short tempo 1 mile cooldown run	3 miles at mid-tempo pace
2	10 min warmup run 3 × 400 10 min cooldown run	1 mile warmup run 1 mile short tempo 1 mile cooldown run	3 miles at mid-tempo pace
3	10 min warmup run 4 × 400 10 min cooldown run	1 mile warmup run 1 mile short tempo 1 mile cooldown run	3.5 miles at mid-tempo pace
4	10 min warmup run 2 × 400, 1 × 800 10 min cooldown run	1 mile warmup run 1.5 mile short tempo 1 mile cooldown run	3.5 miles at mid-tempo pace
5	10 min warmup run 400, 600, 800 10 min cooldown run	1 mile warmup run 1.5 mile short tempo 1 mile cooldown run	4 miles at mid-tempo pace
6	10 min warmup run 5 × 400 10 min cooldown run	1 mile warmup run 1.5 mile short tempo 1 mile cooldown run	4 miles at mid-tempo pace

program (Table 3.2) rather than the Novice program (Table 3.1). The Novice program is for someone who has been inactive and is just beginning to exercise.

Q. *What if I am overweight?*

WEEK	KEY RUN WORKOUT#1	KEY RUN WORKOUT#2	KEY RUN WORKOUT#3
7	10 min warmup run 400, 2 × 800 10 min cooldown run	1 mile warmup run 1.5 mile short tempo 1 mile cooldown run	4.5 miles at mid-tempo pace
8	10 min warmup run 2 × 1000 10 min cooldown run	1 mile warmup run 2 mile short tempo 1 mile cooldown run	4.5 miles at mid-tempo pace
9	10 min warmup run 6 × 400 10 min cooldown run	1 mile warmup run 2 mile short tempo 1 mile cooldown run	5 miles at long tempo pace
10	10 min warmup run 3 × 800 10 min cooldown run	1 mile warmup run 2 mile short tempo 1 mile cooldown run	5 miles at long tempo pace
11	10 min warmup run 200, 400, 600, 800 10 min cooldown run	1 mile warmup run 2 mile short tempo 1 mile cooldown run	5 miles at long tempo pace
12	10 min warmup run 4 × 400 10 min cooldown run	2 miles easy 10 min walk	5-K race

Recovery after each interval = 400 walk/jog.

A. The FIRST running programs are not weight management programs. However, regular physical activity expends energy and can assist you in weight loss. You must also be mindful that excess weight can be stressful to your joints and connective tissue.

Combining a sensible diet with exercise is the safest and most effective way to reach a healthier weight.

If you are more than 30 pounds overweight, walking rather than running is advisable until you have reduced your excess weight. To help reduce stress on your joints, cross-training on non-weight-bearing exercise machines is also recommended until you have reduced your excess weight.

Q. ***Should I get a partner to train with or join a group?***

A. *Yes!* Research shows clearly that compliance with an exercise schedule is better for those who have a training partner or who are part of a group that meets regularly to train. The commitment to others appears to be a powerful motivator.

Q. ***Why does FIRST recommend starting with a 5-K? Many people are joining marathon training groups even though they have no running experience.***

A. FIRST believes that you need to establish a solid fitness base gradually before attempting a long race too soon, which can result in injury. The exhilaration of running a 5-K can be equal to or better than that of walking and running a longer race.

As health educators, we are interested in promoting running as a healthy, lifelong physical activity. Progressing gradually and developing the fitness and endurance for a 5-K before moving on to a 10-K, half-marathon, or marathon is a healthy approach. The physiological development for running peaks after about 8 to 10 years of training. Why not tackle these longer races when you are better prepared physically to do so?

You will have a much better running experience at these longer distances by running shorter races first. Many people are joining a charity training group without any running experience and completing the longer race—half-marathon or marathon—in survival mode. FIRST wants runners to be fully prepared for the race distance that they attempt.

FIRST Success

I never thought I'd have something in common with Oprah Winfrey, George W. Bush, and Will Ferrell, but now I do. I've finished a marathon, and it was all because of Dr. Bill Pierce and his FIRST marathon training program. He helped me achieve my dream of running and completing my first marathon at age 52. I chose the FIRST program because it combined workouts that I thought would give me success . . . and it did!

Each week's workouts got progressively challenging, but I still looked forward to them because I started to see progress. After each workout Dr. Pierce would quickly give me excellent feedback and advice. Even when an injury cropped up more than halfway through the training regimen and I had to stop running, his cross-training advice and encouragement kept me going until I could resume the long runs, injury-free. After crossing the finish line, I couldn't wait to tell him . . . "Thank you, I did it."

Would I follow his training program again? As we say here in Minnesota, "You betcha"!

Diana Pierce (not related but I wish I was!)
NEWS ANCHOR, KARE-TV
MINNEAPOLIS, MINNESOTA

Q. ***As a novice, can I use any of the rest of this manual?***

A: Yes. Once you complete the Novice running program (Table 3.1) and complete your first 5-K, then you can refer to the paces provided in the tables for the Intermediate program (Table 3.2). After completing the Intermediate training program, you will be ready to use the 5-K training program (Table 4.4) found in Chapter 4.

REAL RUNNER REPORT

I am writing to let you know how much I loved your marathon training program, and I would like to thank everyone responsible for making it available.

I started following your program after reading about it in Runner's World. *I got more details on the program from your Web site and followed the workouts you had for the Greenville Marathon. Despite starting a new job that required a lot of travel, I was able to follow the program fairly closely. Although I certainly was not perfect (especially with cross-training workouts), I was surprised how well I could do my long runs after the short but quick runs earlier in the week.*

On December 4, I completed the new Las Vegas Marathon, hoping that my goal of running a sub-4:00 marathon could really happen. My previous PR was around a 4:35. I was able to finish Las Vegas with a 3:56:33 time. Wow! It's such a huge improvement; I can't believe I really did it. Now I'm starting to think that if I work hard enough and continue this program, maybe I can qualify for Boston someday. I also lost a fair amount of weight (I'm not sure how much, but I had to buy all new pants, a size or two smaller). You can't beat that!

Again, thank you so much for making this program available to everyone on the Web. It works so well, and I've passed the word on to almost everyone I meet who is interested in running marathons.

Karen Kewley
PHARMACEUTICAL SALES
APPLETON, WISCONSIN

SECTION II

How to Follow the FIRST Training Program

Three Quality Runs

THE "3" OF THE *"3PLUS2"* TRAINING PROGRAM

Like many runners, I once ran daily, or at least 6 days per week. My training schedule was based primarily on how many miles I would run on a particular day or how many miles I wanted to run each week. In my mid-thirties, partially to train for triathlons but also out of curiosity and a search for variety, I began adding other kinds of training to my schedule. What happened? I found that my fitness level improved. Why? Because rowing 5000 meters or biking hard for 25 miles or swimming 1500 meters the day after a hard running workout was feasible, mentally and physically, whereas another hard running workout would have been difficult and stressful.

My training partner and coauthor, Scott Murr, and I began designing running workouts with a specific purpose. We quickly discovered that 6 days of running couldn't be maintained. By limiting the number of weekly workouts for each type of training, we kept our training fresh and approached each day's workout with more zest. Every day was something different. This approach led to the development of the formal FIRST training programs.

Most runners who incorporate the three quality runs of FIRST training find that their fitness improves as do their race times. What explains this? Most runners focus on the frequency and duration of their training. Their conversations begin with "How many times did you run?" and end

The Runner Writes:

Dear FIRST:

I am a 43-year-old runner from San Antonio, Texas. You may get many of these e-mails, but I wanted to express my appreciation to you for your marathon training program guide and your helpful Web site. I completed my first marathon in 3:42. I was surprised at my time and, with much harder work, completed my second marathon in 3:32. The Boston Marathon bug hit me, but I was not sure how to make myself run any faster.

I did a benchmark of my 10-K speed and was hitting about 7:40 race pace. Of course, I needed to be slightly under that pace for an entire 26 miles to qualify for Boston. The thought overwhelmed me.

When the article on your program came out in *Runner's World,* it captivated me because of the success stories on improving speed. I also have four children, kids' sports activities, various church responsibilities, work, and the list goes on and on. Your program seemed more manageable than most I'd studied. I officially started following FIRST training program in the 18 weeks leading up to the Houston Marathon in January 2006. I followed the program to the letter and never missed any key running day. I always strived to hit my goal pace.

A month or two into your program, I began to gain speed. Instead of maintaining my original 10-K base pace as my guide, I kept ramping up the pace so that my training runs were eventually based on a PMP (planned marathon pace) of 7:25 per mile. Needless to say, my workouts were pretty intense. However, by the end of November, I was hitting all the goals in the various runs based on a 7:25 PMP. This is probably not the way you guys recommend to follow the program, but I really did want to qualify.

I was never injured and rarely gimpy during the entire training time. The owner of my local running specialty store kept discouraging me from limiting my running to 3 days a week; several folks said my long runs were too long with "How many miles did you log this week?" They neglect the importance of *intensity*—the pace of each workout. Try running at the intense paces designated in the tables provided in this chapter and watch your race times improve.

compared with my tempo runs; and fellow runners said I was not logging enough miles. Despite this feedback, I kept following the FIRST plan.

I'm thrilled to say that I finished the Houston Marathon in 3:18:30 and officially qualified for Boston! This was over 13 minutes faster than my previous PR. My average pace was 7:34 per mile. That is faster than my 10-K race pace at the beginning of your training program.

In addition to following your marathon training program, I have really enjoyed the PowerPoint presentations on your Web site. They are very interesting to those who live too far away to attend your seminars.

Sorry for the long e-mail, but I just wanted you to know that your work made a big impact my life this past weekend.

Thanks!

Scott Senter
Banker
San Antonio, Texas

FIRST Replies:

Scott's intense workouts improved his speed and led to his being able to maintain a faster pace for the marathon than what he could previously maintain for 10-K. It's not surprising that other runners chided him for following a low-mileage, three-runs-per-week marathon training program. The program defies conventional thinking about the necessity of piling on the training miles to prepare for a marathon. This chapter supplies you with the appropriate training paces for your current fitness level that will lead to improvement in your fitness level and future running performances.

In the pages to come, you'll find the nuts-and-bolts for your three quality runs per week, the heart of the **"3plus2"** training program. Following are tables that show you how to determine your pace for each run and training schedules for 5-K, 10-K, half-marathon, and marathon races.

THREE QUALITY RUNS: THE SCIENCE

The concept underlying the FIRST training regimen is that each run be performed with a goal of improving one of the primary physiological processes and running performance variables. FIRST conducted training studies in 2003, 2004, and 2005 to test our ***Training with Purpose*** running philosophy. The training programs are designed to help runners train effectively and efficiently and to avoid overtraining and injury.

Maximal oxygen consumption (max VO_2) is a measure of the ability of an athlete to produce energy aerobically. One might say that maximal oxygen consumption gives a runner an idea of how large an engine he or she has to work with. Normally, a higher max VO_2 indicates that more work can be performed during a given time period. This simply means that an individual with a higher max VO_2 should be able to run faster than a comparable runner with a lower max VO_2. A high maximal capacity to deliver oxygenated blood means there is the potential for more muscles to be active simultaneously during exercise. Values typically range between 40 and 80 milliliters per kilogram per minute in terms relative to body weight. Research has shown max VO_2 to increase as much as 20 percent through a combination of endurance and interval training. Max VO_2 and submaximal exercise capacity are limited by different mechanisms. Max VO_2 appears to be related more to cardiovascular factors such as maximal cardiac output, whereas skeletal muscle metabolic factors including respiratory enzyme activity play more of a role in determining submaximal exercise capacity.

Lactate threshold (LT) is a measure of metabolic fitness. Lactate is an organic by-product of anaerobic metabolism, and its accumulation in the blood is used to evaluate the intensity a runner can maintain for extended periods of time—usually 30 minutes or more. Lactate threshold and maximal steady state lactate levels are indications of how well one's muscles are trained to do endurance-type work. Most people, except for the most highly trained athletes, are limited by metabolic fitness rather than cardiovascular fitness. Highly trained endurance athletes become "centrally limited," meaning they can work at extreme heart rates without severe muscle

THREE QUALITY RUNS: THE ESSENTIALS

TYPE OF TRAINING	KEY RUN #1 TRACK REPEATS	KEY RUN #2 TEMPO RUN	KEY RUN #3 LONG RUN
PURPOSE	Improve max VO_2 running speed and running economy	Improve endurance by raising lactate threshold	Improve endurance by raising aerobic metabolism
INTENSITY	5-K race pace or slightly faster	Comfortably hard; 15–45 sec slower than 5-K race pace	Approximately 30 sec slower than goal marathon pace
DURATION OF EACH RUN	10 min or less	20–45 min at tempo pace	60–180 min
FREQUENCY	Repeat shorter segments until quality work totals about 5-K per session	One tempo run per week	One long run per week

fatigue. An untrained individual might reach LT at about 50 to 60 percent of his or her maximum heart rate, whereas a well-trained runner won't reach lactate threshold until about 80 to 95 percent of his or her maximum heart rate.

Running economy is the amount of oxygen being consumed relative to the runner's body weight and the speed at which the runner is traveling. Unnecessary body motion results in an increase in oxygen consumption and thus a decrease in running economy. Running economy can be expressed either as the velocity achieved for a given rate of oxygen consumption or the VO_2 needed to maintain a given running speed. Running at a given submaximal pace and using less oxygen indicates that a runner is more economical or has improved his or her running economy. This determinant in running performance generally takes the longest period of time for measurable improvements.

Training at the appropriate intensity is generally recognized as the most important factor for improving each of the three elements. For that reason, each workout needs to have the appropriate intensity, or running pace, to stimulate the physiological adaptation needed to improve the particular determinant of running performance.

Key Run Workout #1:
Track Repeats

Warmup

Warm up for 15 to 20 minutes with easy jogging followed by four 100-meter strides. Completion of the strides will make the initial track intervals much easier and reduce the shock of going from an easy warmup jog to a near all-out effort on the repeat intervals. Stay comfortable with the strides and focus on good form. You shouldn't be straining during the strides. Gradually accelerate for 80 meters until you reach approximately 90 percent of full speed, and then decelerate over the final 20 meters. Recover for 30 seconds or less, then repeat in the opposite direction.

In Chapter 13, two Key Drills, "butt kicks" and "high knee lifts," that will help your form and flexibility are described and illustrated on pages 205 and 206. These two Key Drills can be incorporated into your warmup strides. After completing two 100-meter strides, begin the third 100 meters by doing "butt kicks" for 20 meters, and then gradually accelerate for 60 meters and decelerate for 20 meters. Recover for 30 seconds, turn around and do the high knee lifts for 20 meters, and then gradually accelerate for 60 meters and decelerate for 20 meters.

The Track Repeats

The track repeats include running relatively short distances of 400 meters to 2000 meters repeatedly, interspersed with brief recovery intervals. Track repeats are designed to improve maximal oxygen consumption, running economy and speed. Most of these workouts total about 5000 meters of fast running per session. Including warmup and cooldown, Key Run Workout #1 typically totals 6 to 7 miles.

Paces for Key Run Workout #1 are provided in Table 4.1.

Caution: Most runners can run the first few repeats faster than the target time. But the challenge is to run the entire workout at the target time with little or no deviation in time for each repeat. The objective is not to run the repeats as fast as you can; you have two other key runs to perform for the week. Do not sacrifice meeting the target times for the tempo and long runs by running the repeats at an exhausting speed that does not provide sufficient recovery for Key Run Workouts #2 and #3.

FIRST Success

About 2 years ago I read about the FIRST "Less Is More" plan for marathon training in ***Runner's World.*** I did my first marathon (Philadelphia) in 2004 but used a traditional plan and ran a 3:49. I noticed that when my weekly mileage crept above 40 miles, my knees and legs seemed to pay the price, particularly when I ran on back-to-back days.

I trained for the Philadelphia Marathon again in the fall of 2005, using yet another traditional plan that had me running high mileage and about 5 days per week. Again, my legs seemed to break down when I needed to log my greatest mileage. About halfway through the program, I switched to the FIRST program and ran a 3:25 in my second marathon. At this point, I set my goal to run a 3:10 to qualify for the Boston Marathon in April 2007.

I work as a physician with very busy days from about 7:30 a.m. to 7:30 p.m.—it's tough to find the time to log the miles necessary for a fast time—so the 3-days-per-week training program is very appealing to me.

I once again prepared for the Philadelphia Marathon in 2006 using the FIRST program exclusively for 16 weeks. This time I based my target paces off of a 6:35 10-K pace. I think I may have missed two tempo runs and one low-mileage long run due to conflicting work commitments. For the first time, my legs felt completely healthy without the tendinitis or shinsplints that usually accompany my training.

I ran the Philadelphia Marathon in 3:09 and qualified for my first Boston Marathon. Your program helped me cut 40 minutes off my time in 2 years and get me the time I needed to qualify for Boston. I would highly recommend your program to any serious runner, particularly those with busy lives outside of their training or those that breakdown with higher weekly mileage.

Thank you.

John Kosteva, MD
ONCOLOGIST
PHILADELPHIA, PENNSYLVANIA

Table 4.1

KEY RUN WORKOUT #1 (TRACK REPEATS) PACES

Improves running economy, running speed, and max VO_2

5-K RACE TIME	400M PACE	600M PACE	800M PACE	1000M PACE	1200M PACE	1600M PACE	2000M PACE
0:15:00	0:01:02	0:01:36	0:02:09	0:02:43	0:03:19	0:04:34	0:05:47
0:15:10	0:01:03	0:01:37	0:02:10	0:02:45	0:03:22	0:04:37	0:05:51
0:15:20	0:01:04	0:01:38	0:02:12	0:02:47	0:03:24	0:04:40	0:05:55
0:15:30	0:01:05	0:01:39	0:02:14	0:02:49	0:03:26	0:04:43	0:05:59
0:15:40	0:01:06	0:01:40	0:02:15	0:02:51	0:03:29	0:04:47	0:06:03
0:15:50	0:01:06	0:01:42	0:02:17	0:02:53	0:03:31	0:04:50	0:06:07
0:16:00	0:01:07	0:01:43	0:02:18	0:02:55	0:03:34	0:04:53	0:06:11
0:16:10	0:01:08	0:01:44	0:02:20	0:02:57	0:03:36	0:04:56	0:06:15
0:16:20	0:01:09	0:01:45	0:02:22	0:02:59	0:03:39	0:04:59	0:06:19
0:16:30	0:01:10	0:01:46	0:02:23	0:03:01	0:03:41	0:05:03	0:06:23
0:16:40	0:01:10	0:01:48	0:02:25	0:03:03	0:03:43	0:05:06	0:06:27
0:16:50	0:01:11	0:01:49	0:02:27	0:03:05	0:03:46	0:05:09	0:06:31
0:17:00	0:01:12	0:01:50	0:02:28	0:03:07	0:03:48	0:05:12	0:06:35
0:17:10	0:01:13	0:01:51	0:02:30	0:03:09	0:03:51	0:05:16	0:06:39
0:17:20	0:01:14	0:01:53	0:02:31	0:03:11	0:03:53	0:05:19	0:06:43
0:17:30	0:01:14	0:01:54	0:02:33	0:03:13	0:03:55	0:05:22	0:06:47
0:17:40	0:01:15	0:01:55	0:02:35	0:03:15	0:03:58	0:05:25	0:06:51
0:17:50	0:01:16	0:01:56	0:02:36	0:03:17	0:04:00	0:05:28	0:06:55
0:18:00	0:01:17	0:01:57	0:02:38	0:03:19	0:04:03	0:05:32	0:07:00
0:18:10	0:01:18	0:01:59	0:02:39	0:03:21	0:04:05	0:05:35	0:07:04
0:18:20	0:01:19	0:02:00	0:02:41	0:03:23	0:04:08	0:05:38	0:07:08
0:18:30	0:01:19	0:02:01	0:02:43	0:03:25	0:04:10	0:05:41	0:07:12
0:18:40	0:01:20	0:02:02	0:02:44	0:03:27	0:04:12	0:05:44	0:07:16
0:18:50	0:01:21	0:02:03	0:02:46	0:03:29	0:04:15	0:05:48	0:07:20
0:19:00	0:01:22	0:02:05	0:02:47	0:03:31	0:04:17	0:05:51	0:07:24
0:19:10	0:01:23	0:02:06	0:02:49	0:03:33	0:04:20	0:05:54	0:07:28
0:19:20	0:01:23	0:02:07	0:02:51	0:03:35	0:04:22	0:05:57	0:07:32
0:19:30	0:01:24	0:02:08	0:02:52	0:03:37	0:04:24	0:06:01	0:07:36
0:19:40	0:01:25	0:02:09	0:02:54	0:03:39	0:04:27	0:06:04	0:07:40
0:19:50	0:01:26	0:02:11	0:02:56	0:03:41	0:04:29	0:06:07	0:07:44
0:20:00	0:01:27	0:02:12	0:02:57	0:03:43	0:04:32	0:06:10	0:07:48
0:20:10	0:01:27	0:02:13	0:02:59	0:03:45	0:04:34	0:06:13	0:07:52
0:20:20	0:01:28	0:02:14	0:03:00	0:03:47	0:04:36	0:06:17	0:07:56
0:20:30	0:01:29	0:02:15	0:03:02	0:03:49	0:04:39	0:06:20	0:08:00
0:20:40	0:01:30	0:02:17	0:03:04	0:03:51	0:04:41	0:06:23	0:08:04
0:20:50	0:01:31	0:02:18	0:03:05	0:03:53	0:04:44	0:06:26	0:08:08
0:21:00	0:01:31	0:02:19	0:03:07	0:03:55	0:04:46	0:06:30	0:08:12
0:21:10	0:01:32	0:02:20	0:03:08	0:03:57	0:04:49	0:06:33	0:08:16
0:21:20	0:01:33	0:02:21	0:03:10	0:03:59	0:04:51	0:06:36	0:08:20
0:21:30	0:01:34	0:02:23	0:03:12	0:04:01	0:04:53	0:06:39	0:08:24
0:21:40	0:01:35	0:02:24	0:03:13	0:04:04	0:04:56	0:06:42	0:08:28
0:21:50	0:01:35	0:02:25	0:03:15	0:04:06	0:04:58	0:06:46	0:08:32
0:22:00	0:01:36	0:02:26	0:03:16	0:04:08	0:05:01	0:06:49	0:08:36
0:22:10	0:01:37	0:02:28	0:03:18	0:04:10	0:05:03	0:06:52	0:08:40

5-K RACE TIME	400M PACE	600M PACE	800M PACE	1000M PACE	1200M PACE	1600M PACE	2000M PACE
0:22:20	0:01:38	0:02:29	0:03:20	0:04:12	0:05:05	0:06:55	0:08:44
0:22:30	0:01:39	0:02:30	0:03:21	0:04:14	0:05:08	0:06:59	0:08:48
0:22:40	0:01:39	0:02:31	0:03:23	0:04:16	0:05:10	0:07:02	0:08:52
0:22:50	0:01:40	0:02:32	0:03:24	0:04:18	0:05:13	0:07:05	0:08:56
0:23:00	0:01:41	0:02:34	0:03:26	0:04:20	0:05:15	0:07:08	0:09:00
0:23:10	0:01:42	0:02:35	0:03:28	0:04:22	0:05:18	0:07:11	0:09:04
0:23:20	0:01:43	0:02:36	0:03:29	0:04:24	0:05:20	0:07:15	0:09:08
0:23:30	0:01:43	0:02:37	0:03:31	0:04:26	0:05:22	0:07:18	0:09:12
0:23:40	0:01:44	0:02:38	0:03:33	0:04:28	0:05:25	0:07:21	0:09:16
0:23:50	0:01:45	0:02:40	0:03:34	0:04:30	0:05:27	0:07:24	0:09:20
0:24:00	0:01:46	0:02:41	0:03:36	0:04:32	0:05:30	0:07:27	0:09:24
0:24:10	0:01:47	0:02:42	0:03:37	0:04:34	0:05:32	0:07:31	0:09:28
0:24:20	0:01:47	0:02:43	0:03:39	0:04:36	0:05:34	0:07:34	0:09:32
0:24:30	0:01:48	0:02:44	0:03:41	0:04:38	0:05:37	0:07:37	0:09:36
0:24:40	0:01:49	0:02:46	0:03:42	0:04:40	0:05:39	0:07:40	0:09:40
0:24:50	0:01:50	0:02:47	0:03:44	0:04:42	0:05:42	0:07:44	0:09:44
0:25:00	0:01:51	0:02:48	0:03:45	0:04:44	0:05:44	0:07:47	0:09:48
0:25:10	0:01:51	0:02:49	0:03:47	0:04:46	0:05:46	0:07:50	0:09:52
0:25:20	0:01:52	0:02:50	0:03:49	0:04:48	0:05:49	0:07:53	0:09:57
0:25:30	0:01:53	0:02:52	0:03:50	0:04:50	0:05:51	0:07:56	0:10:01
0:25:40	0:01:54	0:02:53	0:03:52	0:04:52	0:05:54	0:08:00	0:10:05
0:25:50	0:01:55	0:02:54	0:03:53	0:04:54	0:05:56	0:08:03	0:10:09
0:26:00	0:01:56	0:02:55	0:03:55	0:04:56	0:05:59	0:08:06	0:10:13
0:26:10	0:01:56	0:02:56	0:03:57	0:04:58	0:06:01	0:08:09	0:10:17
0:26:20	0:01:57	0:02:58	0:03:58	0:05:00	0:06:03	0:08:13	0:10:21
0:26:30	0:01:58	0:02:59	0:04:00	0:05:02	0:06:06	0:08:16	0:10:25
0:26:40	0:01:59	0:03:00	0:04:01	0:05:04	0:06:08	0:08:19	0:10:29
0:26:50	0:02:00	0:03:01	0:04:03	0:05:06	0:06:11	0:08:22	0:10:33
0:27:00	0:02:00	0:03:03	0:04:05	0:05:08	0:06:13	0:08:25	0:10:37
0:27:10	0:02:01	0:03:04	0:04:06	0:05:10	0:06:15	0:08:29	0:10:41
0:27:20	0:02:02	0:03:05	0:04:08	0:05:12	0:06:18	0:08:32	0:10:45
0:27:30	0:02:03	0:03:06	0:04:10	0:05:14	0:06:20	0:08:35	0:10:49
0:27:40	0:02:04	0:03:07	0:04:11	0:05:16	0:06:23	0:08:38	0:10:53
0:27:50	0:02:04	0:03:09	0:04:13	0:05:18	0:06:25	0:08:41	0:10:57
0:28:00	0:02:05	0:03:10	0:04:14	0:05:20	0:06:28	0:08:45	0:11:01
0:28:10	0:02:06	0:03:11	0:04:16	0:05:22	0:06:30	0:08:48	0:11:05
0:28:20	0:02:07	0:03:12	0:04:18	0:05:24	0:06:32	0:08:51	0:11:09
0:28:30	0:02:08	0:03:13	0:04:19	0:05:26	0:06:35	0:08:54	0:11:13
0:28:40	0:02:08	0:03:15	0:04:21	0:05:28	0:06:37	0:08:58	0:11:17
0:28:50	0:02:09	0:03:16	0:04:22	0:05:30	0:06:40	0:09:01	0:11:21
0:29:00	0:02:10	0:03:17	0:04:24	0:05:32	0:06:42	0:09:04	0:11:25
0:29:10	0:02:11	0:03:18	0:04:26	0:05:34	0:06:44	0:09:07	0:11:29
0:29:20	0:02:12	0:03:19	0:04:27	0:05:36	0:06:47	0:09:10	0:11:33
0:29:30	0:02:12	0:03:21	0:04:29	0:05:38	0:06:49	0:09:14	0:11:37
0:29:40	0:02:13	0:03:22	0:04:30	0:05:40	0:06:52	0:09:17	0:11:41
0:29:50	0:02:14	0:03:23	0:04:32	0:05:42	0:06:54	0:09:20	0:11:45
0:30:00	0:02:15	0:03:24	0:04:34	0:05:44	0:06:57	0:09:23	0:11:49

Cooldown

After a challenging workout of repeats on the track, a cooldown is important. Jog slowly for 10 to 15 minutes.

How to Follow the Training Schedule for Key Run Workout #1

Track Repeat Example 1: 6 × 800m w/90 sec RI means to repeat an 800-meter run six times, with a recovery interval of 90 seconds. In between the repeats, you recover by walking/jogging for 90 seconds. After the 90 seconds of recovery, you will start the next (#2 of 6) 800-meter run. You run the 800 meters at the same prescribed pace. The goal of the workout is to keep a small range of times for the 800 meters. For example, rather than a set like 3:00, 2:58, 3:04, 3:08, 3:09, and 3:02, shoot for a more consistent range of times, such as 3:02, 3:01, 3:02, 3:02, 3:03, and 3:02. There shouldn't be more than a couple of seconds' difference in your times for the repeat intervals.

Track Repeat Example 2: 5 × 1-K w/400m RI means five repeat runs of 1000 meters (2.5 times around a 400-meter track) with a 400-meter walk/jog as a recovery between repeat runs. Using your prescribed training pace for 1000 meters found in Table 4.1, try running the first repeat at the target pace. Check your time after finishing the first repeat to make sure you aren't running too fast or too slow. Jog 400 meters at a comfortable pace (for most people, this recovery lap will take 2 to 4 minutes) as your recovery. At the end of the jog recovery, begin the second repeat, concentrating on maintaining the prescribed pace. The time for running the five 1-K repeats should vary no more than a few seconds.

The FIRST training program emphasizes to runners the importance of keeping a very small range of times for the entire workout. The target paces should be realistic and challenging, but not so difficult that you are unable to recover for Key Run Workout #2. Our insistence that the entire set of repeats be run within a range of only a couple of seconds pretty much ensures that you won't overdo it.

Key Run Workout #2:

Tempo Run

Warmup

Tempo runs begin with easy running for 1 to 2 miles prior to the faster tempo phase of the workout. As with the strides on the track, the pace should gradually increase during the easy miles, so that you are close to tempo pace by the end of the warmup.

Tempo Portion

The tempo portion of the workout is typically 3 to 5 miles at 10-K pace or slightly slower. For marathon training, the tempo portion is extended to 8 to 10 miles at planned marathon pace.

Paces for Key Run Workout #2 are provided in Table 4.2.

> **How to Follow the Training Schedule for Key Run Workout #2**
>
> **1 mile warmup, 2 miles @ short tempo pace, and 1 mile cooldown** means to start slowly, and gradually pick up the pace, and after 1 mile, run the next 2 miles at the designated pace based on your 5-K race pace (see Table 4.2). This short-tempo pace is approximately 15 seconds slower than your per-mile 5-K race pace. After the 2-mile steady run, slow down and run an easy cooldown mile. In this example, Key Run Workout #2 is a continuous 4-mile run.

Cooldown

A mile to 10 minutes of easy running is recommended for a cooldown after the tempo phase of the run.

Table 4.2

KEY RUN WORKOUT #2 (TEMPO RUN) PACES (PER MILE)

Improves endurance by raising lactate threshold

5-K TIME	SHORT TEMPO	MID TEMPO	LONG TEMPO	EASY
0:15:00	0:05:07	0:05:22	0:05:37	0:06:42
0:15:05	0:05:08	0:05:23	0:05:38	0:06:43
0:15:10	0:05:10	0:05:25	0:05:40	0:06:45
0:15:15	0:05:11	0:05:26	0:05:41	0:06:46
0:15:20	0:05:13	0:05:28	0:05:43	0:06:48
0:15:25	0:05:15	0:05:30	0:05:45	0:06:50
0:15:30	0:05:16	0:05:31	0:05:46	0:06:51
0:15:35	0:05:18	0:05:33	0:05:48	0:06:53
0:15:40	0:05:20	0:05:35	0:05:50	0:06:55
0:15:45	0:05:21	0:05:36	0:05:51	0:06:56
0:15:50	0:05:23	0:05:38	0:05:53	0:06:58
0:15:55	0:05:24	0:05:39	0:05:54	0:06:59
0:16:00	0:05:26	0:05:41	0:05:56	0:07:01
0:16:05	0:05:28	0:05:43	0:05:58	0:07:03
0:16:10	0:05:29	0:05:44	0:05:59	0:07:04
0:16:15	0:05:31	0:05:46	0:06:01	0:07:06
0:16:20	0:05:32	0:05:47	0:06:02	0:07:07
0:16:25	0:05:34	0:05:49	0:06:04	0:07:09
0:16:30	0:05:36	0:05:51	0:06:06	0:07:11
0:16:35	0:05:37	0:05:52	0:06:07	0:07:12
0:16:40	0:05:39	0:05:54	0:06:09	0:07:14
0:16:45	0:05:40	0:05:55	0:06:10	0:07:15
0:16:50	0:05:42	0:05:57	0:06:12	0:07:17
0:16:55	0:05:44	0:05:59	0:06:14	0:07:19
0:17:00	0:05:45	0:06:00	0:06:15	0:07:20
0:17:05	0:05:47	0:06:02	0:06:17	0:07:22
0:17:10	0:05:49	0:06:04	0:06:19	0:07:24
0:17:15	0:05:50	0:06:05	0:06:20	0:07:25
0:17:20	0:05:52	0:06:07	0:06:22	0:07:27
0:17:25	0:05:53	0:06:08	0:06:23	0:07:28
0:17:30	0:05:55	0:06:10	0:06:25	0:07:30
0:17:35	0:05:57	0:06:12	0:06:27	0:07:32
0:17:40	0:05:58	0:06:13	0:06:28	0:07:33
0:17:45	0:06:00	0:06:15	0:06:30	0:07:35
0:17:50	0:06:01	0:06:16	0:06:31	0:07:36
0:17:55	0:06:03	0:06:18	0:06:33	0:07:38
0:18:00	0:06:05	0:06:20	0:06:35	0:07:40
0:18:05	0:06:06	0:06:21	0:06:36	0:07:41
0:18:10	0:06:08	0:06:23	0:06:38	0:07:43
0:18:15	0:06:09	0:06:24	0:06:39	0:07:44
0:18:20	0:06:11	0:06:26	0:06:41	0:07:46
0:18:25	0:06:13	0:06:28	0:06:43	0:07:48
0:18:30	0:06:14	0:06:29	0:06:44	0:07:49

5-K TIME	SHORT TEMPO	MID TEMPO	LONG TEMPO	EASY
0:18:35	0:06:16	0:06:31	0:06:46	0:07:51
0:18:40	0:06:17	0:06:32	0:06:47	0:07:52
0:18:45	0:06:19	0:06:34	0:06:49	0:07:54
0:18:50	0:06:21	0:06:36	0:06:51	0:07:56
0:18:55	0:06:22	0:06:37	0:06:52	0:07:57
0:19:00	0:06:24	0:06:39	0:06:54	0:07:59
0:19:05	0:06:26	0:06:41	0:06:56	0:08:01
0:19:10	0:06:27	0:06:42	0:06:57	0:08:02
0:19:15	0:06:29	0:06:44	0:06:59	0:08:04
0:19:20	0:06:30	0:06:45	0:07:00	0:08:05
0:19:25	0:06:32	0:06:47	0:07:02	0:08:07
0:19:30	0:06:34	0:06:49	0:07:04	0:08:09
0:19:35	0:06:35	0:06:50	0:07:05	0:08:10
0:19:40	0:06:37	0:06:52	0:07:07	0:08:12
0:19:45	0:06:38	0:06:53	0:07:08	0:08:13
0:19:50	0:06:40	0:06:55	0:07:10	0:08:15
0:19:55	0:06:42	0:06:57	0:07:12	0:08:17
0:20:00	0:06:43	0:06:58	0:07:13	0:08:18
0:20:05	0:06:45	0:07:00	0:07:15	0:08:20
0:20:10	0:06:46	0:07:01	0:07:16	0:08:21
0:20:15	0:06:48	0:07:03	0:07:18	0:08:23
0:20:20	0:06:50	0:07:05	0:07:20	0:08:25
0:20:25	0:06:51	0:07:06	0:07:21	0:08:26
0:20:30	0:06:53	0:07:08	0:07:23	0:08:28
0:20:35	0:06:54	0:07:09	0:07:24	0:08:29
0:20:40	0:06:56	0:07:11	0:07:26	0:08:31
0:20:45	0:06:58	0:07:13	0:07:28	0:08:33
0:20:50	0:06:59	0:07:14	0:07:29	0:08:34
0:20:55	0:07:01	0:07:16	0:07:31	0:08:36
0:21:00	0:07:03	0:07:18	0:07:33	0:08:38
0:21:05	0:07:04	0:07:19	0:07:34	0:08:39
0:21:10	0:07:06	0:07:21	0:07:36	0:08:41
0:21:15	0:07:07	0:07:22	0:07:37	0:08:42
0:21:20	0:07:09	0:07:24	0:07:39	0:08:44
0:21:25	0:07:11	0:07:26	0:07:41	0:08:46
0:21:30	0:07:12	0:07:27	0:07:42	0:08:47
0:21:35	0:07:14	0:07:29	0:07:44	0:08:49
0:21:40	0:07:15	0:07:30	0:07:45	0:08:50
0:21:45	0:07:17	0:07:32	0:07:47	0:08:52
0:21:50	0:07:19	0:07:34	0:07:49	0:08:54
0:21:55	0:07:20	0:07:35	0:07:50	0:08:55
0:22:00	0:07:22	0:07:37	0:07:52	0:08:57
0:22:05	0:07:23	0:07:38	0:07:53	0:08:58
0:22:10	0:07:25	0:07:40	0:07:55	0:09:00
0:22:15	0:07:27	0:07:42	0:07:57	0:09:02
0:22:20	0:07:28	0:07:43	0:07:58	0:09:03
0:22:25	0:07:30	0:07:45	0:08:00	0:09:05

Table 4.2 *(continued)*

KEY RUN WORKOUT #2 (TEMPO RUN) PACES (PER MILE)

5-K TIME	SHORT TEMPO	MID TEMPO	LONG TEMPO	EASY
0:22:30	0:07:32	0:07:47	0:08:02	0:09:07
0:22:35	0:07:33	0:07:48	0:08:03	0:09:08
0:22:40	0:07:35	0:07:50	0:08:05	0:09:10
0:22:45	0:07:36	0:07:51	0:08:06	0:09:11
0:22:50	0:07:38	0:07:53	0:08:08	0:09:13
0:22:55	0:07:40	0:07:55	0:08:10	0:09:15
0:23:00	0:07:41	0:07:56	0:08:11	0:09:16
0:23:05	0:07:43	0:07:58	0:08:13	0:09:18
0:23:10	0:07:44	0:07:59	0:08:14	0:09:19
0:23:15	0:07:46	0:08:01	0:08:16	0:09:21
0:23:20	0:07:48	0:08:03	0:08:18	0:09:23
0:23:25	0:07:49	0:08:04	0:08:19	0:09:24
0:23:30	0:07:51	0:08:06	0:08:21	0:09:26
0:23:35	0:07:52	0:08:07	0:08:22	0:09:27
0:23:40	0:07:54	0:08:09	0:08:24	0:09:29
0:23:45	0:07:56	0:08:11	0:08:26	0:09:31
0:23:50	0:07:57	0:08:12	0:08:27	0:09:32
0:23:55	0:07:59	0:08:14	0:08:29	0:09:34
0:24:00	0:08:00	0:08:15	0:08:30	0:09:35
0:24:05	0:08:02	0:08:17	0:08:32	0:09:37
0:24:10	0:08:04	0:08:19	0:08:34	0:09:39
0:24:15	0:08:05	0:08:20	0:08:35	0:09:40
0:24:20	0:08:07	0:08:22	0:08:37	0:09:42
0:24:25	0:08:09	0:08:24	0:08:39	0:09:44
0:24:30	0:08:10	0:08:25	0:08:40	0:09:45
0:24:35	0:08:12	0:08:27	0:08:42	0:09:47
0:24:40	0:08:13	0:08:28	0:08:43	0:09:48
0:24:45	0:08:15	0:08:30	0:08:45	0:09:50
0:24:50	0:08:17	0:08:32	0:08:47	0:09:52
0:24:55	0:08:18	0:08:33	0:08:48	0:09:53
0:25:00	0:08:20	0:08:35	0:08:50	0:09:55
0:25:05	0:08:21	0:08:36	0:08:51	0:09:56
0:25:10	0:08:23	0:08:38	0:08:53	0:09:58
0:25:15	0:08:25	0:08:40	0:08:55	0:10:00
0:25:20	0:08:26	0:08:41	0:08:56	0:10:01
0:25:25	0:08:28	0:08:43	0:08:58	0:10:03
0:25:30	0:08:29	0:08:44	0:08:59	0:10:04
0:25:35	0:08:31	0:08:46	0:09:01	0:10:06
0:25:40	0:08:33	0:08:48	0:09:03	0:10:08
0:25:45	0:08:34	0:08:49	0:09:04	0:10:09
0:25:50	0:08:36	0:08:51	0:09:06	0:10:11
0:25:55	0:08:37	0:08:52	0:09:07	0:10:12
0:26:00	0:08:39	0:08:54	0:09:09	0:10:14
0:26:05	0:08:41	0:08:56	0:09:11	0:10:16
0:26:10	0:08:42	0:08:57	0:09:12	0:10:17

5-K TIME	SHORT TEMPO	MID TEMPO	LONG TEMPO	EASY
0:26:15	0:08:44	0:08:59	0:09:14	0:10:19
0:26:20	0:08:46	0:09:01	0:09:16	0:10:21
0:26:25	0:08:47	0:09:02	0:09:17	0:10:22
0:26:30	0:08:49	0:09:04	0:09:19	0:10:24
0:26:35	0:08:50	0:09:05	0:09:20	0:10:25
0:26:40	0:08:52	0:09:07	0:09:22	0:10:27
0:26:45	0:08:54	0:09:09	0:09:24	0:10:29
0:26:50	0:08:55	0:09:10	0:09:25	0:10:30
0:26:55	0:08:57	0:09:12	0:09:27	0:10:32
0:27:00	0:08:58	0:09:13	0:09:28	0:10:33
0:27:05	0:09:00	0:09:15	0:09:30	0:10:35
0:27:10	0:09:02	0:09:17	0:09:32	0:10:37
0:27:15	0:09:03	0:09:18	0:09:33	0:10:38
0:27:20	0:09:05	0:09:20	0:09:35	0:10:40
0:27:25	0:09:06	0:09:21	0:09:36	0:10:41
0:27:30	0:09:08	0:09:23	0:09:38	0:10:43
0:27:35	0:09:10	0:09:25	0:09:40	0:10:45
0:27:40	0:09:11	0:09:26	0:09:41	0:10:46
0:27:45	0:09:13	0:09:28	0:09:43	0:10:48
0:27:50	0:09:14	0:09:29	0:09:44	0:10:49
0:27:55	0:09:16	0:09:31	0:09:46	0:10:51
0:28:00	0:09:18	0:09:33	0:09:48	0:10:53
0:28:05	0:09:19	0:09:34	0:09:49	0:10:54
0:28:10	0:09:21	0:09:36	0:09:51	0:10:56
0:28:15	0:09:23	0:09:38	0:09:53	0:10:58
0:28:20	0:09:24	0:09:39	0:09:54	0:10:59
0:28:25	0:09:26	0:09:41	0:09:56	0:11:01
0:28:30	0:09:27	0:09:42	0:09:57	0:11:02
0:28:35	0:09:29	0:09:44	0:09:59	0:11:04
0:28:40	0:09:31	0:09:46	0:10:01	0:11:06
0:28:45	0:09:32	0:09:47	0:10:02	0:11:07
0:28:50	0:09:34	0:09:49	0:10:04	0:11:09
0:28:55	0:09:35	0:09:50	0:10:05	0:11:10
0:29:00	0:09:37	0:09:52	0:10:07	0:11:12
0:29:05	0:09:39	0:09:54	0:10:09	0:11:14
0:29:10	0:09:40	0:09:55	0:10:10	0:11:15
0:29:15	0:09:42	0:09:57	0:10:12	0:11:17
0:29:20	0:09:43	0:09:58	0:10:13	0:11:18
0:29:25	0:09:45	0:10:00	0:10:15	0:11:20
0:29:30	0:09:47	0:10:02	0:10:17	0:11:22
0:29:35	0:09:48	0:10:03	0:10:18	0:11:23
0:29:40	0:09:50	0:10:05	0:10:20	0:11:25
0:29:45	0:09:52	0:10:07	0:10:22	0:11:27
0:29:50	0:09:53	0:10:08	0:10:23	0:11:28
0:29:55	0:09:55	0:10:10	0:10:25	0:11:30
0:30:00	0:09:56	0:10:11	0:10:26	0:11:31

A metric version of this table is available at www.furmanfirst.com

Key Run Workout #3: Long Run

Warmup

While there is not a specific warmup for your long run, the early miles of the long run can serve as their own warmup. The recommended long run pace need not be achieved during the first couple of miles.

Long Run

The long run (relative to your goals and your present training mileage) requires steady running from 6 to 20 miles at a pace equal to one's 5-K pace plus 75 to 90 seconds, or 15 to 30 seconds slower than planned marathon pace.

Try starting your training runs a bit slower than the prescribed pace, and then pick up the pace in the middle section of your training run. Try to have a strong finish over the last couple of miles of your long training runs. Faster than recommended pace running during the middle phase of the long run can offset the earlier slower pace, so you can meet the average targeted pace for the entire run.

Paces for Key Run Workout #3 are provided in Table 4.3.

How to Follow the Training Schedule for Key Run Workout #3

15 miles @ MP + 20 sec/mile means to run 15 miles at 20 seconds per mile slower than planned marathon pace. For a runner with a target marathon time of 3:10 or 7:15-per-mile pace, this long run might begin with a 7:55 mile followed by a 7:45 mile, before settling into a 7:35-per-mile pace. After 5 miles of running at a 7:35-per-mile pace, he may want to try the next 3 to 4 miles at 7:25 to 7:30 pace before running the last few miles at 7:35 per mile. Or he may want to hold the 7:35-per-mile pace up through 12 miles and then try to run the last 3 miles faster than 7:35-per-mile pace. You can alternate strategies from one long training run to the next.

Cooldown

Ten minutes of easy walking after a long run serves as a good cooldown. Drinking a sports drink or recovery drink during these 10 minutes will aid your recovery (see Chapter 9 for more on hydration). Stretching later in the day will also help (see Chapter 13).

FIRST TRAINING PACES

FIRST has developed training paces for the Key Run Workouts based on current 5-K race performance. To find the appropriate training pace for a specific distance, refer to the "FIRST Training Paces" tables (Tables 4.1 to 4.3). If you have not run a 5-K recently, you can use Table 2.1 ("Race Prediction Table") to determine comparable performance times for four popular racing distances. The comparability assumes that you are properly trained for that distance.

Each workout specifies the distances to be run and the pace at which they are to be run.

Using Table 2.1: An Example

Let's say that you don't have a recent 5-K time but you do have a recent half-marathon time of 1:55 (8:46-per-mile pace). You would go to Table 2.1 and determine that 24:50 would be a comparable 5-K time. You could then use the time of 24:50 (8:00-per-mile pace) to determine your training paces for the three Key Run Workouts (see Tables 4.1 to 4.3).

Detailed Training Schedules for Four Popular Race Distances

The FIRST's "**3plus2**" training programs for 5-K, 10-K, half-marathon, and marathon distances follow in Tables 4.4 through 4.7, beginning on page 82.

For the four training programs, use your 5-K race pace to select your target training pace for Key Run Workouts #1, #2, and #3 from Tables 4.1 through 4.3. If you don't have a 5-K race finish time, but you have a race finish time from a 10-K, half-marathon, or marathon, use Table 2.1 to predict your 5-K race finish time. That predicted time can be used with Tables 4.1 to 4.3 to determine your target training paces.

If you don't have any race finish times to use for predicting your 5-K race finish time, go to a 400-meter track and run 3 × 1600 meters (4 laps

(continued on page 80)

Table 4.3
KEY RUN WORKOUT #3 (LONG RUN) PACES (PER MILE)
Improves endurance by raising aerobic metabolism

5-K	LONG TEMPO	MP	MP+10	MP+15	MP+20
0:15:00	0:05:37	0:05:33	0:05:43	0:05:48	0:05:53
0:15:05	0:05:38	0:05:35	0:05:45	0:05:50	0:05:55
0:15:10	0:05:40	0:05:36	0:05:46	0:05:51	0:05:56
0:15:15	0:05:41	0:05:37	0:05:47	0:05:52	0:05:57
0:15:20	0:05:43	0:05:38	0:05:48	0:05:53	0:05:58
0:15:25	0:05:45	0:05:40	0:05:50	0:05:55	0:06:00
0:15:30	0:05:46	0:05:41	0:05:51	0:05:56	0:06:01
0:15:35	0:05:48	0:05:42	0:05:52	0:05:57	0:06:02
0:15:40	0:05:50	0:05:43	0:05:53	0:05:58	0:06:03
0:15:45	0:05:51	0:05:45	0:05:55	0:06:00	0:06:05
0:15:50	0:05:53	0:05:47	0:05:57	0:06:02	0:06:07
0:15:55	0:05:54	0:05:50	0:06:00	0:06:05	0:06:10
0:16:00	0:05:56	0:05:52	0:06:02	0:06:07	0:06:12
0:16:05	0:05:58	0:05:54	0:06:04	0:06:09	0:06:14
0:16:10	0:05:59	0:05:57	0:06:07	0:06:12	0:06:17
0:16:15	0:06:01	0:05:59	0:06:09	0:06:14	0:06:19
0:16:20	0:06:02	0:06:01	0:06:11	0:06:16	0:06:21
0:16:25	0:06:04	0:06:03	0:06:13	0:06:18	0:06:23
0:16:30	0:06:06	0:06:06	0:06:16	0:06:21	0:06:26
0:16:35	0:06:07	0:06:08	0:06:18	0:06:23	0:06:28
0:16:40	0:06:09	0:06:11	0:06:21	0:06:26	0:06:31
0:16:45	0:06:10	0:06:13	0:06:23	0:06:28	0:06:33
0:16:50	0:06:12	0:06:15	0:06:25	0:06:30	0:06:35
0:16:55	0:06:14	0:06:18	0:06:28	0:06:33	0:06:38
0:17:00	0:06:15	0:06:19	0:06:29	0:06:34	0:06:39
0:17:05	0:06:17	0:06:21	0:06:31	0:06:36	0:06:41
0:17:10	0:06:19	0:06:23	0:06:33	0:06:38	0:06:43
0:17:15	0:06:20	0:06:25	0:06:35	0:06:40	0:06:45
0:17:20	0:06:22	0:06:27	0:06:37	0:06:42	0:06:47
0:17:25	0:06:23	0:06:29	0:06:39	0:06:44	0:06:49
0:17:30	0:06:25	0:06:30	0:06:40	0:06:45	0:06:50
0:17:35	0:06:27	0:06:32	0:06:42	0:06:47	0:06:52
0:17:40	0:06:28	0:06:34	0:06:44	0:06:49	0:06:54
0:17:45	0:06:30	0:06:36	0:06:46	0:06:51	0:06:56
0:17:50	0:06:31	0:06:38	0:06:48	0:06:53	0:06:58
0:17:55	0:06:33	0:06:39	0:06:49	0:06:54	0:06:59
0:18:00	0:06:35	0:06:41	0:06:51	0:06:56	0:07:01
0:18:05	0:06:36	0:06:43	0:06:53	0:06:58	0:07:03
0:18:10	0:06:38	0:06:45	0:06:55	0:07:00	0:07:05

MP+30	MP+45	MP+60	HMP	HMP+20	HMP+30
0:06:03	0:06:18	0:06:33	0:05:13	0:05:33	0:05:43
0:06:05	0:06:20	0:06:35	0:05:15	0:05:35	0:05:45
0:06:06	0:06:21	0:06:36	0:05:16	0:05:36	0:05:46
0:06:07	0:06:22	0:06:37	0:05:17	0:05:37	0:05:47
0:06:08	0:06:23	0:06:38	0:05:18	0:05:38	0:05:48
0:06:10	0:06:25	0:06:40	0:05:20	0:05:40	0:05:50
0:06:11	0:06:26	0:06:41	0:05:21	0:05:41	0:05:51
0:06:12	0:06:27	0:06:42	0:05:22	0:05:42	0:05:52
0:06:13	0:06:28	0:06:43	0:05:23	0:05:43	0:05:53
0:06:15	0:06:30	0:06:45	0:05:25	0:05:45	0:05:55
0:06:17	0:06:32	0:06:47	0:05:27	0:05:47	0:05:57
0:06:20	0:06:35	0:06:50	0:05:30	0:05:50	0:06:00
0:06:22	0:06:37	0:06:52	0:05:32	0:05:52	0:06:02
0:06:24	0:06:39	0:06:54	0:05:34	0:05:54	0:06:04
0:06:27	0:06:42	0:06:57	0:05:37	0:05:57	0:06:07
0:06:29	0:06:44	0:06:59	0:05:39	0:05:59	0:06:09
0:06:31	0:06:46	0:07:01	0:05:41	0:06:01	0:06:11
0:06:33	0:06:48	0:07:03	0:05:43	0:06:03	0:06:13
0:06:36	0:06:51	0:07:06	0:05:46	0:06:06	0:06:16
0:06:38	0:06:53	0:07:08	0:05:48	0:06:08	0:06:18
0:06:41	0:06:56	0:07:11	0:05:51	0:06:11	0:06:21
0:06:43	0:06:58	0:07:13	0:05:53	0:06:13	0:06:23
0:06:45	0:07:00	0:07:15	0:05:55	0:06:15	0:06:25
0:06:48	0:07:03	0:07:18	0:05:58	0:06:18	0:06:28
0:06:49	0:07:04	0:07:19	0:05:59	0:06:19	0:06:29
0:06:51	0:07:06	0:07:21	0:06:01	0:06:21	0:06:31
0:06:53	0:07:08	0:07:23	0:06:03	0:06:23	0:06:33
0:06:55	0:07:10	0:07:25	0:06:05	0:06:25	0:06:35
0:06:57	0:07:12	0:07:27	0:06:07	0:06:27	0:06:37
0:06:59	0:07:14	0:07:29	0:06:09	0:06:29	0:06:39
0:07:00	0:07:15	0:07:30	0:06:10	0:06:30	0:06:40
0:07:02	0:07:17	0:07:32	0:06:12	0:06:32	0:06:42
0:07:04	0:07:19	0:07:34	0:06:14	0:06:34	0:06:44
0:07:06	0:07:21	0:07:36	0:06:16	0:06:36	0:06:46
0:07:08	0:07:23	0:07:38	0:06:18	0:06:38	0:06:48
0:07:09	0:07:24	0:07:39	0:06:19	0:06:39	0:06:49
0:07:11	0:07:26	0:07:41	0:06:21	0:06:41	0:06:51
0:07:13	0:07:28	0:07:43	0:06:23	0:06:43	0:06:53
0:07:15	0:07:30	0:07:45	0:06:25	0:06:45	0:06:55

MP = marathon pace; HMP = half-marathon pace

Table 4.3 *(continued)*

KEY RUN WORKOUT #3 (LONG RUN) PACES (PER MILE)

5-K	LONG TEMPO	MP	MP+10	MP+15	MP+20
0:18:15	0:06:39	0:06:47	0:06:57	0:07:02	0:07:07
0:18:20	0:06:41	0:06:49	0:06:59	0:07:04	0:07:09
0:18:25	0:06:43	0:06:51	0:07:01	0:07:06	0:07:11
0:18:30	0:06:44	0:06:52	0:07:02	0:07:07	0:07:12
0:18:35	0:06:46	0:06:54	0:07:04	0:07:09	0:07:14
0:18:40	0:06:47	0:06:56	0:07:06	0:07:11	0:07:16
0:18:45	0:06:49	0:06:58	0:07:08	0:07:13	0:07:18
0:18:50	0:06:51	0:07:00	0:07:10	0:07:15	0:07:20
0:18:55	0:06:52	0:07:02	0:07:12	0:07:17	0:07:22
0:19:00	0:06:54	0:07:04	0:07:14	0:07:19	0:07:24
0:19:05	0:06:56	0:07:06	0:07:16	0:07:21	0:07:26
0:19:10	0:06:57	0:07:08	0:07:18	0:07:23	0:07:28
0:19:15	0:06:59	0:07:10	0:07:20	0:07:25	0:07:30
0:19:20	0:07:00	0:07:11	0:07:21	0:07:26	0:07:31
0:19:25	0:07:02	0:07:13	0:07:23	0:07:28	0:07:33
0:19:30	0:07:04	0:07:15	0:07:25	0:07:30	0:07:35
0:19:35	0:07:05	0:07:16	0:07:26	0:07:31	0:07:36
0:19:40	0:07:07	0:07:18	0:07:28	0:07:33	0:07:38
0:19:45	0:07:08	0:07:19	0:07:29	0:07:34	0:07:39
0:19:50	0:07:10	0:07:21	0:07:31	0:07:36	0:07:41
0:19:55	0:07:12	0:07:23	0:07:33	0:07:38	0:07:43
0:20:00	0:07:13	0:07:24	0:07:34	0:07:39	0:07:44
0:20:05	0:07:15	0:07:26	0:07:36	0:07:41	0:07:46
0:20:10	0:07:16	0:07:28	0:07:38	0:07:43	0:07:48
0:20:15	0:07:18	0:07:30	0:07:40	0:07:45	0:07:50
0:20:20	0:07:20	0:07:32	0:07:42	0:07:47	0:07:52
0:20:25	0:07:21	0:07:34	0:07:44	0:07:49	0:07:54
0:20:30	0:07:23	0:07:36	0:07:46	0:07:51	0:07:56
0:20:35	0:07:24	0:07:38	0:07:48	0:07:53	0:07:58
0:20:40	0:07:26	0:07:40	0:07:50	0:07:55	0:08:00
0:20:45	0:07:28	0:07:42	0:07:52	0:07:57	0:08:02
0:20:50	0:07:29	0:07:44	0:07:54	0:07:59	0:08:04
0:20:55	0:07:31	0:07:46	0:07:56	0:08:01	0:08:06
0:21:00	0:07:33	0:07:47	0:07:57	0:08:02	0:08:07
0:21:05	0:07:34	0:07:49	0:07:59	0:08:04	0:08:09
0:21:10	0:07:36	0:07:51	0:08:01	0:08:06	0:08:11
0:21:15	0:07:37	0:07:53	0:08:03	0:08:08	0:08:13
0:21:20	0:07:39	0:07:55	0:08:05	0:08:10	0:08:15
0:21:25	0:07:41	0:07:57	0:08:07	0:08:12	0:08:17
0:21:30	0:07:42	0:07:58	0:08:08	0:08:13	0:08:18

MP+30	MP+45	MP+60	HMP	HMP+20	HMP+30
0:07:17	0:07:32	0:07:47	0:06:27	0:06:47	0:06:57
0:07:19	0:07:34	0:07:49	0:06:29	0:06:49	0:06:59
0:07:21	0:07:36	0:07:51	0:06:31	0:06:51	0:07:01
0:07:22	0:07:37	0:07:52	0:06:32	0:06:52	0:07:02
0:07:24	0:07:39	0:07:54	0:06:34	0:06:54	0:07:04
0:07:26	0:07:41	0:07:56	0:06:36	0:06:56	0:07:06
0:07:28	0:07:43	0:07:58	0:06:38	0:06:58	0:07:08
0:07:30	0:07:45	0:08:00	0:06:40	0:07:00	0:07:10
0:07:32	0:07:47	0:08:02	0:06:42	0:07:02	0:07:12
0:07:34	0:07:49	0:08:04	0:06:44	0:07:04	0:07:14
0:07:36	0:07:51	0:08:06	0:06:46	0:07:06	0:07:16
0:07:38	0:07:53	0:08:08	0:06:48	0:07:08	0:07:18
0:07:40	0:07:55	0:08:10	0:06:50	0:07:10	0:07:20
0:07:41	0:07:56	0:08:11	0:06:51	0:07:11	0:07:21
0:07:43	0:07:58	0:08:13	0:06:53	0:07:13	0:07:23
0:07:45	0:08:00	0:08:15	0:06:55	0:07:15	0:07:25
0:07:46	0:08:01	0:08:16	0:06:56	0:07:16	0:07:26
0:07:48	0:08:03	0:08:18	0:06:58	0:07:18	0:07:28
0:07:49	0:08:04	0:08:19	0:06:59	0:07:19	0:07:29
0:07:51	0:08:06	0:08:21	0:07:01	0:07:21	0:07:31
0:07:53	0:08:08	0:08:23	0:07:03	0:07:23	0:07:33
0:07:54	0:08:09	0:08:24	0:07:04	0:07:24	0:07:34
0:07:56	0:08:11	0:08:26	0:07:06	0:07:26	0:07:36
0:07:58	0:08:13	0:08:28	0:07:08	0:07:28	0:07:38
0:08:00	0:08:15	0:08:30	0:07:10	0:07:30	0:07:40
0:08:02	0:08:17	0:08:32	0:07:12	0:07:32	0:07:42
0:08:04	0:08:19	0:08:34	0:07:14	0:07:34	0:07:44
0:08:06	0:08:21	0:08:36	0:07:16	0:07:36	0:07:46
0:08:08	0:08:23	0:08:38	0:07:18	0:07:38	0:07:48
0:08:10	0:08:25	0:08:40	0:07:20	0:07:40	0:07:50
0:08:12	0:08:27	0:08:42	0:07:22	0:07:42	0:07:52
0:08:14	0:08:29	0:08:44	0:07:24	0:07:44	0:07:54
0:08:16	0:08:31	0:08:46	0:07:26	0:07:46	0:07:56
0:08:17	0:08:32	0:08:47	0:07:27	0:07:47	0:07:57
0:08:19	0:08:34	0:08:49	0:07:29	0:07:49	0:07:59
0:08:21	0:08:36	0:08:51	0:07:31	0:07:51	0:08:01
0:08:23	0:08:38	0:08:53	0:07:33	0:07:53	0:08:03
0:08:25	0:08:40	0:08:55	0:07:35	0:07:55	0:08:05
0:08:27	0:08:42	0:08:57	0:07:37	0:07:57	0:08:07
0:08:28	0:08:43	0:08:58	0:07:38	0:07:58	0:08:08

Table 4.3 *(continued)*

KEY RUN WORKOUT #3 (LONG RUN) PACES (PER MILE)

5-K	LONG TEMPO	MP	MP+10	MP+15	MP+20
0:21:35	0:07:44	0:08:00	0:08:10	0:08:15	0:08:20
0:21:40	0:07:45	0:08:02	0:08:12	0:08:17	0:08:22
0:21:45	0:07:47	0:08:04	0:08:14	0:08:19	0:08:24
0:21:50	0:07:49	0:08:06	0:08:16	0:08:21	0:08:26
0:21:55	0:07:50	0:08:08	0:08:18	0:08:23	0:08:28
0:22:00	0:07:52	0:08:10	0:08:20	0:08:25	0:08:30
0:22:05	0:07:53	0:08:12	0:08:22	0:08:27	0:08:32
0:22:10	0:07:55	0:08:14	0:08:24	0:08:29	0:08:34
0:22:15	0:07:57	0:08:16	0:08:26	0:08:31	0:08:36
0:22:20	0:07:58	0:08:18	0:08:28	0:08:33	0:08:38
0:22:25	0:08:00	0:08:20	0:08:30	0:08:35	0:08:40
0:22:30	0:08:02	0:08:22	0:08:32	0:08:37	0:08:42
0:22:35	0:08:03	0:08:24	0:08:34	0:08:39	0:08:44
0:22:40	0:08:05	0:08:25	0:08:35	0:08:40	0:08:45
0:22:45	0:08:06	0:08:27	0:08:37	0:08:42	0:08:47
0:22:50	0:08:08	0:08:29	0:08:39	0:08:44	0:08:49
0:22:55	0:08:10	0:08:31	0:08:41	0:08:46	0:08:51
0:23:00	0:08:11	0:08:33	0:08:43	0:08:48	0:08:53
0:23:05	0:08:13	0:08:35	0:08:45	0:08:50	0:08:55
0:23:10	0:08:14	0:08:36	0:08:46	0:08:51	0:08:56
0:23:15	0:08:16	0:08:38	0:08:48	0:08:53	0:08:58
0:23:20	0:08:18	0:08:40	0:08:50	0:08:55	0:09:00
0:23:25	0:08:19	0:08:42	0:08:52	0:08:57	0:09:02
0:23:30	0:08:21	0:08:43	0:08:53	0:08:58	0:09:03
0:23:35	0:08:22	0:08:45	0:08:55	0:09:00	0:09:05
0:23:40	0:08:24	0:08:46	0:08:56	0:09:01	0:09:06
0:23:45	0:08:26	0:08:47	0:08:57	0:09:02	0:09:07
0:23:50	0:08:27	0:08:49	0:08:59	0:09:04	0:09:09
0:23:55	0:08:29	0:08:51	0:09:01	0:09:06	0:09:11
0:24:00	0:08:30	0:08:53	0:09:03	0:09:08	0:09:13
0:24:05	0:08:32	0:08:55	0:09:05	0:09:10	0:09:15
0:24:10	0:08:34	0:08:57	0:09:07	0:09:12	0:09:17
0:24:15	0:08:35	0:08:59	0:09:09	0:09:14	0:09:19
0:24:20	0:08:37	0:09:01	0:09:11	0:09:16	0:09:21
0:24:25	0:08:39	0:09:03	0:09:13	0:09:18	0:09:23
0:24:30	0:08:40	0:09:05	0:09:15	0:09:20	0:09:25
0:24:35	0:08:42	0:09:07	0:09:17	0:09:22	0:09:27
0:24:40	0:08:43	0:09:09	0:09:19	0:09:24	0:09:29
0:24:45	0:08:45	0:09:11	0:09:21	0:09:26	0:09:31
0:24:50	0:08:47	0:09:13	0:09:23	0:09:28	0:09:33

MP+30	MP+45	MP+60	HMP	HMP+20	HMP+30
0:08:30	0:08:45	0:09:00	0:07:40	0:08:00	0:08:10
0:08:32	0:08:47	0:09:02	0:07:42	0:08:02	0:08:12
0:08:34	0:08:49	0:09:04	0:07:44	0:08:04	0:08:14
0:08:36	0:08:51	0:09:06	0:07:46	0:08:06	0:08:16
0:08:38	0:08:53	0:09:08	0:07:48	0:08:08	0:08:18
0:08:40	0:08:55	0:09:10	0:07:50	0:08:10	0:08:20
0:08:42	0:08:57	0:09:12	0:07:52	0:08:12	0:08:22
0:08:44	0:08:59	0:09:14	0:07:54	0:08:14	0:08:24
0:08:46	0:09:01	0:09:16	0:07:56	0:08:16	0:08:26
0:08:48	0:09:03	0:09:18	0:07:58	0:08:18	0:08:28
0:08:50	0:09:05	0:09:20	0:08:00	0:08:20	0:08:30
0:08:52	0:09:07	0:09:22	0:08:02	0:08:22	0:08:32
0:08:54	0:09:09	0:09:24	0:08:04	0:08:24	0:08:34
0:08:55	0:09:10	0:09:25	0:08:05	0:08:25	0:08:35
0:08:57	0:09:12	0:09:27	0:08:07	0:08:27	0:08:37
0:08:59	0:09:14	0:09:29	0:08:09	0:08:29	0:08:39
0:09:01	0:09:16	0:09:31	0:08:11	0:08:31	0:08:41
0:09:03	0:09:18	0:09:33	0:08:13	0:08:33	0:08:43
0:09:05	0:09:20	0:09:35	0:08:15	0:08:35	0:08:45
0:09:06	0:09:21	0:09:36	0:08:16	0:08:36	0:08:46
0:09:08	0:09:23	0:09:38	0:08:18	0:08:38	0:08:48
0:09:10	0:09:25	0:09:40	0:08:20	0:08:40	0:08:50
0:09:12	0:09:27	0:09:42	0:08:22	0:08:42	0:08:52
0:09:13	0:09:28	0:09:43	0:08:23	0:08:43	0:08:53
0:09:15	0:09:30	0:09:45	0:08:25	0:08:45	0:08:55
0:09:16	0:09:31	0:09:46	0:08:26	0:08:46	0:08:56
0:09:17	0:09:32	0:09:47	0:08:27	0:08:47	0:08:57
0:09:19	0:09:34	0:09:49	0:08:29	0:08:49	0:08:59
0:09:21	0:09:36	0:09:51	0:08:31	0:08:51	0:09:01
0:09:23	0:09:38	0:09:53	0:08:33	0:08:53	0:09:03
0:09:25	0:09:40	0:09:55	0:08:35	0:08:55	0:09:05
0:09:27	0:09:42	0:09:57	0:08:37	0:08:57	0:09:07
0:09:29	0:09:44	0:09:59	0:08:39	0:08:59	0:09:09
0:09:31	0:09:46	0:10:01	0:08:41	0:09:01	0:09:11
0:09:33	0:09:48	0:10:03	0:08:43	0:09:03	0:09:13
0:09:35	0:09:50	0:10:05	0:08:45	0:09:05	0:09:15
0:09:37	0:09:52	0:10:07	0:08:47	0:09:07	0:09:17
0:09:39	0:09:54	0:10:09	0:08:49	0:09:09	0:09:19
0:09:41	0:09:56	0:10:11	0:08:51	0:09:11	0:09:21
0:09:43	0:09:58	0:10:13	0:08:53	0:09:13	0:09:23

Table 4.3 *(continued)*

KEY RUN WORKOUT #3 (LONG RUN) PACES (PER MILE)

5-K	LONG TEMPO	MP	MP+10	MP+15	MP+20
0:24:55	0:08:48	0:09:15	0:09:25	0:09:30	0:09:35
0:25:00	0:08:50	0:09:17	0:09:27	0:09:32	0:09:37
0:25:05	0:08:51	0:09:19	0:09:29	0:09:34	0:09:39
0:25:10	0:08:53	0:09:21	0:09:31	0:09:36	0:09:41
0:25:15	0:08:55	0:09:23	0:09:33	0:09:38	0:09:43
0:25:20	0:08:56	0:09:25	0:09:35	0:09:40	0:09:45
0:25:25	0:08:58	0:09:27	0:09:37	0:09:42	0:09:47
0:25:30	0:08:59	0:09:29	0:09:39	0:09:44	0:09:49
0:25:35	0:09:01	0:09:31	0:09:41	0:09:46	0:09:51
0:25:40	0:09:03	0:09:32	0:09:42	0:09:47	0:09:52
0:25:45	0:09:04	0:09:34	0:09:44	0:09:49	0:09:54
0:25:50	0:09:06	0:09:36	0:09:46	0:09:51	0:09:56
0:25:55	0:09:07	0:09:37	0:09:47	0:09:52	0:09:57
0:26:00	0:09:09	0:09:39	0:09:49	0:09:54	0:09:59
0:26:05	0:09:11	0:09:40	0:09:50	0:09:55	0:10:00
0:26:10	0:09:12	0:09:42	0:09:52	0:09:57	0:10:02
0:26:15	0:09:14	0:09:44	0:09:54	0:09:59	0:10:04
0:26:20	0:09:16	0:09:46	0:09:56	0:10:01	0:10:06
0:26:25	0:09:17	0:09:48	0:09:58	0:10:03	0:10:08
0:26:30	0:09:19	0:09:50	0:10:00	0:10:05	0:10:10
0:26:35	0:09:20	0:09:52	0:10:02	0:10:07	0:10:12
0:26:40	0:09:22	0:09:54	0:10:04	0:10:09	0:10:14
0:26:45	0:09:24	0:09:56	0:10:06	0:10:11	0:10:16
0:26:50	0:09:25	0:09:57	0:10:07	0:10:12	0:10:17
0:26:55	0:09:27	0:09:59	0:10:09	0:10:14	0:10:19
0:27:00	0:09:28	0:10:01	0:10:11	0:10:16	0:10:21
0:27:05	0:09:30	0:10:03	0:10:13	0:10:18	0:10:23
0:27:10	0:09:32	0:10:05	0:10:15	0:10:20	0:10:25
0:27:15	0:09:33	0:10:07	0:10:17	0:10:22	0:10:27
0:27:20	0:09:35	0:10:09	0:10:19	0:10:24	0:10:29
0:27:25	0:09:36	0:10:11	0:10:21	0:10:26	0:10:31
0:27:30	0:09:38	0:10:13	0:10:23	0:10:28	0:10:33
0:27:35	0:09:40	0:10:15	0:10:25	0:10:30	0:10:35
0:27:40	0:09:41	0:10:16	0:10:26	0:10:31	0:10:36
0:27:45	0:09:43	0:10:18	0:10:28	0:10:33	0:10:38
0:27:50	0:09:44	0:10:20	0:10:30	0:10:35	0:10:40
0:27:55	0:09:46	0:10:22	0:10:32	0:10:37	0:10:42
0:28:00	0:09:48	0:10:24	0:10:34	0:10:39	0:10:44
0:28:05	0:09:49	0:10:26	0:10:36	0:10:41	0:10:46
0:28:10	0:09:51	0:10:28	0:10:38	0:10:43	0:10:48

MP+30	MP+45	MP+60	HMP	HMP+20	HMP+30
0:09:45	0:10:00	0:10:15	0:08:55	0:09:15	0:09:25
0:09:47	0:10:02	0:10:17	0:08:57	0:09:17	0:09:27
0:09:49	0:10:04	0:10:19	0:08:59	0:09:19	0:09:29
0:09:51	0:10:06	0:10:21	0:09:01	0:09:21	0:09:31
0:09:53	0:10:08	0:10:23	0:09:03	0:09:23	0:09:33
0:09:55	0:10:10	0:10:25	0:09:05	0:09:25	0:09:35
0:09:57	0:10:12	0:10:27	0:09:07	0:09:27	0:09:37
0:09:59	0:10:14	0:10:29	0:09:09	0:09:29	0:09:39
0:10:01	0:10:16	0:10:31	0:09:11	0:09:31	0:09:41
0:10:02	0:10:17	0:10:32	0:09:12	0:09:32	0:09:42
0:10:04	0:10:19	0:10:34	0:09:14	0:09:34	0:09:44
0:10:06	0:10:21	0:10:36	0:09:16	0:09:36	0:09:46
0:10:07	0:10:22	0:10:37	0:09:17	0:09:37	0:09:47
0:10:09	0:10:24	0:10:39	0:09:19	0:09:39	0:09:49
0:10:10	0:10:25	0:10:40	0:09:20	0:09:40	0:09:50
0:10:12	0:10:27	0:10:42	0:09:22	0:09:42	0:09:52
0:10:14	0:10:29	0:10:44	0:09:24	0:09:44	0:09:54
0:10:16	0:10:31	0:10:46	0:09:26	0:09:46	0:09:56
0:10:18	0:10:33	0:10:48	0:09:28	0:09:48	0:09:58
0:10:20	0:10:35	0:10:50	0:09:30	0:09:50	0:10:00
0:10:22	0:10:37	0:10:52	0:09:32	0:09:52	0:10:02
0:10:24	0:10:39	0:10:54	0:09:34	0:09:54	0:10:04
0:10:26	0:10:41	0:10:56	0:09:36	0:09:56	0:10:06
0:10:27	0:10:42	0:10:57	0:09:37	0:09:57	0:10:07
0:10:29	0:10:44	0:10:59	0:09:39	0:09:59	0:10:09
0:10:31	0:10:46	0:11:01	0:09:41	0:10:01	0:10:11
0:10:33	0:10:48	0:11:03	0:09:43	0:10:03	0:10:13
0:10:35	0:10:50	0:11:05	0:09:45	0:10:05	0:10:15
0:10:37	0:10:52	0:11:07	0:09:47	0:10:07	0:10:17
0:10:39	0:10:54	0:11:09	0:09:49	0:10:09	0:10:19
0:10:41	0:10:56	0:11:11	0:09:51	0:10:11	0:10:21
0:10:43	0:10:58	0:11:13	0:09:53	0:10:13	0:10:23
0:10:45	0:11:00	0:11:15	0:09:55	0:10:15	0:10:25
0:10:46	0:11:01	0:11:16	0:09:56	0:10:16	0:10:26
0:10:48	0:11:03	0:11:18	0:09:58	0:10:18	0:10:28
0:10:50	0:11:05	0:11:20	0:10:00	0:10:20	0:10:30
0:10:52	0:11:07	0:11:22	0:10:02	0:10:22	0:10:32
0:10:54	0:11:09	0:11:24	0:10:04	0:10:24	0:10:34
0:10:56	0:11:11	0:11:26	0:10:06	0:10:26	0:10:36
0:10:58	0:11:13	0:11:28	0:10:08	0:10:28	0:10:38

Table 4.3 ***(continued)***

KEY RUN WORKOUT #3 (LONG RUN) PACES (PER MILE)

5-K	LONG TEMPO	MP	MP+10	MP+15	MP+20
0:28:15	0:09:53	0:10:29	0:10:39	0:10:44	0:10:49
0:28:20	0:09:54	0:10:31	0:10:41	0:10:46	0:10:51
0:28:25	0:09:56	0:10:33	0:10:43	0:10:48	0:10:53
0:28:30	0:09:57	0:10:35	0:10:45	0:10:50	0:10:55
0:28:35	0:09:59	0:10:36	0:10:46	0:10:51	0:10:56
0:28:40	0:10:01	0:10:38	0:10:48	0:10:53	0:10:58
0:28:45	0:10:02	0:10:40	0:10:50	0:10:55	0:11:00
0:28:50	0:10:04	0:10:42	0:10:52	0:10:57	0:11:02
0:28:55	0:10:05	0:10:44	0:10:54	0:10:59	0:11:04
0:29:00	0:10:07	0:10:46	0:10:56	0:11:01	0:11:06
0:29:05	0:10:09	0:10:48	0:10:58	0:11:03	0:11:08
0:29:10	0:10:10	0:10:50	0:11:00	0:11:05	0:11:10
0:29:15	0:10:12	0:10:52	0:11:02	0:11:07	0:11:12
0:29:20	0:10:13	0:10:55	0:11:05	0:11:10	0:11:15
0:29:25	0:10:15	0:10:57	0:11:07	0:11:12	0:11:17
0:29:30	0:10:17	0:10:59	0:11:09	0:11:14	0:11:19
0:29:35	0:10:18	0:11:01	0:11:11	0:11:16	0:11:21
0:29:40	0:10:20	0:11:04	0:11:14	0:11:19	0:11:24
0:29:45	0:10:22	0:11:06	0:11:16	0:11:21	0:11:26
0:29:50	0:10:23	0:11:08	0:11:18	0:11:23	0:11:28
0:29:55	0:10:25	0:11:11	0:11:21	0:11:26	0:11:31
0:30:00	0:10:26	0:11:13	0:11:23	0:11:28	0:11:33
0:30:50	0:10:30	0:11:26	0:11:36	0:11:41	0:11:46

around the track) with 1 minute recovery between each 1600 meters. During the 1-minute recovery, you can walk around, but don't jog. Try to run the fastest time that you can maintain for all three 1600 meters. That is, the goal is to have little variation in the times of the three 1600s. After you have finished, average the time of the three 1600 repeats and add 15 seconds to that average for a prediction of your 5-K per-mile race pace. You can use that predicted 5-K race finish time to determine your target training paces for the three Key Run Workouts.

For each of the four training programs—5-K, 10-K, half-marathon, and marathon—use Tables 4.1 to 4.3 to find the designated training pace times indicated in Tables 4.4 to 4.7.

MP+30	MP+45	MP+60	HMP	HMP+20	HMP+30
0:10:59	0:11:14	0:11:29	0:10:09	0:10:29	0:10:39
0:11:01	0:11:16	0:11:31	0:10:11	0:10:31	0:10:41
0:11:03	0:11:18	0:11:33	0:10:13	0:10:33	0:10:43
0:11:05	0:11:20	0:11:35	0:10:15	0:10:35	0:10:45
0:11:06	0:11:21	0:11:36	0:10:16	0:10:36	0:10:46
0:11:08	0:11:23	0:11:38	0:10:18	0:10:38	0:10:48
0:11:10	0:11:25	0:11:40	0:10:20	0:10:40	0:10:50
0:11:12	0:11:27	0:11:42	0:10:22	0:10:42	0:10:52
0:11:14	0:11:29	0:11:44	0:10:24	0:10:44	0:10:54
0:11:16	0:11:31	0:11:46	0:10:26	0:10:46	0:10:56
0:11:18	0:11:33	0:11:48	0:10:28	0:10:48	0:10:58
0:11:20	0:11:35	0:11:50	0:10:30	0:10:50	0:11:00
0:11:22	0:11:37	0:11:52	0:10:32	0:10:52	0:11:02
0:11:25	0:11:40	0:11:55	0:10:35	0:10:55	0:11:05
0:11:27	0:11:42	0:11:57	0:10:37	0:10:57	0:11:07
0:11:29	0:11:44	0:11:59	0:10:39	0:10:59	0:11:09
0:11:31	0:11:46	0:12:01	0:10:41	0:11:01	0:11:11
0:11:34	0:11:49	0:12:04	0:10:44	0:11:04	0:11:14
0:11:36	0:11:51	0:12:06	0:10:46	0:11:06	0:11:16
0:11:38	0:11:53	0:12:08	0:10:48	0:11:08	0:11:18
0:11:41	0:11:56	0:12:11	0:10:51	0:11:11	0:11:21
0:11:43	0:11:58	0:12:13	0:10:53	0:11:13	0:11:23
0:11:56	0:12:11	0:12:26	0:11:06	0:11:26	0:11:36

MP = marathon pace; HMP = half-marathon pace

A metric version of this table is available at www.furmanfirst.com

TRAINING WITH PURPOSE: Q&A

Q. *When can I start my FIRST training?*

A. We recommend a base training of 15 miles per week for 3 months prior to beginning any of the FIRST programs; the base training for the marathon training program should be closer to 25 miles per week. In addition to the requisite weekly miles, runners must be capable of long runs of 5 miles for the 5-K training program, 6 miles for the 10-K, 8 miles for the half-marathon, and 15 miles for the marathon training program. If you are a new runner, see Chapter 3 for more details on getting started.

(continued on page 90)

Table 4.4
5-K TRAINING PROGRAM: THE THREE QUALITY RUNS

WEEK	KEY RUN WORKOUT #1	KEY RUN WORKOUT #2	KEY RUN WORKOUT #3
12	10–20 min warmup 8 × 400m w/400m RI 10 min cooldown	1 mile warmup 2 miles @ short tempo pace 1 mile cooldown	5 miles @ long tempo pace
11	10–20 min warmup 5 × 800 w/400 RI 10 min cooldown	1 mile warmup 3 miles @ short tempo pace 1 mile cooldown	6 miles @ long tempo pace
10	10–20 min warmup 2 × 1600 and 1 × 800 w/400 RI 10 min cooldown	1 mile warmup 2 miles @ short tempo pace, 1 mile easy, 2 miles @ short tempo pace 1 mile cooldown	5 miles @ long tempo pace
9	10–20 min warmup 200 (200 RI), 400 (400RI), 600 (400 RI), 800 (400 RI), 800 (400 RI), 600 (400 RI), 400 (400 RI), 200 10 min cooldown	1 mile warmup 4 miles @ mid-tempo pace 1 mile cooldown	6 miles @ long tempo pace
8	10–20 min warmup 4 × 1000 (400 RI) 10 min cooldown	1 mile warmup 3 miles @ short tempo pace 1 mile cooldown	7 miles @ long tempo pace
7	10–20 min warmup 1600, 1200, 800, 400 (400 RI) 10 min cooldown	1 mile warmup 1 mile @ short tempo pace, 1 mile easy, 1 mile @ short tempo pace, 1 mile easy, 1 mile @ short tempo pace 1 mile cooldown	6 miles @ long tempo pace

WEEK	KEY RUN WORKOUT #1	KEY RUN WORKOUT #2	KEY RUN WORKOUT #3
6	10–20 min warmup 10 × 400 w/1:30 RI 10 min cooldown	1 mile warmup 4 miles @ mid-tempo pace 1 mile cooldown	8 miles @ long tempo pace
5	10–20 min warmup 6 × 800 w/1:30 RI 10 min cooldown	1 mile warmup 2 miles @ short tempo pace, 1 mile easy, 2 miles @ short tempo pace 1 mile cooldown	7 miles @ long tempo pace
4	10–20 min warmup 4 × 1200 w/400 RI 10 min cooldown	1 mile warmup 3 miles @ short tempo pace 1 mile cooldown	7 miles @ long tempo pace
3	10–20 min warmup 5 × 1000 w/400 RI 10 min cooldown	1 mile warmup 2 miles @ short tempo pace, 1 mile easy, 1 mile @ short tempo pace, 1 mile easy, 2 miles @ short tempo pace 1 mile cooldown	7 miles @ long tempo pace
2	10–20 min warmup 3 × 1600 w/1:00 RI 10 min cooldown	1 mile warmup 3 miles @ short tempo pace 1 mile cooldown	6 miles @ long tempo pace
1	10–20 min warmup 6 × 400 w/1:00 RI 10 min cooldown	1 mile warmup 3 miles easy 1 mile cooldown	**5-K race**

RI = Rest interval, which may be a timed rest/recovery interval or a distance that you walk/jog after each track repeat.

Table 4.5
10-K TRAINING PROGRAM: THE THREE QUALITY RUNS

WEEK	KEY RUN WORKOUT #1	KEY RUN WORKOUT #2	KEY RUN WORKOUT #3
12	10–20 min warmup 8 × 400m w/400m RI 10 min cooldown	1 mile warmup 3 miles @ short tempo pace 1 mile cooldown	6 miles @ long tempo pace
11	10–20 min warmup 5 × 800 w/400 RI 10 min cooldown	1 mile warmup 2 miles @ short tempo pace, 1 mile easy, 2 miles @ short tempo pace 1 mile cooldown	7 miles @ long tempo pace
10	10–20 min warmup 2 × 1600 and 1 × 800 w/400 RI 10 min cooldown	1 mile warmup 4 miles @ mid-tempo pace 1 mile cooldown	8 miles @ long tempo pace
9	10–20 min warmup 200 (200 RI), 400 (400 RI), 600 (400 RI), 800 (400 RI), 800 (400 RI), 600 (400 RI), 400 (400 RI), 200 10 min cooldown	1 mile warmup 2 miles @ short tempo pace, 1 mile easy, 1 mile @ short tempo pace, 1 mile easy, 2 miles @ short tempo pace 1 mile cooldown	9 miles @ long tempo pace
8	10–20 min warmup 4 × 1000 w/400 RI 10 min cooldown	1 mile warmup 4 miles @ short tempo pace 1 mile cooldown	10 miles @ long tempo pace
7	10–20 min warmup 1600, 1200, 800, 400 w/400 RI 10 min cooldown	1 mile warmup 5 miles @ mid-tempo pace 1 mile cooldown	8 miles @ long tempo pace

WEEK	KEY RUN WORKOUT #1	KEY RUN WORKOUT #2	KEY RUN WORKOUT #3
6	10–20 min warmup 10 × 400 w/1:30 RI 10 min cooldown	1 mile warmup 3 miles @ short tempo pace 1 mile cooldown	10 miles @ long tempo pace
5	10–20 min warmup 6 × 800 w/1:30 RI 10 min cooldown	1 mile warmup 1 mile @ short tempo pace, 1 mile easy, 2 miles @ short tempo pace, 1 mile easy, 1 mile @ short tempo pace 1 mile cooldown	8 miles @ long tempo pace
4	10–20 min warmup 4 × 1200 w/400 RI 10 min cooldown	1 mile warmup 3 miles @ short tempo pace 1 mile cooldown	10 miles @ long tempo pace
3	10–20 min warmup 5 × 1000 w/400 RI 10 min cooldown	1 mile warmup 6 miles @ mid-tempo pace 1 mile cooldown	8 miles @ long tempo pace
2	10–20 min warmup 3 × 1600 w/1:00 RI 10 min cooldown	1 mile warmup 3 miles @ short tempo pace 1 mile cooldown	7 miles @ long tempo pace
1	10–20 min warmup 6 × 400 w/1:00 RI 10 min cooldown	1 mile warmup 3 miles easy 1 mile cooldown	**10-K race**

RI = Rest interval, which may be a timed rest/recovery interval or a distance that you walk/jog after each track repeat.

A metric version of this table is available at www.furmanfirst.com

Table 4.6
HALF-MARATHON TRAINING PROGRAM: THE THREE QUALITY RUNS

WEEK	KEY RUN WORKOUT #1	KEY RUN WORKOUT #2	KEY RUN WORKOUT #3
18	10–20 min warmup 12 × 400m (90 sec RI) 10 min cooldown	2 miles easy, 3 miles @ short tempo pace 1 mile easy	Distance: 8 miles Pace: HMP + 20 sec/ mile
17	10–20 min warmup 400, 600, 800, 1200, 800, 600, 400 (400 RI) 10 min cooldown	5 miles @ mid-tempo pace	Distance: 9 miles Pace: HMP + 20 sec/ mile
16	10–20 min warmup 6 × 800 (90 sec RI) 10 min cooldown	2 miles easy, 3 miles @ short tempo pace 1 mile easy	Distance: 10 miles Pace: No specific pace; Easy/relaxed effort run
15	10–20 min warmup 1200, 1000, 800, 600, 400, 200 (200 RI) 10 min cooldown	5 miles @ mid-tempo pace	Distance: 9 miles Pace: HMP + 20 sec/ mile
14	10–20 min warmup 5 × 1-K (400m RI) 10 min cooldown	1 mile easy, 3 miles @ short tempo pace 1 mile easy	Distance: 9 miles Pace: HMP + 20 sec/ mile
13	10–20 min warmup 3 × 1600 (1 min. RI) 10 min cooldown	6 miles @ long tempo pace	Distance: 11 miles Pace: HMP + 30 sec/ mile
12	10–20 min warmup 2 × 1200 (2:00 RI), 4 × 800 (2:00 RI) 10 min cooldown	1 mile easy, 2 miles @ mid-tempo pace 1 mile easy, 2 miles @ mid-tempo pace 1 mile easy	Distance: 10 miles Pace: HMP + 20 sec/ mile
11	10–20 min warmup 6 × 800 (1:30 RI) 10 min cooldown	5 miles @ mid-tempo pace	Distance: 12 miles Pace: HMP + 30 sec/ mile
10	10–20 min warmup 2 × (6 × 400) (1:30 RI) (2:30 RI between sets) 10 min cooldown	1 mile easy, 2 miles @ mid-tempo pace 1 mile easy 2 miles @ mid-tempo pace 1 mile easy	Distance: 8 miles Pace: HMP + 20 sec/ mile

WEEK	KEY RUN WORKOUT #1	KEY RUN WORKOUT #2	KEY RUN WORKOUT #3
9	10–20 min warmup 1 mile (400m RI), 2 miles (800m RI), 2 × 800m (400m RI) 10 min cooldown	5 miles @ mid-tempo pace	Distance: 13 miles Pace: HMP + 30 sec/mile
8	10–20 min warmup 3 × (2 × 1200) (2:00 RI) (4:00 RI between sets) 10 min cooldown	6 miles @ mid-tempo pace	Distance: 10 miles Pace: HMP + 20 sec/mile
7	10–20 min warmup 1-K, 2-K, 1-K, 1-K (400m RI) 10 min cooldown	5 miles @ mid-tempo pace	Distance: 14 miles Pace: HMP + 30 sec/mile
6	10–20 min warmup 3 × 1600 (400 RI) 10 min cooldown	6 miles easy & relaxed effort	Distance: 10 miles Pace: HMP + 20 sec/mile
5	10–20 min warmup 10 × 400 (400 RI) 10 min cooldown	5 miles @ mid-tempo pace	Distance: 15 miles Pace: HMP + 30 sec/mile
4	10–20 min warmup 3 × 2000 (400 RI) 10 min cooldown	1 mile easy, 2 miles @ mid-tempo pace 1 mile easy, 2 miles @ mid-tempo pace 1 mile easy	Distance: 10 miles Pace: HMP + 20 sec/mile
3	10–20 min warmup 2 × 3200 (400 RI) 10 min cooldown	5 miles @ mid-tempo pace	Distance: 12 miles Pace: HMP + 20 sec/mile
2	10–20 min warmup 5 × 1-K (400m RI) 10 min cooldown	2 miles easy, 3 miles @ short tempo pace 1 mile easy	Distance: 8 miles Pace: HMP + 20 sec/mile
1	10–20 min warmup 6 × 400 (400 RI) 10 min cooldown	3 miles, easy & relaxed effort	**Half-marathon race day** Distance: 13.1 miles Pace: race pace

HMP = Half-marathon pace

RI = Rest interval, which may be a timed rest/recovery interval or a distance that you walk/jog after each track repeat.

A metric version of this table is available at www.furmanfirst.com

Table 4.7
MARATHON TRAINING PROGRAM: THE THREE QUALITY RUNS

WEEK	KEY RUN WORKOUT #1	KEY RUN WORKOUT #2	KEY RUN WORKOUT #3
16	10–20 min warmup 3 × 1600m (1 min RI) 10 min cooldown	6 mile run: 2 miles easy, 2 miles @ short tempo pace, 2 miles easy	13 miles @ MP + 30 sec/mile
15	1 mile warmup 4 × 800 (2 min RI) 10 min cooldown	7 mile run: 1 mile easy, 5 miles @ MP, 1 mile easy	15 miles @ MP + 45 sec/mile
14	10–20 min warmup 1200, 1000, 800, 600, 400, 200 (all with 200 RI) 10 min cooldown	7 mile run: 1 mile easy, 5 miles @ long tempo pace, 1 mile easy	17 miles @ MP + 45 sec/mile
13	10–20 min warmup 5 × 1-K (400m RI) 10 min cooldown	6 mile run: 1 mile easy, 4 miles @ mid-tempo pace, 1 mile easy	20 miles @ MP + 60 sec/mile
12	10–20 min warmup 3 × 1600 (1 min RI) 10 min cooldown	6 mile run: 2 miles easy, 3 miles @ short tempo pace, 1 mile easy	18 miles @ MP + 45 sec/mile
11	10–20 min warmup 2 × 1200 (2 min RI); 4 × 800 (2 min RI) 10 min cooldown	5 miles @ mid-tempo pace	20 miles @ MP + 45 sec/mile
10	10–20 min warmup 6 × 800 (1:30 RI) 10 min cooldown	8 mile run: 1 mile easy, 6 miles @ long tempo pace, 1 mile easy	13 miles @ MP + 15 sec/mile

WEEK	KEY RUN WORKOUT #1	KEY RUN WORKOUT #2	KEY RUN WORKOUT #3
9	10–20 min warmup 2 × (6 × 400) (1:30 RI) (2:30 RI between sets) 10 min cooldown	6 mile run: 2 miles easy, 3 miles @ short tempo pace, 1 mile easy	18 miles @ MP + 30 sec/mile
8	10–20 min warmup 1 mile (400m RI), 2 miles (800m RI), 2 × 800m (400m RI) 10 min cooldown	6 mile run: 1 mile easy, 4 miles @ mid-tempo pace, 1 mile easy	20 miles @ MP + 30 sec/mile
7	10–20 min warmup 3 × (2 × 1200) (2 min RI) (4 min between sets) 10 min cooldown	10 miles @ MP	15 miles @ MP + 20 sec/mile
6	10–20 min warmup 1-K, 2-K, 1-K, 1-K (400m RI) 10 min cooldown	6 mile run: 1 mile easy, 5 miles @ mid-tempo pace	20 miles @ MP + 30 sec/mile
5	10–20 min warmup 3 × 1600 (400 RI) 10 min cooldown	10 miles @ MP	15 miles @ MP + 10 sec/mile
4	10–20 min warmup 10 × 400 (400 RI) 10 min cooldown	8 miles @ MP	20 miles @ MP + 15 sec/mile
3	10–20 min warmup 8 × 800 (1:30 RI) 10 min cooldown	5 miles @ mid-tempo pace	13 miles @ MP
2	10–20 min warmup 5 × 1-K (400m RI) 10 min cooldown	6 mile run: 2 miles easy, 3 miles @ short tempo pace, 1 mile easy	10 miles @ MP
1	10–20 min warmup 6 × 400 (400 RI) 10 min cooldown	3 miles @ MP	Marathon day: 26.2 miles @ MP

RI = Rest interval, which may be a timed rest/recovery interval or a distance that you walk/jog after each track repeat.

MP = Marathon pace

A metric version of this table is available at www.furmanfirst.com

Q. *I have never done this type of training. How do I get started?*

A. During the base training, gradually become familiar with the track repeats and tempo runs. By introducing just one of the faster-paced workouts at a time, you can avoid too great a training overload at one time. During the base training and introduction to the FIRST training approach, these faster-paced workouts do not have to be run at a pace as fast as prescribed by FIRST for the training program. Use the 3-month base training to gradually work up to your FIRST training paces.

Q. *Can I use my goal race times to determine my training paces?*

A. It is important that training paces be determined from actual race time performances, which represent the runner's current fitness level. It needs to be emphasized that you should run the paces based on your current fitness and not your goal race times. To do otherwise may increase your risk of a running-related injury.

We have coached runners who insist on trying to run training paces consistent with their goal race times rather than those determined from recent race performances. The problem that these runners encounter is trying to maintain their ambitious training paces over several workouts. They may be able to meet the faster-than-their-current-fitness level for Key Run Workout #1 and maybe even Key Run Workout #2, but then fall apart in Key Run Workout #3. In Chapter 10, we address running-related injuries due to overly ambitious training paces. The benefits of the FIRST program result from completing all the workouts week after week.

Q. *What if the workout paces are too fast for me?*

A. Most runners participating in the FIRST "**3plus2**" training program for the first time indicate that the paces for the three key workouts are faster than what they have been accustomed to running on a regular basis, but generally, they have been able to eventually meet the target paces. Adjust the pace so that you can complete the entire workout with little variation in the pace. This is a key component of the Key Run Workouts. Completing the entire workout with little variation in the pace is preferable to running a few of the early repeats or the early portion of the tempo and long run at a much faster pace than what you can maintain for the latter half of the workout.

Q. ***How important is it to stick to the prescribed paces?***

A. It is important to stay as close as possible to the prescribed paces—neither slower nor faster than the specified times. Running slower will not provide the stimulation necessary for adaptation; running faster will jeopardize your chances of successful completion of the next Key Workout. Fatigue and extreme physiological stress can result from crossing the training threshold. Furthermore, too fast a pace can lead to overtraining and possible injury.

Q. ***When should I adjust the paces for faster workouts?***

A. Adjustments to training paces can be made after races that produce a new standard or after completing all three weekly workouts at the specified paces with the perceived exertion judged to be easy to moderate. If your race time indicates a faster training pace or if you can easily achieve all three weekly workout times, try a faster pace for the next week's workouts.

Q. ***Why are there different recovery intervals?***

A. The workouts are designed to have a variety of distances and paces. Similarly, the recovery times for repeats are varied. The reason for training at different distances and intensities is that the body adapts when it is pressed to respond to an overload. Different types of overload elicit different physiological responses. These workouts are designed to stimulate the key physiological mechanisms needed for improved running performance. Recovery periods can increase or decrease the stress of the workouts. Varying the stressors—distance, pace, and recovery period—is a mechanism for producing changes in the workload and stimulating physiological adaptations.

Q. ***Which key workout is the toughest?***

A. Some runners find the track intervals difficult but find the long run pace easy. Conversely, some runners find the track intervals easy and are very challenged by the long tempo and long run paces. Some runners have more speed than endurance, and vice versa.

Runners in the FIRST "**3plus2**" training program often report that the tempo run workouts are the most difficult. They generally require running at a pace that is somewhat uncomfortable for about a half-hour. Similar to the track intervals, one of the goals of the tempo run is to keep an even pace throughout the workout. If there is a disparity in the pacing, it is preferable to increase the pace so that you finish strong, rather than vice versa.

Q. ***Will my fitness improve more with distance or with intensity (speed)?***

A. Training volume and intensity are critical factors in improving fitness. Runners often find it challenging to find the right balance of volume and intensity. By running a lot of miles each week, it becomes difficult to run at a pace fast enough to stimulate the physiological adaptations needed to get faster. By running very fast for each run, it is difficult to get the total mileage necessary for building endurance. That's why FIRST has designed and incorporated three purposeful key workouts with different distances and paces to develop a balance of endurance and speed.

Q. ***Isn't the FIRST "3plus2" training program low on total training miles?***

A. There are many differences in individuals' abilities to tolerate training mileage. These differences are influenced by physiology, anatomy, biomechanics, and years of running experience. Typically, smaller, lighter, and younger runners are able to tolerate more miles. These runners become the elite performers who can run hard, run often, and run long. However, many runners—aging runners in particular—find that they cannot tolerate high-mileage weeks built on 5 to 7 days of running. For them, reducing the number of days of running per week is appealing and effective. Runners who have limited training time or an injury, or those just looking for a fresh approach to training, may find that quality training can help them achieve faster performances while fitting their training into a balanced lifestyle. Because the FIRST program is lower on training miles than other traditional running programs, it is attractive to those in the aforementioned categories. However, the FIRST "**3plus2**" training program is NOT lower on training volume. A portion of the weekly total of aerobic training is achieved from aerobic modes of training other than running. Cross-training is an integral part of the program (see Chapter 5).

Q. ***Can I run only three times per week?***

A. We have conducted training studies that permitted runners to supplement our basic program with additional runs if they wished. Most runners in these studies chose not to do extra runs after the first few weeks because they found that they could perform the three key workouts better with a day of recovery from running in between workouts. There were no differences in improvement between those who ran only 3 days per week and those who did supplemental easy runs. For that reason, we designed the "**3plus2**" program to include the three quality runs and two cross-training workouts. An optional cross-training workout is also permitted.

Running more than three times per week may be beneficial. Most running programs include running 5 to 7 days per week. For reasons stated throughout this book, we find that much can be accomplished by running three times per week without the accompanying risks of injury.

Q. ***How does hill training fit into the "3plus2" training program?***

A. The FIRST training program emphasizes the importance of maintaining the proper pace for all key workouts. It is understood that the pace for a tempo run and long run will be affected by hills.

More time will be lost on the uphills than gained on the downhills, but the two should even out roughly on an out-and-back or loop course. There is no easy rule for adjusting pace times for hills since the steepness, total elevation gain, etc., would have to be calculated. Try to simulate race course terrain with your training terrain, if possible. If your key race is a hilly course, then train by using hills in longer runs as well as tempo runs. If you live in a flat area, you can treat bridges, overpasses, and parking decks as hills to incorporate hill training into your training.

Since I grew up in West Virginia, running up and down hills was an everyday occurrence. And today, since I live in the Piedmont region of South Carolina, it's impossible to run, save for a running track, without encountering hills. Hills certainly add stress to your training. That stress can make you a stronger runner. Learning to run hills efficiently takes practice.

Stress from hills not only taxes the cardiorespiratory system, but it also stresses the muscles and connective tissue. Plantar fasciitis and Achilles tendinitis can develop from excessive hill running. Be sure to stretch your calves before and after hill running. I like running hills, but because of my tight calves, I must limit the amount of time spent going up and down. Scott likes running hills. In fact, one of his fastest marathons (2:48) was the Smoky Mountain Marathon in Tennessee.

If you are headed to Boston in April, be sure to include hill training in your preparation. Be prepared to run several miles of uphill after miles of long, gradual downhill running that fatigues the quads. Top that off with more downhill and you have some wobbly Boston finishers.

Q. ***How does aging affect my ability to use the FIRST training programs?***

A. Older runners report that recovery from a hard workout takes longer than it once did and that they need a day of rest from running after each day of running. Our coaching and studies find that these runners like the FIRST approach.

5

Essential Cross-Training

THE "2" OF THE "3PLUS2" TRAINING PROGRAM

My coauthor, Scott Murr, likes to say that he is a fit person who runs, rather than a runner who is fit. I suppose that, as physical educators, we are not as singularly focused as many running coaches and authors. We are concerned about total fitness—cardiorespiratory endurance, muscular strength, muscular endurance, flexibility, body composition, coordination, and balance. We have found that cross-training not only contributes to improved running but also enhances total fitness.

I was a Division I collegiate basketball player who continued playing seriously after college on AAU teams and, briefly, in Spain. I eventually gave up playing basketball when I found it conflicted with my marathon training. There was only so much time and energy for training. Injuries, which interfered with running, occurred too frequently on the basketball court. So I became a single sport person in pursuit of personal best times at all distances.

However, I missed participating in a variety of activities. I became concerned about my overall fitness, since I had given up weight training and other sports in my single-minded pursuit of running success. I was fortunate that Scott, my running partner, was knowledgeable about cross-training from his triathlon training. He introduced me to cross-training for triathlons. After training for a few triathlons, I felt that my fitness was more well-rounded, I ran faster, and I enjoyed the variety of activities.

Swimming, biking, and rowing were cross-training activities that I could do at a high intensity while maintaining a schedule of quality runs. I confess that I now do less aerobic cross-training than I recommend for optimal performance, but that's because I also play tennis regularly. As I said, there's only so much time and energy.

The Runner Writes:

Dear FIRST:

I have never trained like this before, and I never understood how to train for a marathon until I got involved with FIRST. This is by far the best program I have ever attempted.

I really enjoyed the cross-training requirement. I have never focused on cross-training and never did anything more than run. Cross-training helped me to get fitter without so much wear on my knees and legs. I cross-trained two or three times a week throughout the program. I primarily swam and then spent the rest of my time on a stationary bike or stairclimber.

Overall, I enjoyed the FIRST approach, and my dedication to the FIRST training program was the number one reason I improved my marathon PR from 3:25 to 3:10.

Scott Infanger
FIRST 2005 marathon training study participant
Nashville, Tennessee

FIRST Replies:

Scott Infanger's remarkable improvement was influenced by his faithful inclusion of cross-training in his training regimen. The FIRST **"3plus2"** training program includes three key runs a week, each designed to improve a crucial component of running performance. However, the training program is not just 3 days of running per week. Two key cross-training workouts per week are required, and these contribute to a high level of aerobic fitness,

This chapter lays out the cross-training activities that will best complement your running. Scott Murr describes how to get the most benefit from each cross-training mode. Capitalizing on his knowledge as an 11-time finisher of Ironman Triathlons—six in Kona, Hawaii—we have included a description of our recommended cross-training workouts and their advantages and disadvantages.

Below is a letter from a participant in our marathon study who found cross-training to be just what he needed to improve his marathon performance.

which is critical to running performance. The "plus2" component of the **"3plus2"** program is critical to the FIRST approach to training.

Although Scott had run five marathons before joining the FIRST study, we did not feel that he had reached his potential. With each training program he had tried, he had experienced injuries that interfered with his training. He was able to run hard; he just couldn't tolerate the running volume. The FIRST program was ideal for him. He enjoyed swimming and biking. Because he swam and biked at a high intensity, he was able to increase his fitness. When we tested Scott in the lab after 15 weeks, we recognized that his significant improvement meant his goal of qualifying for Boston (3:10) was realistic. I counseled him on pacing and told him that if he ran a smart race, he could achieve his goal. He followed that advice and met his goal with 9 seconds to spare!

FIRST's training programs all adhere to established "principles of training" (see Chapter 3). The "specificity" principle asserts that the best way to develop fitness for running is to train the energy systems and muscles as closely as possible to the way they are used while running and racing. Thus, the best way to train for running is to run, for swimming is to swim, and for weight lifting is to lift. This principle can be taken too far. For example, many runners just run, and their runs have no specific purpose. For that reason, we also promote variety. Ample evidence suggests that cross-training can help improve running performance.

CROSS-TRAINING: THE ESSENTIALS

- Cross-training is typically defined as an exercise program that uses several modes of training to develop a specific component of fitness, in this instance, aerobic fitness.
- Each week, perform two FIRST cross-training workouts **(XT#1 and XT#2)**.
- Replace easy run days (junk mileage) with cross-training.
- Cross-training helps to reduce the risk of injuries.
- Cross-training allows for a tremendous volume of central circulatory training without overuse of a particular muscle group.
- Cross-training allows for a greater daily training intensity. Even though the same muscle groups are utilized, they are being used differently.
- Non-weight-bearing cross-training activities give the legs and running muscles a well-deserved break, promoting recovery.
- Cross-training provides variety in the training regimen.
- Cross-training workouts can be based on time rather than distance.

CROSS-TRAINING Q&A

Q. *How often should I cross-train?*

A. Supplement the three Key Run Workouts with a minimum of two cross-training workouts per week ("**3plus2**"). The number of cross-training sessions depends on the total training volume that is reasonable for your fitness level and the time you have available for training, as well as on the amount of running that you are doing. Some runners are able to tolerate and benefit from four or more cross-training workouts per week.

Below is an example of a "**3plus2**" training program weekly schedule.

DAY 1	DAY 2	DAY 3	DAY 4	DAY 5	DAY 6	DAY 7
Cross-Train (XT#1)	Key Run Workout #1	Cross-Train (XT#2)	Key Run Workout #2	Off	Key Run Workout #3	Optional Cross-Train or Rest

Q. *How long should cross-training sessions be?*

A. Rather than a 30- to 45-minute easy run, you can cross-train at a higher intensity for the same duration. When cross-training, it is best to base workouts on time rather than distance. Just as with running, you can have short, intense cross-training workouts made of short, high-intensity work intervals interspersed with rest bouts, or you can have workouts that mirror tempo workouts—a hard 20- to 25-minute effort—or you can have a workout that imitates the long run—a 2- to 3-hour, moderate-intensity workout.

Q. *How do I measure the intensity of my cross-training workouts?*

A. Many of the aerobic fitness machines have some built-in measure of work output or speed that you can use to judge your effort. Perceived exertion is also a valid measure of exercise intensity. In other words, a 45-minute Spinning workout at a moderate cadence with little resistance may be an "easy" workout, while a 30-minute Spinning workout with a faster cadence and moderate resistance may be a "hard" workout.

For Cross-Training Workouts #1 and #2, we ask runners to use perceived exertion to determine the intensity. It is very difficult without knowing an individual's fitness for a specific exercise mode or piece of equipment to recommend a specific workload. For instance, leg strength influences your workload on the bike, and swimming technique greatly influences your lap times in the pool. Because heart rates vary for the same perceived effort from one mode to another, we do not use heart rates for determining intensity.

Q. *Can I cross-train and run on the same day?*

A. Yes. Even though the "**3plus2**" program designates running and cross-training workouts on separate days, the individual seeking a high-volume training regimen can supplement the "**3plus2**" training program with additional cross-training workouts on running workout days. Most runners will not be eager to add extra training after the intense FIRST run workouts. Similarly, cycling or swimming can be good cooldown recovery activities after a run. They are also ways of extending a run workout without extending the time of running-related muscular and connective tissue stresses.

Q. *What are the best cross-training activities for runners?*

A. It is important to choose activities that complement your running. Be sure to give your running muscles a break. Activities such as swimming, rowing, and biking all give good cardiovascular benefits without stressing your lower legs and running musculature. These are non-weight-bearing activities that help give the legs and running muscles a well-deserved rest, promoting recovery.

Cross-training is an integral part of the FIRST training approach. It is important that you avoid "all-or-nothing" thinking. It takes time to get a feel for new activities. And, as with running, it is important to learn to pace yourself in the various modes of cross-training.

MODES OF CROSS-TRAINING

Below are descriptions of cross-training workouts that will enhance your running. Scott Murr has coached many triathletes and has helped many runners use cross-training to complement their training. He has drawn on his own experience as a competitive triathlete from sprint triathlons to the Ironman distance to develop effective training workouts. As we have described throughout this book, substituting different modes of aerobic training for running workouts can have multiple benefits, including reduced likelihood of an overuse injury, increased recovery time for running muscles, variety in training, and even increased training intensity.

Select one workout from **XT#1** and one from **XT#2**. Perform each weekly. You can choose the same workout each week from each category, or you can choose to perform a different workout in the same mode (e.g., two cycling workouts) or workouts of different modes (e.g., one swimming and one cycling) from week to week. You can also choose to do the same mode for **XT#2** as for **XT#1** or vary the modes for the two cross-training workouts. Whatever works for you. Changing modes of cross-training workouts adds variety and helps keep the FIRST training program fresh.

Cycling

Cycling is a non-weight-bearing and low-impact aerobic exercise that develops aerobic fitness while allowing leg recovery from the demands of running. It helps develop the quadriceps, which can balance out the strengthening of the hamstrings and calves that results from running. Cycling can also increase hip and knee joint flexibility. Because there is no pounding with cycling, runners often recover quickly, so cycling does not interfere too much with the demands of the Key Run Workouts. Performing intervals on a bike can also help increase leg turnover for running while contributing to improved running speed. High-power bike intervals work the leg muscles even harder than uphill running, but without the impact of hard running. Cycling can be done outdoors or indoors on a stationary trainer or bike.

For runners who cycle, cadence is important. Most runners who cycle tend to "push a big gear" with a low cadence when cycling. Cycling is probably more beneficial when runners work on quick pedaling at a cadence of 80 to 100 pedal revolutions per minute (rpm). For strength workouts, the cadence should range from 80 to 90 rpm. For tempo and recovery efforts, the cadence should range from 90 to 100 rpm.

Advantages and Disadvantages of Outdoor Cycling

Be aware that if you choose to bike outdoors as a means of cross-training, cycling is much more expensive than running. While running in the rain or cold may not be the most fun, most runners are able to run regardless of the weather. Cycling in the rain is no fun and can be quite risky. Although cyclists generally have fewer injuries than runners, there is always a safety issue when cycling outdoors. When a cyclist does have a wreck, it can be serious.

Advantages and Disadvantages of Indoor Cycling

Indoor bike workouts may be a safer option than cycling outside. They can be safe, social, and fun. Indoor bike workouts do not require expensive equipment—just a fitness center membership. With an indoor bike workout, runners are able to go at their own effort levels while still doing a group workout. Opportunities for indoor bike workouts are not influenced by the weather.

However, there are a couple of drawbacks to indoor bike workouts, depending on the type of indoor bike you use. Technique can be an important issue, so FIRST suggests that you check with your local fitness specialists regarding proper setup and use of a particular stationary bike. Because of the variety of indoor bikes, you may not be able to duplicate exact workloads and workouts.

Swimming

Many runners who begin swimming do so as the result of a running injury. Swimming is an excellent non-impact way to improve overall fitness. It increases upper-body strength and endurance while taking much of the stress off the legs. Swimming stretches the hamstrings and increases ankle flexibility, which may aid running performance. It also allows the body to stay active, yet recover from a hard run.

It's important to remember that swimming requires much more technique than running. An unfit swimmer can typically outswim a fit runner. Runners need to learn how to swim in a streamlined fashion. Once you feel comfortable moving through the water, you can then start building endurance. There is no doubt that swimming well requires time, commitment, and focused practice, but proper swimming technique is very achievable for most runners.

While form and technique are important for running, they are much more so for swimming. Because most new swimmers do not have good swim technique, they often tire before they are able to get a good cardio workout from swimming—the reason they do not swim regularly!

Tips for Runners Who Swim

These following tips are for runners who swim rather than for competitive swimmers.

- Rather than swim with a fast arm turnover, strive to keep the strokes long and relaxed. Distance per stroke is more important than the number of strokes per minute. Concentrate on getting as much distance per stroke as you can. Count the number of strokes you take for one length of the pool; try to get your stroke count under 20 (for a 25-meter pool).
- Develop good breathing technique—remember to exhale completely with your face in the water before rolling your head to the side to breathe. If you find that you are getting out of breath quickly, ask a swim instructor to offer some tips on your swim stroke.
- Since runners are accustomed to using their legs for propulsion, many runners who start swimming kick too hard. Swimming is primarily an upper-body activity, since kicking provides around 10 percent of the forward propulsion.

Many runners kick hard because their kick is inefficient. Their kicking is inefficient because they have tight and inflexible ankles. Consequently, most runners do not like kick sets. But kick sets not only help with aerobic fitness, they also help improve your ankle and lower leg flexibility. Scott has found that this has helped his running.

Swimming can be a great cross-training workout if you can be patient and stick with it. If you want to incorporate swimming as part of your training, FIRST suggests that, just as with your runs, you have a plan for your swim workout.

A reasonable goal for a runner would be to stay in the water for 30 minutes and move as much as possible. For example, swim one lap, rest 15 seconds, kick one lap using a kickboard, rest 15 seconds, and repeat this sequence for 30 minutes. You could look at this as an interval workout in the water.

Most runners hate kicking because they often feel like they are working hard while making little progress down the pool. Commit yourself to the kicking: You will get better and so will your lower leg and ankle flexibility.

If you don't give up on swimming, you will make quick gains. Just as with your running, set a goal for each workout. For example, the first short-range goal might be to swim 400 yards or meters nonstop, gradually increasing your goal to 1500 yards or meters.

Deep Water Running

Deep water running (DWR) involves running while partially submerged in neck-deep water without being able to touch the bottom of the pool. DWR simulates running on land, but with no impact and no weight on the joints. DWR is probably the most recommended activity for the injured runner.

You can wear a flotation device, such as an aquajogger belt, but it will reduce the work intensity. DWR uses the same motion as running on land and is the most biomechanically specific form of cross-training for the runner.

Because water is more resistant than air, DWR results in a lower leg turnover or stride cadence. This may be a disadvantage. Since DWR may "train" a slower neuromuscular firing pattern than typical running, FIRST suggests using it as a cross-training mode only when you are injured.

Tips for Deep Water Running

1. Try to simulate normal running style.
2. Raise your knees up to about hip height, then push down and slightly backward with your foot.
3. Bend your arms in a 90-degree angle and swing them from the shoulder.
4. Avoid leaning forward from the waist. Keep your hips in line under your shoulders.
5. Keep a loosely closed fist and let your legs move you forward.
6. Keep your abs tight to support your back.

Rowing

Rowing is a good cross-training choice for runners. Rowing machines are widely available in health clubs and fitness centers. Most runners are able to quickly learn the motion required.

Rowing is a total-body, non-weight-bearing exercise. It works both the upper and lower body, taking the major muscles through a wide range of motion, which promotes good flexibility.

Because it is an indoor activity, rowing can be done anytime. Finally, rowing is self-paced, so runners of all abilities can use it to develop their fitness.

Elliptical Fitness Machines and Stairclimbers

Combining running, cross-country skiing, and stairclimbing, elliptical fitness machines (EFX) are increasingly popular in health clubs. Cross-training on an EFX allows runners to duplicate running-like workouts in both time and intensity. Because EFX are weight-bearing modes that simulate running (without the pounding), this mode is not recommended for cross-training in the FIRST "**3plus2**" training program. FIRST promotes cross-training in non-weight-bearing modes in an attempt to give the running muscles a recovery opportunity.

Stairclimbers help build quadriceps strength, which helps with hill running. Because stairclimbing is also a weight-bearing exercise, this mode is also not recommended for cross-training in the FIRST training program.

If you choose an elliptical cross-trainer or stairclimber, for proper use of the equipment and a higher-intensity workout, avoid holding onto the handrails.

FIRST CROSS-TRAINING WORKOUTS

The primary purposes of cross-training in the FIRST training approach are to help keep your overall aerobic fitness high and to help your running muscles recover from the stress of high-intensity running. Therefore, we suggest that your two cross-training workouts be at a moderate to hard effort level and done in non-weight-bearing modes of exercise. You can use "perceived effort" (see next page) as a reference for cross-training

FIRST Cross-Training Perceived Effort Scale

1 2 3 4 5

The levels on this scale are in a range from 1 to 5.

Effort Level 1: Easy. No increase in breathing rate; can go all day.

Effort Level 2: Easy to moderate. Mild increase in breathing rate.

Effort Level 3: Moderate to hard. Noticeable increase in breathing.

Effort Level 4: Hard. Noticeable increase in breathing; difficult to talk in full sentences.

Effort Level 5: Very hard. Breathing hard; unable to talk.

effort level or intensity. We recommend an easy cross-training day after Key Run Workout #3 to serve as an active recovery day.

Since different fitness centers have different equipment, the cross-training workouts refer to general types of equipment. Some cross-training suggestions are for stationary bikes typically found in fitness centers, while some suggestions are for Spinning bikes. Rowing and swimming are the other modes of cross-training exercise we recommend.

Cross-Training Workout #1 (XT#1)

Choose one of the following workouts for XT#1:

1. **Mode:** Stationary cycling (45 minutes; any upright stationary fitness bike is fine)

   Workout: 8 minutes easy spinning, 30 minutes moderate, 7 minutes easy; cadence about 95 to 100 rpm

2. **Mode:** Stationary cycling (45 to 60 minutes)

   Workout: Constant Spin workout of 45 to 60 minutes of fast cadence at more than 100 rpm. After 10 minutes, adjust the resistance to a perceived effort (PE) level of 2. This should not be a very taxing workout, but you should be sweating by 30 minutes. Reduce the resistance to a PE level of 1 for the last 5 minutes.

3. **Mode:** Stationary cycling and running (45 minutes)

Workout: 5 minutes easy as a warmup; increase cadence to 100+ rpm and maintain that cadence for 30 minutes (because of the faster cadence, the effort level will be a 3 on the perceived effort scale); and 10 minutes of *easy* running afterward as a cooldown

4. **Mode:** Pool: No swimming but kicking (about 20 to 30 minutes)

   Workout: Most runners hate kicking because they are so bad at it. Kicking will help your running. Kick 1 length of a 25-meter or 25-yard pool; rest 30 seconds. Repeat this 20 times. Use a kickboard and hold it out in front of you. You do not need to put your face in the water. Focus on kicking from the hips rather than the knees.

5. **Mode:** Pool: Swimming (about 20 to 30 minutes)

   Workout: 1 length fast, 1 length easy; 2 lengths fast, 2 lengths easy; 3 lengths fast, 3 lengths easy; 2 lengths fast, 2 lengths easy; 1 length fast, 1 length easy. Rest 1 minute. Repeat entire sequence two more times.

6. **Mode:** Rowing (30 minutes)

   Workout: 5 minutes easy rowing, then 1 minute hard effort, 1 minute easy effort, 2 minutes hard, 1 minute easy; 3 minutes hard, 1 minute easy; 4 minutes hard, 1 minute easy; 3 minutes hard, 1 minute easy; 2 minutes hard, 1 minute easy; 1 minute hard, 3 minutes cooldown

Cross-Training Workout #2 (XT#2)

Choose one of the following workouts for XT#2:

1. **Mode:** Stationary cycling (45 minutes)

   Workout: 10 minutes easy spinning as a warmup, alternate resistance between a PE level of 4 for 1 minute with 4 minutes of fast spinning at a PE level of 1. Repeat this six times. Finish with 5 minutes easy as a cooldown.

2. **Mode:** Stationary cycling (50 minutes)

   Workout: 10 minutes easy spinning as a warmup, 15 minutes moderate to hard, 5 minutes easy; 15 minutes moderate to hard, 5 minutes easy as recovery; all with cadence of about 95 to 100 rpm

3. **Mode:** Stationary cycling and rowing (50 minutes)

   Workout: 5 minutes easy spinning, then alternate 5 minutes hard/fast rowing and 5 minutes easy but fast spinning (more than 100 rpm). Repeat this row/bike sequence four times, and finish with 5 minutes spinning as a cooldown.

4. **Mode:** Stationary cycling and running (50 minutes)

   Workout: 10 minutes easy spinning, 30 minutes moderate, cadence about 95 to 100 rpm. Follow immediately with 10 minutes easy running.

5. **Mode:** Stationary cycling and running (about 60 minutes)

   Workout: 10 minutes easy spinning as a warmup, 15 minutes at a resistance of PE level 3, jog 1 mile at your long run pace; repeat this sequence two times. Finish with 10 minutes easy spinning as a cooldown.

6. **Mode:** Swimming (about 20 to 30 minutes)

   Workout: Swim 8 lengths. Follow immediately by kicking 2 lengths. Rest 1 minute. Repeat this sequence five times.

Optional Cross-Training Workouts (Optional XT)

Any of the following workouts can be used for an optional cross-training workout.

1. **Mode:** Rowing (35 minutes)

   Workout: 5 minutes easy rowing, 10 minutes moderate to fast; 5 minutes easy, 10 minutes moderate to fast; 5 minutes easy

2. **Mode:** Spinning bike (50 minutes)

   Workout: 5 minutes easy spinning; 40 minutes fast cadence (about 95 to 100 rpm); 5 minutes relaxed spinning as a cooldown

3. **Mode:** Rowing or stationary cycling—your choice (46 minutes)

   Workout: 5 minutes easy as a warmup; then 1 × 4 minutes fast, 4 × 1 minutes fast, 3 × 2 minutes fast, 2 × 3 minutes fast, 4 × 1 minutes fast, all with 1 minute easy recovery; 5 minutes easy as a cooldown

4. **Mode:** Stationary bike (60 minutes)

   Workout: 20 minutes easy, 20 minutes moderate; 20 minutes easy

5. **Mode:** Swimming (20 minutes)

   Workout: 20 minutes of a combination of continuous swimming and kicking

A Word on Weight Training

Weight training, or strength training, is *not* considered cross-training in the FIRST training program. The FIRST approach considers cross-training an activity designed to complement the high-quality run training and to provide an aerobic workout without pounding on the legs. FIRST does recommend strength training for runners (see Chapter 12), but not as part of cross-training.

CROSS-TRAINING: FINAL COMMENTS

The Principle of Variation

The variation principle comes into play in several different ways in the FIRST training program. After quality run training, we recommend that you cross-train (the variation principle) to give your running muscles a chance to recover. You should also use training cycles to vary the intensity and volume of your training (the variation principle again) to help achieve peak levels of fitness.

We also recommend changing exercises or activities periodically so that you don't overstress a part of your body—another form of variation. Changing activities also helps you maintain your interest in running.

It may appear that two of our principles, specificity and variation, are incompatible. The specificity principle states that training must be specific to the desired adaptation, but the variation principle seems to assert the opposite: You should train by using a variety of activities. Really, however, it's all a matter of degree. Yes, more specific training is better to the extent that you can tolerate it, but it can become exceedingly boring and risky. Thus, some variety that involves the same muscle groups is a useful change.

While some running-related injuries require a total break from any exercise, many running injuries require rest only from running (active rest), allowing for a similar volume of training while injured as when injury-free. In other words, even when you're injured, you may be able to keep exercising the same amount of time per week by using cross-training.

Cross-training reduces your risk of injuries. If running is your only mode of exercise, the same muscles are always stressed in the same way, increasing the likelihood of injury. Cross-training allows for a tremendous volume of central circulatory training without overusing a particular muscle group. Cross-training also allows for a greater daily training intensity. Even though the same muscle groups are utilized, they are being used differently. Higher intensity throughout a training program increases caloric output, too, so you can achieve and maintain optimal body fat percentages much more easily.

Cross-training provides variety in your training regimen. A variety of aerobic-oriented activities utilize and stress a greater muscle mass, and you can achieve more balanced overall fitness.

With cross-training, you have more flexibility with your workouts, too: For instance, if the roads are icy, you can swim; if the pool is closed, you can cycle or walk. This helps you avoid boredom and burnout and keeps up your zest for training. Training in more than one sport is great for motivation, and the variety enhances your desire to train. While the FIRST training approach is "run less," it is not "train less." The FIRST training approach specifies high-quality running and cross-training so that total weekly exercise typically remains the same when you switch to the **"3plus2"** training program from another running program.

6

The "3plus2" Training Week

To benefit fully from the FIRST training program, you'll need to perform *all five* workouts each week. The cumulative training effect of the workouts over 12 to 18 weeks translates into improved fitness, more speed, and better endurance. In this chapter, you will find the results of three FIRST training studies that demonstrated significant improvements in runners' fitness profiles and race performances.

Emily Kolakowski participated in our 2005 marathon training study and experienced an improvement of 26 minutes in her marathon time. On the next page, she describes the aspects of the program that benefited her.

(continued on page 115)

The Runner Writes:

Dear FIRST:

The FIRST training program improved my running dramatically. It helped me to become a stronger, faster, and more efficient runner with each week of training. The intensity of my running was the first improvement I noticed. Prior to this training program, I had been more concerned with the total weekly mileage important for long distance runners. The speed and intensity of the workouts had been somewhat ignored. Adding speed workouts to increase the intensity of training made a difference.

The fact that we were limited to running only on non-consecutive days allowed for proper recovery time between workouts for me. The intensity was challenging. The cross-training component helped to make non-running days an active recovery instead of a passive one. Overall, I felt more recovered by running on non-consecutive days. Allowing for that day in between really prepared me to focus and make the next key run really count.

At first, it was hard to get used to running only 3 days a week. Once I adjusted to the new routine, I loved it! I felt recovered before each key run. The cross-training eliminated the boredom factor. The variety in the Key Run Workouts was such a refreshing addition to the training. I had not had much variety in my previous training. The FIRST program really challenged me at the perfect intensity. I am still amazed at how on target the workout paces were, consistently, for all 16 weeks of training.

I was lacking the amount of variety I included in my weekly workouts prior to the FIRST program. Three days a week of three different key runs and 3 days of cross-training really helped to keep all the workouts fun and interesting. It was also encouraging to know that the cross-training was helping to improve fitness and giving the running muscles a break.

More important, I was ecstatic to see my marathon time go from 4:21:23 to 3:55:18.

Emily Kolakowski
Participant in the FIRST 2005 marathon training study and clinical exercise physiologist
Bethesda, Maryland

FIRST Replies:

Emily's comments typify what we have heard from many runners who have used our training program.

- Most runners judge their training by how many miles they run per week.
- Most runners do not focus on speed and getting faster.
- Most runners' workouts lack variety.
- Most runners do not allow for sufficient recovery, which is necessary for quality workouts.
- Most runners do not realize the value of cross-training. It enhances fitness and adds variety.

We also hear from many runners using our program that they find the training paces challenging, but they are surprised to find that they can meet those targets with good efforts and proper recoveries. The *gradual* progression of stress and overload is what stimulates improvement in the cardiorespiratory system and muscular tissue responsible for running performance.

The FIRST **"3plus2"** training program is designed to improve your racing times by increasing your overall fitness. FIRST's ***Training with Purpose*** philosophy means that each training session, with its well-defined goals, is aimed at improving one of the three major determinants of performance. The three Key Run Workouts each week are the foundation of the FIRST training approach. These workouts are designed to stimulate adaptations to improve the three primary physiological determinants of running performance: maximal oxygen consumption, lactate threshold, and running economy. The individually tailored workouts are based on the runner's current fitness level. For each of three key runs—track repeats, tempo run, and long run—FIRST prescribes specific paces and distances.

While the FIRST **"3plus2"** training program reduces the amount of running that you do weekly, it does not limit your training to 3 days per week. There has been a misconception by some runners that the FIRST

(continued)

The Runner Writes *(continued)*

training program is only 3 training days per week. The total training volume of the program includes three key running workouts and a minimum of two key cross-training workouts.

We recognize that most training books have chapters with comprehensive regimens for stretching, strength training, and form drills. In keeping with our philosophy of getting the optimal benefits from a minimal time commitment, we have selected what we consider the most beneficial and essential stretches (Chapter 13), resistance training exercises (Chapter 12), and running drills (Chapter 13) for you to include in your program. These four stretches, five strength training exercises, and two drills will take only a few minutes each week, but the return on your time investment in terms of performance and reduced risk of injury is significant.

We, as runners, are well aware that stretching, strength training, and form drills are typically neglected. Runners assume that more time spent running will be more beneficial than devoting some of their limited time to supplemental training exercises. However, once those same runners are injured, they spend much of their rehabilitation time cross-training, strength training, and stretching, all components of the FIRST training approach.

Often, runners, in their zeal to get faster, engage in risky training that may not contribute to health and strength. Through repetition, many runners will incur overuse injuries and create muscular imbalances. We want to build fitter and healthier runners, not just faster ones. Smart training can help you be faster, fitter, and healthier. Chapters 4 and 5 provide the essentials of our running program designed to promote faster running while contributing to your overall health and prolonging your running career.

The information included in the later chapters about stretching, strength training, form, year-round training, and nutrition are of utmost importance as well. If you want to become a well-balanced runner, you must follow a complete program that contributes to a balanced approach to training.

THE "3PLUS2" TRAINING WEEK

THE "3PLUS2" TRAINING PROGRAM

DAY 1	DAY 2	DAY 3	DAY 4	DAY 5	DAY 6	DAY 7
Cross-Train (XT#1)	Key Run Workout #1	Cross-Train (XT#2)	Key Run Workout #2	Off	Key Run Workout #3	Optional Cross-Train or Rest

Day 1

Key Cross-Training Workout #1 (XT#1) (see page 106)

Day 2

Key Run Workout #1: Track Repeats (see Chapter 4 for details)

- Warm up with 15 to 20 minutes of easy running
- Key Workout (see Table 4.1 for paces and Tables 4.4 through 4.7 for training schedules)
- Cool down with 10 to 15 minutes of easy running

Day 3

Key Cross-Training Workout #2 (XT#2) (see page 107)

Day 4

Key Run Workout #2: Tempo Run (see Chapter 4 for details)

- Warm up with 1 mile; start with easy running and warm up to tempo pace
- Key Workout (see Table 4.2 for paces and Tables 4.4 through 4.7 for training schedules)
- Cool down with 1 mile of easy running

Day 5

Rest day

Day 6

Key Run Workout #3: Long Run (see Chapter 4 for details)

- Start with easy running and gradually increase to long run pace (see Table 4.3 for paces and Tables 4.4 through 4.7 for training schedules)

Day 7

Rest day or *optional* cross-training (see page 108)

RESULTS OF FIRST TRAINING STUDIES

In Chapter 1, we described the methods of our FIRST training studies in considerable detail. Based on their running histories and fitness and running goals, we chose approximately 25 runners for each of the three studies. We were careful to include a good representation of males and females, young and old, and a wide range of running experiences. (See Table 6.1.) In all three studies, we provided 16 weeks of individualized training for the participants.

All research participants were given specific training distances and intensities, each chosen to stimulate improvement in one of three performance variables: maximal oxygen consumption, lactate threshold, and running speed at peak oxygen consumption. In each study, all the runners completed laboratory pre- and post-tests to gauge improvement, including hydrostatic weighing to estimate body composition and a progressive maximal treadmill running test to determine maximal oxygen consumption, lactate threshold, and running economy.

A 16-week study in the fall of 2003 showed that runners could achieve improvement in all three running performance variables by following a three-quality-runs-per-week training program. The participants were given three running workouts—interval repeats on the track, a tempo run, and a long run—to perform weekly. Any additional training—running or cross-training—was left to the participant's discretion.

To further test the effectiveness of this training approach, we conducted a marathon training study in 2004 that restricted runners to just three runs per week. Runners were encouraged to do two additional cross-training workouts, but the cross-training was not mandatory.

In 2005, we replicated the 2004 marathon training study with one change; the participants were required to complete two aerobic cross-training workouts per week.

Having coached and worked with runners for 20-plus years, we discovered that most recreational and age-group runners, even those who race regularly at distances from 5-K to the marathon, do not train scientifically or with a purpose. We hypothesized that by adhering to training paces and distances determined by their fitness levels, runners in our studies would improve one or more of their key running performance variables.

Table 6.1
SUMMARY OF RESULTS FROM FIRST STUDIES

	2003	2004	2005
FEMALES	7	10	8
MALES	15	12	9
AGES	23–63 years	25–56 years	24–52 years
AVERAGE AGE	F = 41.7 M = 40.1	F = 34.8 M = 36.7	F = 35 M = 35.4
% IMPROVEMENT OF MAX VO_2	4.8	4.2	5.4
% IMPROVEMENT OF RUNNING SPEED AT LACTATE THRESHOLD	4.4	2.3	5.6
% IMPROVEMENT OF RUNNING SPEED AT PEAK VO_2	7.9	2.4	2.1
RANGE OF MARATHON FINISH TIMES FOR FEMALES	—	3:56–4:44	3:41–4:49
AVERAGE MARATHON FINISH TIMES FOR FEMALES	—	Median = 4:17:02 Mean = 4:20:42	Median = 3:56:18 Mean = 4:02:22
RANGE OF MARATHON FINISH TIMES FOR MALES	—	2:56–4:51	2:57–4:19
AVERAGE MARATHON FINISH TIMES FOR MALES	—	Median = 3:46:19 Mean = 3:49:23	Median = 3:42:51 Mean = 3:35:24
NUMBER OF FIRST-TIME MARATHON FINISHERS	—	8 (3F, 5M)	3 (2M, 1F)
AVERAGE TIME OF FIRST-TIME MARATHONERS	—	F = 4:03:07 M = 3:48:49	F = 4:03:34 M = 3:46:22
NUMBER OF PERSONAL BEST TIMES (FOR THOSE WHO HAD RUN A MARATHON PREVIOUSLY)	—	7 of 13 (53.8%)	12 of 14 (85.7%)

After the results of the laboratory pre-test were evaluated, individually tailored workouts for the 16-week training program were developed. Each week included three key runs to be performed on non-consecutive days. The distance and pace of the individually prescribed workouts were based on the initial laboratory assessment and the subject's most recent race time or track performance.

All study participants reported to us weekly on their run results (time, distance, and the perceived difficulty of each workout). We responded to each report and advised each runner about any needed changes in his or her training program. Additionally, in the 2003 and 2004 studies, the FIRST staff met with the subjects at the end of each month to receive and give feedback about the training program. Because the participants in the 2005 study were from 11 different states, it was not logistically possible to meet during the 16-week period.

The post-test laboratory assessments were conducted after 15 weeks and were replications of the pre-test assessments.

Results

Pre- and post-training, three variables were compared to determine the effects of the 16-week training program: max VO_2, running speed at lactate threshold, and running speed at max VO_2.

As a group, the runners showed improvement over the 16 weeks of training on all three variables related to running performance, all statistically significant. Individually, all runners improved on at least one of the running performance variables. The results are displayed in the summary table (Table 6.1).

Running only 3 days a week, veteran marathoners who were accustomed to training 5 or 6 days a week improved their physiological profiles from the laboratory assessment, as well as improving their marathon performances. ***Training with Purpose*** means having workouts designed to specifically target the determinants of running performance. The FIRST running studies confirm that ***Training with Purpose*** is an efficient and effective philosophy to getting fitter and faster.

7

Rest and Recovery

Every serious runner I know has, at some point, believed that the path to faster times was simply more and more running. At first, those increases in training volume result in improvements. *Voilà,* more must be even better. However, not only does all of the excessive running lead to a performance plateau, but slower times accompany the strenuous training efforts as well. In 1980, having missed a couple of long training runs and wanting to reassure myself that I was ready for Boston, I ran a fast 20-miler at marathon pace a week prior to Patriot's Day. Throughout that training run, I could picture myself having a great Boston because I felt so light and speedy. My training exuberance resulted in sore legs that were still aching during my warmup on race day and that completely failed me before I surrendered to the EMS wagon.

That embarrassing failure at Boston taught me a lesson that coauthor Scott Murr often quotes: "It is better to be 10 percent undertrained than 1 percent overtrained when you step to the start line." Our common errors in trying to gain that extra fitness upset the ideal balance of training and recovery. These errors contributed to our discovering a training approach that led to the creation of the **"3plus2"** training program.

The Runner Writes:

Dear FIRST:

The FIRST program absolutely improved my running. I reached my goal of running a 3:10 marathon (my previous PR was 3:25) and qualifying for Boston, and I felt great during the marathon.

The FIRST training program helped me feel very comfortable the entire race. I'm thrilled with the results, and I don't think I could have done it without the FIRST training program.

It was not hard for me to follow the advice not to run 2 days in a row. I felt that I needed a day off of running after almost every workout, but I wasn't so wiped out that I couldn't cross-train hard on the non-running days. I like the built-in rest periods and days off from running. That helped me feel good for every run.

Aaron Colangelo
Participant in the FIRST 2005 marathon training study and attorney
Washington, D.C.

FIRST Replies:

Aaron's success with a carefully designed training program of quality training and quality recovery exemplifies the importance of balancing these two key training components. Aaron found that he could maintain a faster pace on the key run days by having recovery days.

Previously, Aaron had run more frequently, but with less intensity and less variation in his pace. During his participation in our study, Aaron swam and biked for his cross-training workouts, and even though he worked hard on those days, which improved his cardiorespiratory fitness, cross-training gave his running muscles the needed recovery to run hard the next day.

Aaron followed the FIRST program for 16 weeks, exactly as it was intended. His results were remarkable. We were thrilled when we watched him cross the marathon finish line under 3:10.

Quality rest and recovery are crucial components in the FIRST training program.

REST AND RECOVERY: THE ESSENTIALS

- Quality Training + Quality Nutrition + Quality Rest = Quality Results
- Recovery is important and has a place in every training schedule.
- Rest and recovery should be defined in a training program just as the workouts are described.
- Successful runners are those who have recovered the best.
- The rate of recovery is influenced by many factors, which include age, fitness level, life stressors, health level, diet, sleep, and exercise background/experience.
- A prerace rest period needs to be planned and must be structured in order to be effective.
- Once you have completed a key workout or a race, it is important to recover from that physical stress.
- Just as runners complete tapers prior to racing, they should gradually return to quality training.
- Keep written records of your daily physical activities.
- The FIRST approach to recovery includes two important components: rest and nutrition.

1. Rest

Allowing the body to rest from intense run workouts is paramount for improving.

Sleep may be the most important recovery technique. Sleep allows the body an opportunity to regenerate; the body releases growth hormones that aid and repair stressed muscles from hard workouts/races.

Active, yet low-intensity, exercise such as non-weight-bearing swimming, rowing, and cycling allows the stressed running muscles an opportunity to recover. It is during the recovery that the adaptation from the training stimulus (the hard run) occurs. That adaptation, or improvement, helps you run faster.

2. Nutritional Recovery

Diet is the other important factor in recovery. A sound diet is essential for a healthy athlete. Carbohydrates are important and necessary for glycogen-depleted muscles. Dehydration can delay or prolong recovery. Hydration with carbohydrate calories immediately after exercise has been shown to speed recovery. See Chapter 11 on nutrition for more information on this important recovery component.

REST AND RECOVERY: Q&A

Q. ***What about "streakers"—runners who haven't missed a day for years or those who run a marathon every week?***

> **A.** Many runners use the words *rest* and *recovery* with disdain. These runners have the idea that runners are "tough" and think that rest and recovery are signs of weakness. However, rest and recovery are training tools that should be included in any training program. "Streakers" and others who are overloading without recovery are vulnerable to injury and illness. Besides depressing their immune systems and increasing their susceptibility to running-related maladies, they will not be able to perform to their potential. Streakers are typically more concerned with their streak than they are with their performance potential.

Q. ***When is it important to rest and recover?***

> **A.** Once you have completed a key workout or a race, it is important to recover from that training stimulus. The FIRST training approach balances rest and recovery with quality runs. The day following a Key Run Workout is intended to be a rest day for your weight-bearing running muscles. The idea is to allow your legs a chance to recover so that your next key run can be a quality, productive run.

Q. ***What influences the rate of recovery?***

> **A.** Your rate of recovery is influenced by many factors, which

include your age, your fitness level, your exercise background and experience, life stressors, your health level, your diet, and sleep.

Q. ***What is overload?***

A. Overload is a planned, systematic and progressive increase in training stress in order to improve fitness and/or performance. Running at a pace faster than that to which you are accustomed or running a distance farther than normal is considered overload. A cycle of overload and recovery enables runners to gradually improve their fitness and performance. This cycle must be carefully structured so that the overload does not exhaust or injure. The recovery must be sufficient to permit the next overload workout.

Finding the appropriate balance of overload and recovery is essential for improvement. We have developed training schedules with prescribed distances and paces to provide the stress needed to stimulate adaptation to the overload. By gradually increasing your pace or distance, your body will continue to adapt, and you will become fitter.

Q. ***How should a recovery be structured during a training period?***

A. Recovery during training can refer to recovery in a workout or between workouts.

With the FIRST training approach, runners perform three Key Run Workouts in any order throughout the week; however, they need to allow for recovery between the key workouts. We recommend that runners cross-train on other days of the week. The idea is to allow the primary running muscles an opportunity to recover so that an optimal training load can be applied at the next scheduled run workout. Combined with sound nutrition, non-running days allow the opportunity for muscle glycogen to be replenished.

By resting prior to a stressful run (FIRST Key Run Workouts or a race), you can perform the run at the necessary intensity. We have found that most runners who try to maintain their 5-days-per-week running routine are unable to complete the Key Run Workouts at the prescribed intensities. A non-running day prior to your key run serves as a mini-taper.

Q. ***How should recovery be structured for a prerace event?***

A. If you are training to race and you want to run your best, it is important to allow your body to recover from the stresses of prolonged training periods. You cannot maintain your normal training, say, 40 miles a week, and then go straight into a 10-mile race and expect to run a PR.

Prerace rest does not necessarily mean one or two days without running or exercise before race day. A prerace rest period must be significant and structured. In a structured training schedule, training builds up gradually (with built-in recovery periods) until some specified period before the target race, when the training load usually peaks. Then, a taper begins, with a reduced training load—2 weeks before a marathon and 1 week before a 5-K or 10-K is common. The taper allows your body to recover fully, so that you are fully prepared to race and can reasonably expect to perform at or near your best. All FIRST training programs include a taper prior to a race.

Q. ***How should postrace recovery be structured?***

A. Once you have completed a race, it is important to recover from that stress. Improvement occurs during the recovery phase and not during the workout itself. Your rate of recovery is influenced by many factors. One key recovery factor is postrun hydration/nutrition (see Chapter 11 on nutrition for post-exercise/race recommendations).

Due to the stress of a race, you can't expect to return to prerace levels of training immediately. Your body needs time to recover. An immediate return to high-level training may lead to a reduced level of performance and possible injury.

After a race, take a complete rest from running (anything from 2 or 3 days for a 10-K to a week or more for a marathon). This is a

FIRST Success

I wanted to let you know that your 3-days-a-week running plan worked for me. My marathon goal was 3:10:00. I ran a 3:08:39 at the Lincoln Marathon this weekend. The 3:10 had been eluding me for the last couple of years, and I needed to try something new. This apparently worked. Thank you for showing me that 100 to 120 miles per week is not required to reach my running goals.

I followed the 16-week plan fairly closely. I changed up some of the days for the long runs to coordinate with my schedule, and I built up to 23 miles for my longest—otherwise the track workouts and the tempos I did as scheduled. I mountain biked once a week for 45 minutes to an hour and did "circuit training" in my basement on the other days. My circuit training consisted of pushups, situps, other ab stuff, arm curls, weighted knee bends, calf lifts, and stretching for about 50 minutes once or twice a week.

Jason K. Babcock, PE
ENGINEER
WAVERLY, NEBRASKA

good time to cross-train: You can stay active while minimizing any additional stress to the primary running muscles. Your return to training should be gradual. If your peak level of training before the race was 40 miles per week, return at 20 miles a week, and, over the next 2 to 3 weeks, gradually build up to your previous levels.

Here are some postrace recovery guidelines for resuming FIRST "**3plus2**" training:

After a 5-K race: Substitute an easy run for Key Run Workout #1 (Track Repeats) the following week. If your energy levels have returned to normal, then resume normal training with Key Run Workout #2 (Tempo Run). Continue with your normal cross-training. Reduce the intensity if you are experiencing postrace fatigue.

After a 10-K race: Same as after a 5-K race. In addition, reduce the intensity of Key Run Workout #2 to 90 percent of your normal effort.

After a half-marathon: If you raced an all-out effort, then reduce the intensity of your workouts for the next 2 weeks. Rest the day immediately following the race. Resume cross-training but substitute easy runs for Key Run Workouts #1 and #2 during the week following the race. One week later, make the long run half of your normal distance, and run at an easy pace. The second week after the half-marathon, resume regular training if you feel rested and have no lingering muscle or joint aches.

After a marathon: You need to take a week off from running. *Yes,* we mean it! Follow the off week with a week of easy running, and in the third week, begin doing your workouts, but at no more than 90 percent effort. If you have no aches and pains after 3 weeks, then you can return to regular workouts.

REST AND RECOVERY: THE SCIENCE

As we saw in the Q&A on page 123, one basic principle of training is *overload.* Overload is a planned, systematic, and progressive increase in training stress in order to improve fitness and/or performance. In other words, train hard and become fatigued, then rest and recover while your body adapts to an increased workload. Repeating this cycle of overload, fatigue, recovery, and adaptation makes you fitter and faster. However, there is a limit to one's capacity to endure and adapt. The progressive overload must be done gradually.

An overload for runners can mean running farther, more often, or faster. It is important that these stressors be increased gradually and separately, and care must be taken not to increase multiple stressors simultaneously. In other words, overload only one variable at a time.

Other non-training stressors can add to your overload. These non-training stressors include altitude, colds and allergies, poor dietary habits, environmental extremes, travel, stressful work situations and personal

FIRST Success

I wanted to write and give you a firsthand testimonial to the effectiveness of your marathon training program. I have been reading and followed your FIRST program for the National Marathon held on March 25th in Washington, D.C. I would like to report that I completed my first marathon in 3:22:17. In the past, I tried to follow other recommended marathon training programs, but I always reinjured my iliotibial band and, needless to say, had to abandon the completion of my first marathon. It is nice to know that research exists to prove that more miles are not necessarily better.

Your program limited the pounding on my knees, increased my stamina, and enabled me to complete my first marathon. I am planning on running another marathon in September and plan to follow the program you developed again.

In addition, due to the training program, I knocked a minute off my best 10-K time and completed the Capitol Hill Classic in 41:17.

Pete Bockelman
SPORTS MARKETING
WASHINGTON, D.C.

relationships. Pay attention to elevated outside stressors, and recognize when it might not be a good time to increase your training load.

While to a certain extent it is true that more training will make a runner faster, crossing your threshold of tolerance for increased stress will result in fatigue that exceeds your body's ability for adaptation. Highly competitive, goal-oriented runners may succumb to the temptation to dedicate themselves to incessant training, expecting of significant performance improvements. But those dedicated efforts can actually prove unproductive.

The key to getting faster is to combine the appropriate amount of training (quality training) with adequate rest and recovery. Increasing the overload at a rate that exceeds your body's ability to adapt causes staleness and even exhaustion. This condition of *overtraining* results in an impaired ability to train and perform. If any component of your training program—frequency, intensity, or duration—is increased too rapidly, or if your program does not provide adequate recovery from increased demands, you will not be able to adapt and your performance will decline. Recovery and rest are essential components of any runner's training program.

Runners are told to listen to their bodies. Recognizing the signs and symptoms of overtraining early, and intervening in the cycle with increased rest before fatigue becomes chronic, is important. Symptoms of overtraining include mood disturbances, irritability, sleep disturbances, increased susceptibility to colds, appetite changes, and a struggle to maintain standard training performances. Rest and recovery are essential to help you counteract the fatigue created by the training overload, which in itself is necessary for adaptation.

8

Year-Round Training

We get a lot of messages from runners asking (1) how to train between marathons that are less than 8 weeks apart, (2) if it's okay to run a half-marathon 3 weeks before a marathon, and (3) whether a 10-K can be substituted for a long training run. Clearly, many runners want to race often, even when it jeopardizes optimal performances. As runners, we understand the interest in racing often. However, it is difficult to achieve peak performance when you race too frequently.

At our public lectures, runners bemoan their poor race performances and want to know why their performances are what they are. When questioned, they begin listing all of their recent races. I, in turn, ask why they run so many races. It's often because they have a favorite race they do every year, they want to accompany friends to a race, they had a bad race and want to vindicate it, or they believe that they may earn an age-group award (probably a day when there are multiple races in the area!). I find it difficult to persuade runners to choose a race schedule for the year that permits serious training for just a few key races and plan training appropriately.

(continued on page 132)

The Runner Writes:

Dear FIRST:

I discovered your program in *Runner's World* magazine. I am 39 years old and I have been prone to injury in the past. This week, I completed my fourth marathon. I had been following the Jeff Galloway running methods, and I found that allowing sufficient rest in between workouts helped me this year in avoiding any real injuries. I ran the New York City Marathon last week as a guide for the Achilles Club. I helped guide a blind runner. We were on target for 3:40; however, at mile 22, he started to cramp up, and we finished in 3:53. I felt good after finishing, and by today, most of the soreness is gone. I could see your program working very well for athletes with disabilities who have to depend on other, sighted runners to run. Most Achilles runners get out three to four times max per week. I would like to know what your opinion is on starting back in to train for another marathon, and at what week we would start on your program. We are looking to run a fast marathon in the next few months and, hopefully, qualify for Boston. Any feedback you can give us would be greatly appreciated.

Yours truly,

Joe O'Brien
Engineer
Somers, New York

FIRST Replies:

We were pleased to hear from Joe about another group that could benefit from the FIRST training approach. We admire his willingness to assist disabled athletes in reaching their goals. We recommended that Joe take a week off from running after the marathon and then follow our recovery plan.

Assuming that, after a week, there are no injuries or lingering irritations from the marathon, it is safe to return to gentle running. After a week of easy running, during the third week after the marathon, you can start running more vigorously, but not at 100 percent of your intensity or duration—maybe at 80 to 90 percent. In the fourth week, you can resume your regular training, but you should still be careful. Resume your regular training for another month and then, if you are eager to run another marathon, you can begin the 18-week training program. Beginning the marathon preparation only 2 months after an all-out marathon effort is pushing the limits of what we believe to be prudent and ideal. The FIRST training approach allows for only two marathons in a 12-month period.

Marathon training is stressful, even with our method that emphasizes recovery, so be cautious about jumping right back into the next marathon training cycle. After the post-marathon recovery month, we recommend 2 to 3 months of serious training before beginning the next 18-week marathon training preparation. The time off provides a break from the mental stress associated with the marathon preparation. It is also a good time to run a shorter race and capitalize on the strong base built for the marathon.

We receive a lot of inquiries about how much time is needed between marathons. This question is one of the toughest to answer because there are many factors that enter into the equation. Some individuals recover more rapidly than others. The differences in recovery are influenced by the intensity of the effort and the weather conditions—running in warm conditions when a lot of fluids were lost slows recovery.

We are aware of individuals who have run marathons every week of the year. One runner who contacted us had run marathons for more than 50 months consecutively. In all sports, there are individuals who have special abilities. These individuals may have special recovery capabilities. However, their constant racing may prevent their attaining an optimal performance.

For most individuals, we believe that running more than two marathons per year risks their being overtrained, injured, and prevented from the proper preparation needed for a solid performance. We realize that sometimes, runners enter a marathon with the attitude that it is a long training run; thus it does not entail the same stress as an all-out effort, and the recovery needed will be shorter. However, a marathon is still 26.2 miles of running. Even if you do not run up to your maximum capability, you still need a recovery from the biomechanical stress.

I find that the spring is a good time to focus on a couple of 5-Ks and/or 10-Ks and to incorporate shorter track repeats and faster tempo runs—maybe even a half-marathon. Fall provides lots of choices for marathons and, usually, ideal weather for long training runs.

Of course, there are marathons in the spring and shorter races in the fall. The point is that each season needs a particular focus. During a year when I run Boston in the spring, I will focus my weekends on long runs and limit spring races. You need to be flexible. We suggest that you identify two to four key races a year and then focus on training for them. Low-priority races typically do not fit well into a planned training schedule. I have runners tell me that they are going to run their favorite 10-K in April, even though they are training for Boston. By racing a week or two before Boston, they jeopardize their Boston performance. Conversely, by racing the following weekend, they invite injury. Year-round training needs year-round planning.

The letter on page 130 is from a runner asking about how soon to begin training for a marathon after just having completed one—one of our more common questions. The letter is interesting for another reason: the service that Joe O'Brien is providing to fellow runners.

YEAR-ROUND TRAINING: THE ESSENTIALS

- For optimal performances, develop a year-long training and racing plan.
- Choose races in advance and develop a training schedule for each race.
- Include a variety of racing distances.
- Develop a plan that includes a variety of training periods.
- Follow a 12-week training schedule for 5-Ks and 10-Ks.
- Follow a 16- to 18-week training schedule for half-marathons and marathons.
- Build in recovery periods after races.
- Target no more than two marathons per year.

FIRST Success

Gentlemen,

I'm another satisfied "noncustomer" (we just used the "free" FIRST program out of *Runner's World*). I used your plan and stuck to it religiously, even through the really fun speedwork. Since my partner and I had some marathon experience and our PRs were separated by nearly 40 minutes, we modified the plan a bit. That is, we "averaged" our different paces, figuring we'd get my partner his PR and get me an easier day. Plan worked to perfection. . . . Carl cut 27 or so minutes from his previous PR, and I had an "enjoyable" race. ***Both*** of us felt better, both during and after the race. Recovery seems to be going better than in any previous marathon.

I've been telling people about the plan. Having seen my positive experience, many of my "midpack" friends are extremely interested in finding the secret. Your plan is by no means an easy way out, just a great way to train efficiently and intelligently.

After my previous "last" marathon, it took me a year to forget the pain and start training for another. Your plan gave me a reason, and the hope, to do so. Now, I've signed up for my next, a short 6 days after completing my "best." We will now try to get both my partner and myself a PR in Akron next fall.

Thanks!

Steve Brandstetter
CONSTRUCTION ESTIMATOR
WYOMING, OHIO

YEAR-ROUND TRAINING: Q&A

Q. ***Should I train the same way all year long?***

A. High school, collegiate, and elite runners have distinct running seasons. For high school and collegiate competitors, these seasons often consist of cross-country in the fall, indoor track in the winter, outdoor track in the spring, and base training in the summer. In the case of elite runners, their competitive schedules include the summer European track circuit and often a fall or spring road race, which, for the long distance runners, means a major marathon. Thus, these competitors have specific championship races as goals, which determine their training schedules for their three or four annual peak performances. Conventional wisdom from exercise physiologists and elite coaches over the past 50 years suggests that training for these peak performances should be divided into distinct training periods, typically referred to as *periodization.*

Q. ***Should the age-group runner use periodization?***

A. Most age-group runners like to race often. We have found in our training studies and coaching that most runners are reluctant to sacrifice participation in their favorite road races to focus their training on a particular goal. They want to race every month or more often while training for a personal best or to qualify for Boston. Unfortunately, trying to race all of the local events is not compatible with formulating a long-range plan with distinct phases. Many age-group and club runners attempt to maintain a year-round peak in performance. That attempt not only leads to eventual injury or burnout, it also does not permit the type of training that will lead to an optimal performance. However, a modified periodization model can permit year-round competition with a focus, while keying on several specific races and goals.

Q. ***How can the age-group runner have training phases compatible with racing goals?***

A. You can divide the year into cycles for one key race or up to four key races, one in each season. Race distances should allow ample time for recovery before the next cycle begins. FIRST does not recommend a four-race year that would include all marathons or even a combination of marathons and half-marathons. FIRST would recommend no more than two marathons a year—one in

FIRST Success

Dear FIRST,

I just wanted to thank you for the program!

I improved from a 3:31 marathon (in the fall of 2005) to my new PR of 3:17 in yesterday's Vienna Marathon.

The great thing about it wasn't even the time, but the fact that I felt very strong even in the last 5 miles (which had been my weak point in my previous three marathons), being able to keep a steady pace throughout the whole race all the way to the finish line.

Thanks again! I will continue with the FIRST program for my next marathon.

With best regards,

Wolfgang Schmid
LOGISTICS CONSULTANT
VIENNA, AUSTRIA

the fall and one in the spring, for example—for optimal race performance.

Q. ***What is an example of a year-round racing plan that incorporates different training phases?***

A. A training plan that includes a winter 5-K, a spring 10-K, a late summer or early fall half-marathon, and a fall marathon provides different types of training that stimulate the physiological adaptations that determine running performance. Training programs must produce the appropriate stimulation to produce workload adaptation. That is, for the 5-K, there must be more emphasis on intensity for shorter distances, and for the marathon, there must be more emphasis on endurance.

If a marathon is in your yearlong plan, consider that an 18-week training plan, in addition to 2 to 4 weeks of recovery, covers 5 months. Developing specific training for shorter races and preparing for them specifically and properly requires several months. It is easy to see why developing a yearlong plan is important.

Q. *How can the FIRST three-quality-runs-per-week model be used for a year-round racing plan?*

A. The three basic workouts—track repeats, tempo runs, and long runs—can be used year-round as the basic training plan. You will notice that the plans outlined in Chapter 4 are similar in structure, but the training distances are modified according to the race distance. Running the track repeats and tempo runs at a slightly faster pace becomes more important for the 5-K and 10-K preparation, and running the long runs at a slightly faster pace becomes more important for the half-marathon and marathon training.

Q. *What are the benefits of a training plan?*

A. A training plan makes it easier to select your workouts. No matter what training schedule you are following, your plan will detail your workout. You will not have to think about planning a workout when you step on the track or pavement, since you will already have a plan. Having a structured plan has been one of the aspects of the FIRST training programs that runners have most enjoyed.

Just as with any planning, adjustments may be needed at times due to injury, illness, fitness level, or other uncontrollable variables. The occasional adjustment to a plan, however, is far simpler than the daily decisions you must make about each training session when you have no plan.

SHORT- AND LONG-TERM PLANNING

Runners benefit from a training plan, both short-term and long-term. Having a plan that outlines training and racing for the coming year increases the likelihood that your training schedule will include different emphases.

A training plan helps to ensure that you follow a structured program. Breaking the training process into phases with specified workouts over well-defined periods provides identified targets. These targets serve as training goals, and you can use these training goals to give yourself a measure of accountability. Runners participating in FIRST programs repeatedly report that they like structure and accountability.

REAL RUNNER REPORT

I recently ran my second marathon (Atlanta Thanksgiving Day Marathon) and used the FIRST marathon program published in Runner's World. *My time was 3:03:50, which was 6:10 faster than when I ran the same marathon 4 years ago. In the 3 years since my first marathon, I have trained for three marathons (Boston twice and NYC once) and have been injured each time (two stress fractures and a strained quadriceps muscle). I stuck very strictly to the running portion of the program but was not always diligent on the cross-training (all cross-training was cycling, the sport in which I have been competing for the past 20 years).*

A few interesting observations:

- *Your program fits my lifestyle perfectly—I am 37 years old with two young children and a busy professional career.*
- *During the entire training program, I never became worn down or tired, and I never had any hint of an injury. I felt fresh on almost all of my runs.*
- *I replaced the second 20-mile run with a 22-mile run.*
- *Although I was a little sore at the end of the marathon, my legs were fine in a couple of days (after the first marathon, I was so sore that I could barely walk for about 7 days).*
- *The Atlanta Marathon is a very hilly marathon, and my goal is to go sub-3:00 on a more reasonable marathon course.*
- *I have been trying to come up with a 3-day-a-week program because I felt there were too many "junk" days in most programs, but you guys came up with a great solution before I could work out the kinks of my schedule.*

Needless to say, I am a big believer in your program! I now plan to run Boston and will begin training in the next few weeks. If you ever need someone to promote the FIRST methodology, feel free to contact me.

Scott F. Bass
PRIVATE WEALTH ADVISOR
ATLANTA, GEORGIA

SECTION III

Performance Factors

9

Running Hot and Cold

I am the butt of many jokes by my running friends about visits to postrace medical tents. Throughout my first 10 years of marathoning, I suffered numerous bouts of hyperthermia and hypothermia. Those bouts planted me in the medical tent with one or two IVs being administered on at least three occasions. I wonder whether there is a need for a running book evaluating medical tent services. I could vouch for the good treatment at Marine Corps in Washington, D.C.; Boston; Las Vegas; Tucson; Wolgast, Germany; and probably a city near you.

Why such poor toleration of environmental stress? Stupid or masochist? Actually, I planned someday to write a running book and thought that I needed to experience every condition that runners might encounter, so that I could comment on them firsthand.

What did I learn? First, being hydrated is very important; second, adjusting your planned pace prior to the race is wise, if conditions are not conducive for a peak performance; and third, when you begin to exhibit symptoms of a heat-related condition, don't ignore them.

Typically, in the summer, we receive messages from runners similar to the one on page 142 asking how to adjust training in the heat and humidity.

THE ESSENTIALS: RUNNING HOT AND COLD

- Ideal conditions for running performance are 45° to 60°F and low humidity.
- Heat and cold above and below the ideal have adverse effects on running times.
- Heat is the most dangerous and most difficult environmental condition to combat.

The Runner Writes:

Dear FIRST:

Good morning. I read the *Runner's World* article about your program, and I downloaded your training schedule to use in northern Virginia for my Marine Corps Marathon preparation.

How do you adjust, if at all, pacing for long runs (marathon pace plus) and tempo runs (10-K-plus) during high heat and humidity conditions?

There's been no escape from 90°F-plus temperatures and high humidity this summer in the Washington, D.C., area, and I've not been able to maintain either recommended pace without having my heart rate approach 96 percent or more of my anaerobic threshold.

Curt Smith
Northern Virginia

FIRST Replies:

Curt's question is one that many runners in the South and East face in the summer months. In the western part of the country, the low humidity and wide range of temperature throughout the day provide cooler times of day for running workouts without wilting. However, in the regions of the country with high humidity, it is not possible to run as fast in the summer months with the challenging environmental conditions. So, how do runners in these regions adjust their summer running?

There are tables that show the performance decrement due to heat. There's no question that heat and humidity will slow your pace. However,

- Properly hydrate before, during, and after workouts in hot conditions.
- Avoid comparing training and racing times in the heat to times run in ideal conditions.
- Reduce exercise intensity in very hot conditions. When temperatures exceed 90°F or when the sum of temperature (°F) and humidity (percent) exceeds 135, runners should modify their workouts.

the principle of specificity of training dictates that you need to run as close to race pace as possible. Because you will most likely not be running your fall marathon in the extreme heat and humidity that you will experience in the summer, it is not particularly valuable to train in very high temperatures that cause you to run 30 seconds per mile slower than your normal training pace.

To combat this problem, Scott Murr and I prepare during the summer for fall marathons by running early in the morning, when the temperatures are typically 68° to 72°F with little radiant heat, even though the humidity is high. There will still be a performance decrement, but the neuromuscular and biomechanical training will not be much different from your fall training and racing. You can expect to run a little slower than your normal targeted pace. As long as your effort is challenging, but doable, you will be getting the benefits you are seeking. Running in the afternoons with a 90°F-plus heat index does not permit the faster running needed for training specificity, at least not safely.

Another option that is available to those who live near higher elevations is to take a weekend drive to find cooler temperatures for the long run. Fortunately, Greenville, South Carolina, is less than a half-hour from the hills of the North Carolina Piedmont. We frequently do our summer long runs 30 minutes away, in the scenic, cooler, shaded hills—but we still do them early in the morning.

- During hot weather, train in the early morning, when the temperatures are coolest.
- Acclimatize to heat for 7 to 14 days when warm weather begins. (See the Q&A below.)
- You can minimize the adverse effects of cold with proper clothing and accessories.

RUNNING HOT AND COLD: THE SCIENCE

Adapting to the Environment

Your body adapts to the heat through increased bloodflow to the skin, increased sweating, and a higher core temperature. You need to replace the sweat lost though regular hydration. Only water that evaporates results in significant cooling; the sweat running off your body reduces your body heat very little. Higher humidity reduces the rate of evaporation. Wet skin does not sweat as much as dry skin; therefore, "pour it in, don't pour it on." In other words, drink water rather than pouring it on the top of your head.

Generally, even in cold weather, the significant amount of heat produced as a result of exercise will more than maintain core temperature. Only after extended exercise with the depletion of glycogen stores and the resultant fatigue will there be a risk that the body does not produce enough heat to maintain a sufficient core temperature. At that time, the risk of hypothermia can become a concern.

RUNNING HOT AND COLD: Q&A

Q. *What is a "hot" environment?*

A. As a runner, when the temperature begins to climb over 60°F, you can expect the temperature to influence your running, i.e., 1 to 2 percent loss of running efficiency for each 1.5°F increase in temperature. This performance decrement becomes more pronounced as the race distance increases. Add increased humidity to an already warm day, and the impact on your running is even more pronounced. Your expected performance goals must be adjusted when you encounter high temperatures and humidity.

Q. ***How important is hydration in countering the effects of heat?***

A. Very important. The answer to this question could easily take up an entire chapter. Hydration becomes a key factor in running performance in those sessions lasting more than 1 hour. A 2 to 3 percent water loss will result in a significant performance decrement.

Q. ***How can you be sure that you are drinking enough, but not too much?***

A. Make sure that your urine output is plentiful and the color is clear or pale yellow before you begin your run. If you are losing more than 1.5 percent of your body weight during a run, you are losing too much fluid through sweat, and you need to drink more before and during your run.

Q. ***How do you acclimatize to the heat?***

A. Heat acclimatization requires exercising in the heat. Sitting in a hot environment, even for extended periods of time, will not result in the adaptations necessary for exercising in the heat. Your body learns to sweat more effectively and to tolerate liquid replacement as you train in hot environments. It takes 10 to 14 days for your body to completely acclimatize to elevated environmental temperatures, although initial adaptations occur in the first 5 days.

Q. ***What's a runner to do when it's hot?***

A. You will not be able to sustain as fast a pace as normal in the heat even after acclimatization. In Key Run Workout #1, you may need to take longer recovery intervals. In Key Run Workouts #2 and #3, you may not be able to maintain the prescribed pace for the specified distance. Run the specified distance at an effort you perceive as moderate to hard. When running in hot, humid conditions, be smart and listen to your body.

To cope with the heat, try running in the early morning, when temperatures are coolest. Another option is to run indoors on the treadmill. The lower temperature and humidity of the indoor environment will enable you to run at a faster pace than the outdoor heat would permit. However, if you are training for a summer race, even if it is in the early morning, running indoors all the time will not provide the acclimatization you'll need to run in hot, humid conditions on race day. Mixing outdoor running for acclimatization with indoor running for speed may be a good race preparation strategy. Consider the specificity principle: Try to train in conditions similar to those in which you will be racing.

Q. *Is hydration important in cold weather?*

A. Most individuals tend to take in less liquid when they are exposed to a cold environment, even when exercising. Just as in the heat, thirst is a very poor measure of your need for fluids.

Fluid replacement in a cold environment is important, but it typically won't be as obvious to you as it would be in warm conditions.

Also, just because it's cold, don't forget the sunscreen!

10

Running Injuries

Like many runners, I suffered miserably with plantar fasciitis and Achilles tendinitis because I kept training through the soreness and pain. Both injuries are devilish to eliminate, especially when you continue training after detecting the symptoms. The more inflamed the tissue, the longer the recovery. Now, I take preventive and rehabilitative measures at the first hint of an irritation. With an appropriate training program and a conservative approach to irritations, downtime from running can be kept to a minimum. However, runners tend to ignore symptoms or hope that they will go away. That rarely happens if you keep running.

My most sobering moment with injury occurred 2 days after running the Las Vegas Marathon. As I sat down at the breakfast table, I experienced a sharp pain in my back. After several days of severe pain, I managed to get back to my normal activities. I had what I thought was a hamstring strain until an MRI showed that I had a herniated disk. It didn't respond to rest or steroidal injections; surgery was required.

My neurosurgeon explained that there was no guarantee that I would be able to run or play tennis after surgery, and, if I could, running might be limited to a few miles at a time. After surgery, I began to think that his

(continued on page 150)

The Runner Writes:

Dear FIRST:

I first read about your program in the August 2005 issue of *Runner's World*. I'm 43 and have run eight marathons and many halfs in the last 10 years, but I have suffered Achilles heel injuries the last few years on a more traditional 45- to 50-mile peak training program. After missing my Boston qualifying goal at the Napa Marathon by 5 minutes (and I really dragged the last 4 miles) in early 2005, I decided to try your FIRST marathon training program. Despite the fact that there are many people who are skeptical of the results (especially in the online forums), I thought the program made sense for me.

Please thank everyone who helped with the program and the research. I was able to shave 6 minutes off my PR and beat my goal of 3:20 with a finish time of 3:18 at the Silicon Valley Marathon today. That qualifies me for Boston, though right now I'm not sure I feel much like running another marathon!

I followed the program to the letter, and it gave me a structure and discipline that was great. I also had enough recovery time to make it work, and I remained injury-free. The speed workouts were tough, and I struggled with them at first, but eventually, I got stronger and faster. I can't say I was ever totally comfortable with them, but I knew they would help out on race day. I also cross-trained by cycling on hilly terrains on weekends.

On race day, the last few miles were still hard, but I had the mental and physical toughness to get me through it and stay on pace.

I encourage you guys to write a book on this program. I first read about your program in *Runner's World*. If you need endorsements or case studies, I would be happy to help!

Thanks again for helping me achieve an important goal.

Zack Urlocker
Software executive
Santa Cruz, California

***FIRST* Replies:**

We took Zack's advice and wrote this book!

Many runners have reported that reducing the number of days and miles has been the answer to their particular injuries. By eliminating the injuries, these runners are able to train with the intensity needed to improve their fitness and running performance. It is gratifying that our program is enabling runners to pursue and achieve running goals that, because of previous injuries, they thought no longer attainable.

We spend much of our time answering questions about injuries. Runners want to know how to continue running even though they are injured. Actually, if we could educate runners to increase their training gradually and to respond to injuries at the earliest onset of symptoms, most of the downtime from running could be avoided and the treatments relatively minor and successful. We have found it difficult to convince runners to reduce their running as soon as they incur an irritation. When runners contact us about an injury and we ask how long they have been having problems, the answer is often "months."

We insist that runners in our training studies inform us immediately about any symptom of injury. We immediately have them reduce their distance and pace. If that doesn't help to relieve the problem, we reduce the frequency of running. We also suggest other conservative treatments along with the reduced training. By following those guidelines, we have been able to help runners continue their training with only minor modifications rather than a significant training interruption.

In the main text of this chapter, we have answered commonly asked questions about injuries, and we describe in some detail the most common running injuries, the causes, the signs and symptoms, and the treatments.

gloomiest projection just might be true. I began with walking; after 6 weeks, I added swimming, progressed to biking, and finally tried running. It was a slow and frustrating process that seemed like two steps forward, one step backward for about 18 months. However, I gradually built up my speed and distance, and I completed a marathon 30 months after my surgery.

During that rehabilitation time, I worked closely with a physical therapist and adopted an attitude that I would diligently follow the therapist's directions and would accept and appreciate whatever physical activity I could do. After 10 years of varied training and eight postsurgery marathons, I still truly appreciate each run, and I realize I can't take for granted that I will always be able to participate in an activity I enjoy immensely.

Did running contribute to my herniated disk? My neurosurgeon said that there was no way to know the cause of the injury. Repetitive strenuous activities can contribute to back problems, but many other activities, such as 25 years of competitive basketball, could have been the source of the trauma. It could have been a congenital condition that I share with my mother. I mention the back surgery to give an example of how important rehabilitation under supervision is, and how progressing gradually can result in full recovery.

My recommendation as a result of my struggles with injuries is to pay close attention to your body and seek a professional opinion and treatment early after signs and symptoms of injury. Keep your body in good shape. The stretches, strength training exercises, and form drills we've included in this book can be done in a reasonable amount of time and will not only improve performance but also provide a good injury defense.

On page 148 is a letter from a California runner who used the FIRST "**3plus2**" marathon training program to qualify for Boston while remaining injury-free.

RUNNING INJURIES: THE ESSENTIALS

- Most runners will incur a running-related injury at some point in their running career that will interfere with their running.

- The majority of these injuries will be associated with the anatomy at or below the knee.
- The majority of the injuries are related to doing too much, too fast or too soon.
- Modify training until the injuries have mended.
- The sooner and more aggressively injuries are treated, the sooner they will be repaired.

RUNNING INJURIES: Q&A

Q. *What are acute injuries?*

A. Strains, partial tears of muscle, and sprains, partial tears of ligaments and tendons, usually occur as a result of a fall, a twisting movement, or a forceful, explosive movement. The immediate application of compression and ice and elevation of the injured area will reduce the inflammation and swelling. Seek medical help if the pain or swelling is severe. Rest the affected part until pain and swelling are greatly reduced or absent. Begin a return to activity by strengthening the injured area, followed by a gradual return to full activity.

An injury does not necessarily preclude activity altogether. You may be able to bike or swim, depending on the specific location of the injury.

Q. *What are overuse injuries?*

A. Running contributes to repetitive stress on muscles, tendons, and bones. Without adequate recovery, overuse injuries, such as patellofemoral pain syndrome (runner's knee), Achilles tendinitis, plantar fasciitis, and shinsplints, can develop. The body can recover from most of this stress, but only if it has adequate time for the tissue to adapt, compensate, and strengthen. Just how fast the adaptation occurs is related to age, overall conditioning, and the gradual progression of increased training.

Q. *How much running is too much?*

A. Frequency and duration of running are two of the factors that determine the overall stress. Adding days of running must be balanced against the increased likelihood of injury. The length of runs must be increased gradually. Too much, too often leads to injury.

Q. *Is training intensity associated with injuries?*

A. Intense training is a fundamental part of the FIRST approach. Intensity brings the greatest gains in performance while at the same time presenting the opportunity for injury. How to balance the use of intensity with the prevention of overuse injuries is one of the challenges that all runners face. You must increase the intensity (pace) *gradually.* Just because you are capable of running faster doesn't mean that you should be doing so in each workout. The FIRST approach is not based on how fast you can complete each run. Distance and intensity should not be increased at the same time. Manipulate only one of the three primary training variables—frequency, duration and intensity—at a time. Increasing more than one variable at a time significantly increases your risk of injury. However, once you have suffered an overuse injury, the primary treatment will be to reduce intensity.

Q. *How can overuse injuries be prevented?*

A. To prevent overuse injuries, you need a prudent, well-defined program of running. FIRST's 3-days-a-week program design is ideal for runners who may be injury-prone. With the appropriate intensity and mileage determined for each workout, you can attain improved running performance while reducing your risk of injury. Elite runners who are willing to bear the risks of injury associated with greater intensity, frequency, and duration of effort are not likely to find our approach appealing. Conversely, for the average competitive runner, the costs, measured in pain and lost training days, of pushing to the limits are not likely to be worth the marginal improvements.

Q. ***How do I know if I have a biomechanical or anatomical problem?***

A. These two categories are not mutually exclusive, and one can lead to the other. A specialist may need to examine both your stride and the biomechanical structure of the lower half of your body. Gait analysis using high-speed video or digital techniques is effective, but it can be costly. Talk to your sports medicine physician about what is available in your area. There may be a clinic for runners that can assist you in this endeavor.

Q. ***What about nonsteroidal anti-inflammatory medicine in treating or preventing running injuries?***

A. Nonsteroidal anti-inflammatory drugs (NSAIDs) are very useful in reducing the inflammation associated with different types of running injuries. Their use is often indicated during the recovery from overuse injuries, but they should not be used to permit training by masking the inflammation. You should treat these as medicine and not as performance boosters. Treating them as the latter may lead to greater injury and other complications.

Q. ***Do I need orthotics?***

A. Orthotics are inserts placed in the shoe to correct certain biomechanical problems, such as overpronation or flat feet. Orthotics may be helpful to a runner with bad alignment who is suffering from pain and repeated injuries. A sports medicine doctor can evaluate whether orthotics will be beneficial to you.

Q. ***How does excess body weight affect running injuries?***

A. Body weight has a big impact on running performance and injuries. Carrying too much body weight reduces performance and puts significant additional strain on your joints, ligaments, and muscles.

Q. *What are the most common running injuries?*

A. Below, we describe seven common running injuries and how to treat them.

Runner's Knee

Runner's knee is a term that refers to several conditions associated with pain around the front of the knee. This pain is often a result of a misalignment that causes irritation to the underside of the kneecap.

Signs and symptoms: Generally, mild irritation at the joint itself will occur. There may be localized swelling and redness. If left untreated, the inflammation can become painful to the point that any running or walking downhill or climbing stairs results in strong pain in the joint.

Treatment: Since this condition is due to overuse, reducing the current training regimen is usually warranted. You won't need to stop activity, but you may need to substitute other forms of exercise until the inflammation is cured. Any activity that puts strain on the knee will slow healing. Hill running may have to be greatly reduced or eliminated. Low-impact activities like elliptical training, deep water running, or swimming can be substituted. Absolute rest may be required in extreme cases, but this is uncommon.

Strengthening the quadriceps (thigh muscles) is an important goal. Stretching the hamstrings, along with the calf muscles, may permit complete straightening of the knee in a normal fashion.

Ice is still one of the best ways to deal with inflammation following a workout. After your workout, complete about a 10-minute cooldown stretch of the lateral thigh, hamstrings, and calves. Immediately begin icing the knee. Fill a plastic bag with ice and apply this directly to the kneecap; hold it in place with an elastic wrap. Keep the ice on for 20 minutes, and follow this routine after every workout.

Iliotibial Band Syndrome

Iliotibial band syndrome (ITBS) is the most common cause for pain located on the lateral aspect of the knee. Like many running injuries, ITBS takes weeks to reach a level that begins to affect training. Sometimes, a runner has had no signs or symptoms but is struck with lateral knee pain while running on a road with a sloped shoulder.

Overpronation can result in stress on the iliotibial band. Weak thigh muscles, hamstrings, and quadriceps often are related to the risk for ITBS, as are weak gluteal muscles.

Signs and symptoms: The most common complaint of the runner will be a sharp or burning pain on the lateral aspect of the knee. Typically, pain begins after running a certain distance and is likely to worsen as the run continues. Following the run, the pain may disappear but will return during the next training session. As the condition worsens, the pain may become prominent sooner during the run and eventually even during walking, particularly when climbing stairs. Redness and swelling over the lateral aspect of the knee develop occasionally.

Treatment: Rest, ice massage, and nonsteroidal anti-inflammatory medicine can address the acute symptoms. After the pain subsides, you should begin stretching the iliotibial band. Your quadriceps, hamstrings, and hip muscles will need strengthening to prevent a recurrence.

To stretch the ITB, lie on your side with both legs bent in running position. Bend the bottom leg as you bring it toward your chest. Move the top leg back toward your butt so that the running position of your legs is as exaggerated as possible. Hold this position for 30 seconds, then flip sides and repeat.

In severe cases, a physician might prescribe a steroid injection.

Shinsplints

When the connective tissue, tendons and ligaments, of the lower leg become inflamed, the condition is what we call shinsplints.

Beginning runners are the most likely to be affected. Several factors that may lead to shinsplints include hard running surfaces, worn-out shoes, uneven running surfaces, flat feet, and excessive hill running. All of these can contribute to microtears in the connective tissue that develops into inflammation because of inadequate recovery from excessive stress.

Signs and symptoms: The pain of shinsplints may seem minor initially, and it is not easy to locate exactly. It's generally felt in the lower third of the tibia, where the muscles attach to the bone. The pain may seem to appear at about the same distance into every run, and it may improve or get worse as the run continues. Usually, it will disappear several minutes to hours after the run is over. If left untreated, the pain is likely to increase over time and become constant, triggered even by slow walking. If you can point to a particular point on your leg where the pain is triggered by touch, you may have a stress fracture that needs attention by a physician

Treatment: Since shinsplints are primarily an overuse injury, the treatment is similar to that for other overuse injuries. Try rest from running, ice massage, nonsteroidal anti-inflammatory medication, and stretching the muscles of your lower leg.

Well-conditioned muscle fatigues more slowly; therefore, the more you strengthen your leg muscles, the better your chances of avoiding shinsplints.

Stress Fractures

The stress from running on the feet and legs makes these areas extremely susceptible to microscopic injuries to the bone that do not have time to heal. Eventually, the bone begins to fail, and small cracks can be seen with x-rays or other images. Increases in mileage—particularly, sudden increases—can bring about bone damage that your body can't repair quickly enough, leading to stress fractures. Your muscles may get fatigued with training and absorb shock more poorly, requiring your bones to bear more of the shock of impact. Harder surfaces, such as concrete, also increase the likelihood of injury. Runners who do not take in enough calcium or who have other conditions that might weaken bones are more susceptible to stress fractures. Females are at greater risk of stress fractures than males due in part to their smaller muscle mass and inadequate calcium intake.

Signs and symptoms: The pain associated with stress fractures is usually more localized than it is with shinsplints. Tenderness and swelling may be present at the fracture site. Your doctor may use a bone scan or other diagnostic imaging to diagnose a stress fracture.

Treatment: Rest may take care of the problem. If the injury is not too serious, typically, 4 to 8 weeks without running (during which you'll have to use cross-training) should be sufficient.

Achilles Tendinitis

Inflammation of the Achilles tendon is primarily due to overuse, complicated by anatomical or biomechanical problems. Muscle inflexibility, overpronation, and weak lower leg muscles can all contribute to inflammation and injury of the Achilles tendon. A single extreme stress may also result in injury and pain.

Signs and symptoms: Acute tendinitis is defined by the rapid onset of a sharp or burning pain. Squeezing the tendon results in a sharp pain. As the tissue warms up, the pain may decrease. It may be possible to rub the tendon between your thumb and index finger and feel a gritty sensation—a sign of inflammation.

Achilles tendinitis is one of the major causes of heel pain. A lump may form in the belly of the tendon or just to the side of where the tendon attaches to the heel bone. Early-morning walking may result in debilitating pain for several steps, but the pain may subside with continued walking.

Treatment: Rest is the key to healing Achilles tendon problems. Reduce training volume by 50 percent and continue at this level until the pain is completely gone. Nonsteroidal anti-inflammatory medication may be taken for 7 to 10 days to help decrease the inflammation. Ice massage three or four times a day for 20 minutes is also a great way to reduce the inflammation. When the pain has disappeared, begin increasing your training by 5 to 10 percent each week, until you have returned to pre-injury volume.

You can place a ¼-inch-thick felt heel pad in the shoe of the injured side. This will reduce the tension on your Achilles tendon. You may need to keep this in your shoe for several months.

Achilles tendinitis responds well to conservative stretching. Wall leans held for 30 seconds with the leg straight and then for 30 seconds with the knee bent slightly work well. Use a watch to be sure that you are stretching for the correct amount of time. Alternate legs until you have completed three cycles of stretches with each leg. Do this three or four times a day. Stretch only until you begin to feel discomfort; never permit the stretch to become painful.

Inspect your shoe for excessive wear. Seek advice from a person who is trained in selecting running shoes based on foot mechanics. Also consider the use of orthotics, as described above.

If conservative treatment does not improve the pain significantly, more aggressive forms of therapy may be necessary, even including casts and physical therapy. You must be patient here. Severe cases of Achilles tendinitis can take many months to resolve.

If you ignore treatment for the injury or if you continue to run through the pain, damage to the tendon can weaken the connective tissue so that it is unable to withstand the additional forces of jumping, running, or climbing stairs, making a rupture possible. A ruptured tendon requires surgery and casting for 12 months, followed by several months of physical therapy.

Plantar Fasciitis

One of the hallmark injuries of runners around the world is *plantar fasciitis*, commonly called heel pain. Inflammation occurs where the plantar fascia, a bundle of connective tissue in the sole of the foot, attaches to the heel bone, eventually causing pain and a change in training habits.

Repeated stresses on the foot during the footstrike result in plantar fascia strain. This strain is exaggerated during fast running and hill running: Both cause the fascia to stretch. Running on the beach's soft sand can quickly inflame the fascia. If the volume of training and, in particular, the type of training described above, is too great for the recuperative powers of the tissues, a cycle of plantar fasciitis may begin.

Signs and symptoms: The universal symptom for plantar fasciitis is a sharp pain felt in the heel and arch during the first few steps in the morning. The plantar fascia contract during the night's rest, and the first few steps begin the painful stretching process. Sitting for long periods during the day may result in the same pain in the arch.

FIRST Success

After completing my fourth marathon in June 2005 with disappointing results (my first one not showing improvement), I needed to find a marathon training program that decreased my high susceptibility to injury, but still increased my speed and endurance. I fortunately saw the 3-day training plan article in the August 2005 ***Runner's World*** and decided to give it a chance. I tried the FIRST program, and although I missed a couple weeks due to illness, I was still able to improve my PR from 3:30 to 3:15 at the Las Vegas Marathon in December. Even more important to me, I achieved the seemingly impossible goal of qualifying for the Boston Marathon.

Philip Cushman
U.S. AIR FORCE
LITCHFIELD PARK, ARIZONA

The pain of plantar fasciitis may get better during warmup for a training session, and it may remain at a reduced level throughout the session. As you begin cooling down, the pain may begin to increase, and it may be quite severe over the next few hours.

Treatment: The first level of treatment is conservative. It consists of relative rest, icing, stretching, heel pads, off-the-shelf orthotics, massage, and nonsteroidal anti-inflammatory medication. Massage can help to stretch the fascia. One common way to massage the bottom of your foot is to roll it over a can, a round stick, or a ball. Early treatment should resolve the inflammation for the large majority of runners.

More aggressive levels of treatment might include steroid injections, custom orthotics, night splints, and physical therapy. Steroids can have an immediate positive effect on the pain of plantar fasciitis. The pain is likely to return, though, if appropriate followup treatment is not maintained. Orthotics may be necessary to control foot motion and support the arch during footstrike and toe-off. Night splints will keep the plantar fascia from contracting overnight.

Chronic Calf Tears

Another common injury among runners is chronic calf muscle tears. These tears result in knots in the calf as surrounding tissues tear and scar tissue develops.

Signs and symptoms: While the knots probably develop over time, they tend to make their presence known suddenly, when a sharp tightness occurs in the calf. The tightness can stop you in your tracks. Runners often describe this onset as viselike pressure in the calf.

Treatment: Cross-friction massage must be applied to the knots to stretch the damaged fibers and to relieve the pressure exerted on the muscle. You must stretch both the soleus and gastrocnemius muscles regularly (see Chapter 13 on stretching). We recommend doing these stretches both before and after running. It is important to begin all workouts with 10 to 15 minutes of easy running, gradually increasing the pace before any intensive running.

Final Comments on Running Injuries

One of the primary goals of the FIRST program is to promote lifelong running enjoyment. Injury prevention is critical in meeting this goal. Since overuse injuries are the major culprit in ending many runners' careers, reducing the total volume of training by eliminating unnecessary or "junk" miles should have a favorable outcome for injury prevention.

Our program requires higher-intensity training to help you reach your goals. This training is tailored to your individual abilities as defined by your current performance levels, while allowing for 4 days without running each week. These off days permit recovery from previous workouts, leaving you fresh for the next training run and reducing overuse problems. However, you must carefully monitor your own body—particularly the knees, ankles, and feet—for signs and symptoms of overuse injuries. Be prepared to take immediate action to keep an injury from progressing to more severe levels.

11

Running Nutrition

We cannot overemphasize the importance of good nutrition for performance and overall health. I grew up eating an all-American diet, meaning lots of fat, sugar, and praise from grandmothers and aunts for "cleaning my plate" and asking for seconds. After several years of inconsistent marathon finishes and gastrointestinal distress following 10-Ks, I made drastic changes in my dietary habits. I adopted a strict low-fat, plant-based diet. Immediately, my training and racing improved, as well as my comfort while running. The GI distress disappeared, and I began finishing marathons without my energy levels tumbling drastically. More important, my blood fats were reduced, and my heart disease risk ratios improved. I also found it much easier to maintain a steady and desirable weight.

I have observed many runners who train vigorously and assiduously, but fail to reach their potential because of poor eating habits. Conversely, I have seen runners in our training studies improve dramatically because of improved nutrition as much as dedicated and smart training. Just as we mentioned in Chapter 7 on rest and recovery, Quality Training + Quality Nutrition + Quality Rest = Quality Results.

(continued on page 165)

The Runner Writes:

Dear FIRST:

My training diet in the past has had some serious holes in it. I really don't mind reading labels and taking the time and discipline to "clean up" my diet. What has been very difficult for me in the past is to actually "count" calories or control portions. This is not to say that I would not attempt to do this in the future; it has just been the most difficult aspect of my training diet in the past.

What I have done is come up with my own training diet that has seemed to get me down to my target race weight. What I don't know is whether it is providing the proper carbs to my body for optimum performance. My training diet relies in great part on simple overall principles that I adhere to every day. This comes at the expense of counting calories every day. These principles are (1) eliminate all breads, pastas, and potatoes unless 24 to 48 hours prior to a long run (15 miles or more); (2) no desserts except for fat-free yogurt; (3) no fast food except for salads; (4) dinners are predominantly grilled steaks, chicken, or fish with vegetables.

Again, I simply live by these wide, sweeping principles and eat whatever portion I need to feel "full." This can translate into some large portions for dinner at times.

Any specific ideas you have for nutrition? My normal rest weight is 160 pounds when I'm not watching my diet (but still training). I like to run marathons at 143 to 145 pounds. In the past, the way I've gotten down to race weight is with intensive training and a lower-carb diet. This is not to say I'm doing Atkins—I will still carbo load before long runs—but my daily diet consists of no breads, pastas, starches, or desserts (except for yogurt), etc. I eat lots of grilled steak, fish, chicken, and vegetables. The only daily "carb" intake would be a bowl of cereal every morning. I know I need carbs to supplement my training and performance, but I can't seem to get down to race weight without limiting my daily intake. Any ideas?

Nick Ford
Director of operations
Columbus, Ohio

FIRST Replies:

Second only to requests for specific running advice are the many requests we receive for nutritional counseling. Most of the runners attending our lectures and participating in our training studies indicate that they are confused about dietary guidelines or have difficulty adhering to them. Unfortunately, the avalanche of books touting unsound dietary schemes has not made it easier for runners like Nick to be well-informed with accurate nutritional advice.

There are many philosophies concerning every aspect of nutrition, weight loss, and competition. Runners seem to have strong ideas about nutrition, but they are also willing to experiment. Human variability ensures that no one nutrition program works for everyone; however, there are some basic principles of nutrition that are well-grounded in research. Wholesome nutritional habits are essential for runners to be appropriately fueled for their energy needs.

Let's examine Nick's dietary practices. We endorse some of his dietary principles and suggest modification to others.

His first principle to "eliminate all breads, pastas, and potatoes unless 24 to 48 hours prior to a long run (15 miles or more)" should be reconsidered.

Carbohydrates—ultimately, glucose molecules—are the cornerstones supporting the body's energy needs, whether for brain function or the finish of a race. The body can make the glucose it needs, but that is often at the expense of protein taken from body stores. To keep his body from converting protein into glucose, Nick needs a high-carbohydrate diet (60 to 70 percent of calories coming from carbohydrates) built on *unrefined* carbohydrates. Many grocery stores offer whole wheat pasta and bread options that would be a good addition to Nick's diet.

Nick's second principle of "no desserts except for fat-free yogurt" is reasonable, since most desserts are simple sugars. Complex or unrefined carbohydrates are healthier choices for your carbohydrate sources. Unrefined carbohydrates tend to slow the rate of release of glucose from the gut, which may help curb hunger and appetite over time. Minimizing or avoiding

(continued)

The Runner Writes *(continued)*

simple sugars will help avoid a roller-coaster effect in blood glucose levels. Adding fruits as a dessert choice would be a healthier option. Fruits, like other unrefined carbohydrates, add lots of important vitamins and minerals and, in some cases, fiber.

Intense training requires that carbohydrates be replaced daily. Since the FIRST training approach is based on high-quality running, it is important that your daily diet be based predominantly on complex (unrefined) carbohydrates.

Nick's third principle is "no fast food except for salads." Fast food (typically fried) presents challenges for a healthy diet. However, it may be difficult for runners to completely avoid fast food options. When you find it necessary to eat at a fast food place, salads can be healthy options. Make sure you skip the high-fat dressings and "crispy" chicken that often negate the value of the healthy salad choice. Other healthful choices include fruits and baked items such as potatoes.

Eating "dinners (that) are predominantly grilled steaks, chicken, or fish with vegetables" was Nick's final dietary principle. While we do not specifically promote a completely vegetarian diet, for health reasons, we do promote a primarily plant-based diet. There are many entrées that could be substituted for his dependence on meat as the center of a meal.

Most high-protein foods are also high in fat. Plant-based sources of protein eliminate the extra fat that usually accompanies animal protein. In addition, with plant proteins, you get complex carbohydrates. While much emphasis today has been placed on the need for and role of protein, the primary source of energy for endurance athletes is complex carbohydrates.

"Portion distortion" has made it difficult for Americans to recognize what is a reasonable amount of food to consume. Larger servings, plates, cartons, and bottles have made it a challenge to understand what a normal serving size is. Losing weight is a matter of balancing caloric intake (the food you eat) with caloric expenditure (daily metabolism and calories burned by exercise).

Nick's letter on page 162 is typical of the many we receive asking whether we can give nutritional advice that will aid running performance. This chapter is devoted to answering those many letters.

RUNNING NUTRITION: THE ESSENTIALS

- A well-balanced diet is recommended for all healthy adults; just because you exercise and run does not mean you can eat anything you want.
- A runner's diet should be based primarily on complex (unrefined) carbohydrates, which includes whole grains, fruits, and vegetables.
- Sixty to 70 percent of your calories should come from carbohydrate sources, with only 10 percent from simple carbohydrates.
- Protein should account for 10 to 20 percent of total calories and should be selected from vegetables and lean cuts of meat. Vegetable protein is just as effective as animal protein in meeting your daily requirements, but it has the advantage of reducing saturated fat intake. Include beans, whole grains, nuts, and seeds as good sources of vegetable protein in your diet.
- Fat calories should account for 15 to 25 percent of your total caloric intake.
- Trans fatty acids (common in snack and processed foods) should be avoided due to their significant negative impact on blood cholesterol.
- Healthy eating will meet all of your needs as a runner, with only minimal changes needed prior to competition.
- Your diet must provide the energy needed for successful participation in a vigorous training program.
- Once you have reached your optimal training weight, you must fine-tune your caloric intake to maintain your desired target weight.
- Not eating enough will result in an inability to complete the

quality workouts in the FIRST training program, and it may result in loss of lean body weight.

- Eating a variety of foods ensures that you'll take in a variety of nutrients.

RUNNING NUTRITION: Q&A

Q. *Why should I consume so many carbohydrates?*

A. A nutritious diet plan is based around a selection of fruits, vegetables, and whole grains, which have carbohydrates as a major component. By selecting primarily unrefined carbohydrate products, runners decrease their risk for several chronic diseases, including diabetes, heart disease, and cancer. Carbohydrates supply the immediate energy needs of the body and are the major source for glycogen, which is the storage form of carbohydrates in the body. A high-carbohydrate diet ensures the runner a full glycogen load for training and competition.

Q. *What is the glycemic index, and should I concern myself with it?*

A. Nick's caution regarding carbohydrates is not completely unfounded. Some carbohydrates raise your blood sugar level more than others. The glycemic index is a measure of how a carbohydrate source affects your blood sugar level.

Foods with a high glycemic index release sugar into the bloodstream faster than foods with a lower glycemic index. In general, refined carbohydrates and simple carbohydrates (sugars) have a higher glycemic index than complex carbohydrates (starches). Unrefined grains such as brown rice and whole grain breads and cereals tend to have a lower glycemic index than refined carbohydrates. Fruits and vegetables also have a low glycemic index. Other examples of carbohydrates with lower glycemic index values are whole wheat pastas, whole grain breads, bran cereals, grapes, fresh and dried apricots, apples, grapefruit, oranges, baked beans, lentils, corn, peas, chickpeas, green beans, and low-fat yogurt.

After an intense workout or race, you might choose to consume high-glycemic foods to get your blood glucose level up quickly, so as to assist in replenishing muscle glycogen and aid recovery.

Q. ***Will consuming more protein increase my running performance?***

A. Protein does not provide a significant amount of energy when you run or work out. Protein is the major building material of the body and is essential for tissue growth and repair. A diet based on 15 percent protein will meet both of these needs. The body cannot store protein; any extra is converted into carbohydrates or fat, with little being used for your immediate energy needs.

Q. ***Is the protein from meat better than proteins from plant sources?***

A. Protein is protein, regardless of the source. Animal protein has been called high-quality protein because it contains all 20 amino acids needed by humans. Soy is the only plant source that contains all 20 amino acids. Therefore, vegetarians must mix and match their food selections throughout the day to ensure that they receive all 20 amino acids from their diet. For example, a combination of beans and rice, sometimes called complementary protein sources, will supply all of the essential amino acids. For health, more of your protein should be derived from plant sources so as to reduce fat intake. While we are not necessarily advocating a totally vegetarian diet, we are suggesting that endurance athletes and runners adopt a primarily plant-based diet.

Q. ***Why are polyunsaturated fats preferable to saturated fats?***

A. There are numerous studies linking saturated fat with chronic diseases, especially heart disease. Polyunsaturated fats have been associated with a decrease in the risk for this disease. By combining unsaturated fats with a low-fat diet, you will have an optimal disease-fighting menu. A healthy runner is typically a faster runner.

Q. ***What are trans fatty acids (TFAs), and why are they considered so bad?***

A. Trans fatty acids are created during the hydrogenation process of corn or other oils to increase shelf life and meet consumer tastes. TFAs are known to reduce the good cholesterol, HDL, while increasing the bad cholesterol, LDL. TFAs have also been shown to damage the blood vessels, increasing the risk of atherosclerosis and heart disease.

Q. ***How much fluid does a runner need to consume?***

A. It is important to stay adequately hydrated. Drink enough during the day to keep your urine clear. Two hours before a workout, drink 16 ounces of your preferred sports drink or water. Two hours is ample time for the fluid to be cleared from the stomach and for the kidneys to remove the excess. Thirst is not a reliable way of determining your hydration needs. Therefore, you need to follow a schedule for drinking.

You should consume a quantity of fluid that is just equal to your fluid loss from sweating and breathing during exercise. Sweat rates vary from runner to runner and with the weather conditions. Weighing yourself before and after a run is a good way to determine your sweat loss during exercise. If you are losing more than 1.5 percent of your body weight during a run, you are losing too much fluid through sweat, and you need to drink more before and during your run.

You need to practice drinking during your training, both to train your body to handle fluids during exercise and to learn what is a comfortable amount for you to drink while working out. The longer the event, the more important it is to follow the schedule, especially when fluid loss from sweating is exceeding your system's ability to handle added fluids.

Q. *What fluid is best to drink?*

A. Prior to race day, contact the event promoters to find out what types of fluid replacement are available. During your long runs, practice with the race day drink to get used to it. If you can't tolerate the event drink, be prepared to drink water or carry your own drink. You do not want to find out on race day that your stomach can't handle the event drink.

Q. *What about using energy gels? Are they better?*

A. Gels taken with water provide essentially the same nutrients as a sports drink. For runners concerned about race finish time, grabbing a cup of sports drink from an aid station is going to be quicker and more convenient than opening a gel and also drinking a cup of water.

Q. *Can I drink too much water?*

A. Yes, especially during prolonged exercise. Many runners have heard the mantra "hydrate, hydrate, hydrate." Hydration is good and important, but during long runs, some runners drink too much fluid. This results in a dilution of the body's sodium stores, leading to hyponatremia. Hyponatremia is a life-threatening condition that has been responsible for several marathoners' deaths over the past years. Use your weight loss during exercise as a guide for fluid replacement.

Q. *Why should I worry about hyponatremia?*

A. Hyponatremia has become a major topic of concern in marathons over the past few years. Hyponatremia is an abnormally low concentration of sodium in the blood. Too little sodium can cause cells to malfunction, and extremely low sodium levels can be fatal.

To make sure that you consume enough fluid for a workout or race, you need to know your sweat rate. Weigh yourself nude before and after your long runs at the pace and under the conditions anticipated for your race. As a general rule, for every pound lost through sweating, you want to make sure that you drink 16 ounces. (Or, in metric terms, for every kilogram lost through sweating, you should drink around 1 liter.)

The popularity of the marathon has resulted in the participation of runners with a vast divergence of talent. Marathon times have increased to an average of over 4 hours, with many runners still on the road 5 to 6 hours after the start. Many of these runners have trained with groups that stress the importance of fluid intake throughout the course of the race. Due to the low workload related to their pace, these runners actually gain water weight as a result of consuming more water than is lost by sweating. This results in lower sodium concentrations in their blood and could potentially lead to hyponatremia. Because the symptoms may resemble those of dehydration, hyponatremia victims are often given liquids, only worsening their condition.

Q. ***Should I take a mineral/vitamin supplement?***

A. In general, a balanced diet will meet the needs of most runners. Due to the stress of high-quality training, taking a multivitamin with minerals once a day is fine and has not been shown to pose any health risks as long as you avoid megadoses. Because you are getting vitamins and minerals from the foods you eat, try to find a vitamin that contains no more than 100 percent of the Daily Value for any vitamin.

Q. ***What about other supplements?***

A. There are numerous supplements on the market, many with seemingly convincing claims of supporting research. All of the FIRST faculty members are runners. Some FIRST faculty may take a multivitamin, but as athletes interested in a healthy, safe, and prolonged approach to running, none takes nor recommends dietary supplements.

Q. ***How many calories do I need to consume daily?***

A. The quick answer is, "as many as you burn daily." A complete answer is not so easy. Body size and activity level play a significant factor in determining daily caloric needs. A simple way to estimate your daily caloric needs is to multiple your body weight (in pounds) by 11.3. Then, add an additional 100 calories for each mile of running.

For example, a 135-pound runner who ran 5 miles would need approximately:

135 × 11.3 = 1525 + 500 (for 5 miles) = 2025 calories

A 160-pound runner who ran 15 miles would need approximately:

160 × 11.3 = 1808 + 1500 (for 15 miles) = 3308 calories

These are estimates, and they will require fine-tuning by each individual.

Q. ***What is an ideal body weight for a runner?***

A. You should be more concerned about body composition than body weight. For long distance running, extra body weight puts significant stress on the legs. Extra weight also increases the overall workload on the body, thereby decreasing running economy. For most male runners, a body composition of 8 to 15 percent fat would be an achievable goal, while female runners should aim for a range of 16 to 25 percent body fat.

Q. ***Do I need special nutrition for competition? How about carbohydrate loading?***

A. Exercise increases the energy requirements of the body up to 25 times those of normal expenditure. Your body converts all carbohydrates to glucose, which may be used immediately as fuel or stored for later use. Glycogen is the storage form of glucose in the body, and it is mostly stored in your skeletal muscles and liver. Your body has a limited storage capacity for glycogen, which may be rapidly depleted during strenuous exercise.

During exercise that feels "easy," more than half of the calories used for energy come from stored body fat. As exercise intensity increases to "moderate," the body begins to burn less fat and utilize more glycogen. Long runs tend to deplete glycogen. The term "hitting the wall" is used to describe the effect that glycogen depletion has on a runner.

Once your stored glycogen is depleted, your body shifts back to burning fat. Since converting fat to energy cannot be done as efficiently as using glycogen for energy, your pace decreases.

One aim of training is to increase the pace at which you can run while burning fat. In other words, your "easy" pace becomes a faster pace. By burning fat rather than glycogen, you put off glycogen depletion longer; you put off "hitting the wall." Appropriate training increases the pace you can maintain before your crossover from fat burning to carbohydrate burning occurs. And this helps to save glycogen that will be needed farther down the road.

If you maintain a diet that is high in complex carbohydrates, it is not necessary to "carbo load." As you begin a taper, your activity level will decline, and as a result, you will burn fewer of your carbohydrate stores. Your normal high-carbohydrate diet (60 to 70 percent of total calories coming from carbohydrates), combined with a decrease in activity (for your taper), will result in "carbohydrate loading." The day prior to your race should also be high in carbohydrates, but refined carbohydrates may be a better choice at that time because of their reduced fiber content.

The most efficient energy yield from stored glycogen occurs with an even running pace. A fast pace early in the race speeds the depletion of glycogen and leads to "hitting the wall."

Q. ***What should I eat prior to competition?***

A. Individuals must determine the type and quantity of food to eat before a race, as well as when they will consume the meal. To work out your personal plan, begin with the information below, and vary the type, quantity, and timing of meals through trial and error on long distance training days. Maintain an accurate log of these variables and your long run performances to determine your most effective and agreeable prerace meal plan.

For a simple way to estimate your caloric needs on race morning, use this formula:

(Hours before race) × (body weight in pounds) =
(number of calories to eat)

For example, if you wake up at 6:00 a.m. and your race is at 8:00 a.m., that's 2 hours. So, for a 150-pound runner, that's:

2 × 150 = 300 calories

Typically, consuming 300 to 500 calories 3 hours before a half-marathon or marathon, followed by 100 to 150 calories of sports drink an hour prior to the race, should supply adequate prerace fuel.

For shorter races lasting less than an hour (5-K and 10-K), fewer, if any, prerace calories are necessary.

Q. ***Do I need to ingest energy during the race?***

A. Running a marathon or half-marathon may deplete your glycogen stores, resulting in your "hitting the wall." To prevent it, you need to consume carbohydrates during the race, not only to replace glycogen stores in your muscle but also to maintain the necessary level of blood glucose. You can meet this goal with 6 to 8 ounces of sports drink every 30 to 35 minutes or, on warmer days, every 20 to 30 minutes. Some runners like to use energy gels during marathons. Consuming an energy gel with water every hour can also help maintain adequate blood glucose levels.

Even though you may have 90 or more minutes of stored carbohydrates, you need to begin taking in a sports drink early in the race in order to "spare" your stores of glycogen.

Q. ***What should I consume after a workout or race?***

A. The workout or race is over, and you are feeling exhausted. Now is the time to start replenishing the glycogen and fluids lost during the race. Sports drinks are a good option. Your body is a "carbohydrate sponge" immediately after intense and exhausting exercise. Glycogen resynthesis from carbohydrates consumed after exercise takes place most rapidly during the first 30 minutes after exercise. Foods with a high glycemic index may speed up the replenishment of glycogen in skeletal muscle due to the rapid rise in glucose and insulin. The first 2 hours following exercise is when your body is most "spongelike." During this time, try to take in solid foods that are high in carbohydrates, such as bagels, bananas, or pudding.

The body is able to replace glycogen stores in approximately 22 hours after a hard workout, if enough carbohydrates are consumed during this time. Research indicates that muscle glycogen replenishment is most rapid during the first 2 hours after a hard workout. A 165-pound (75-kilogram) runner should consume approximately 90 grams of carbohydrates per hour for the first 2 hours following a workout and then follow the guidelines in this chapter for daily carbohydrate intake. High glycemic carbohydrate drinks are a good source of carbohydrates during the initial 2-hour period.

FINAL THOUGHTS ON RUNNING NUTRITION

Running, like all activities carried out by the body, requires energy. If there are several ways to meet your body's energy needs, the question becomes, "What is the best diet?" The shelves of bookstores are filled with volumes, all claiming to offer the "best" diet. This book is not a sports nutrition manual, nor is there room to explore the biochemistry of nutrition. If you need more specific dietary information, we recommend consulting a sports nutritionist.

REAL RUNNER REPORT

I just ran the California International Marathon (Sacramento) and followed the FIRST training program. It was a huge success, as I improved my time by 10 minutes: from 3:59 to 3:49. Not great times, but fine for me. I ran my fastest marathon, 3:30, in 1983, when I was in grad school. I lost interest in running but started running marathons again in 2000. Since then I have lost 25 pounds and, with this last outing, improved my time by about an hour.

Two years ago, I did 3:59 and thought I could go faster. So, I followed Pete Pfitzinger's Advanced Marathoning program, but the heavy mileage seemed to create more fatigue (I am 51 years old) and eventually led to injury. I had decided to try to run 3 days a week, and then I heard about your program. The FIRST approach involved much more intensity than I had planned but, in addition to the obvious cardiovascular improvement, I think the speedwork helped with eccentric strengthening. I had little of the intense quad fatigue in the last 10-K that I had previously experienced. As a consequence, I ran the last 21-K only 21 seconds slower than the first.

I think you have developed a great program, especially for the aging runner. Thanks so much.

Kevin D. Salyer
PROFESSOR OF ECONOMICS
UNIVERSITY OF CALIFORNIA–DAVIS

SECTION IV

Supplemental Training

12

Strength Training for Runners

Nowhere is the adage "Use it or lose it" more relevant than with your muscles. Running tends to employ one set of muscles over and over while neglecting others. Runners must also combat the loss of muscle mass that is a natural part of the aging process. It is imperative that we do strength exercises as we age to diminish that loss of muscle tissue.

For your overall fitness and good health, you should exercise the major muscles groups in your back, chest, shoulders, arms, torso, and legs. To enhance your running, we have described five strength training exercises that can be performed in a relatively short period of time. They will also contribute to better running and injury prevention in the long run.

I like feeling stronger not only for sports but also for everyday activities. Two or three times per week, in about 20 to 30 minutes, I do a circuit of exercises that works my large muscle groups. Typically these strength training sessions are not on Key Run Workout days. My training partner and coauthor Scott Murr likes to do his strength training on the same days he runs. I recommend establishing a strength training routine that fits your weekly schedule. Regardless of your strength training schedule, consistency is the key.

Below is a letter from a runner inquiring about how much lower body *weight* training to include in his marathon training. We recommended that he follow our *strength* training plan for runners.

The Runner Writes:

Dear FIRST:

I'm e-mailing you from San Antonio and plan to utilize the FIRST training program for a January 2006 marathon in Houston, Texas. I've completed two marathons with a PR of 3:32. At 43 years old, my ultimate goal is to reach 3:20 and qualify to run in Boston. With four kids, organized sports for the kids, a job, and church responsibilities, time is a precious commodity. Unfortunately, long weekend runs that begin at 4:30 a.m. are just part of the package.

I typically train for a marathon by running four or five times a week and I also try to include three mornings of weights at a local gym. It is really overwhelming. I'm 6 feet tall and weigh 145 (a typical runner build). Lifting weights helps me keep some weight on my body and provides some definition. My routine has been to lift weights on Monday, Wednesday, and Friday, doing upper body, legs, and back, and then arms.

This brings me to my simple question about the FIRST training program. Do you guys recommend doing a leg weight workout (i.e., squats, lunges, thigh extensions, etc.) on one of the days between a training run? This would fall on a Wednesday in my routine. If you do, is it a simple low-weight workout or more of a standard workout? I'm typically a little sore the day following a leg workout. Would I be defeating the purpose of your FIRST training program by incorporating the weight training (especially the leg workouts), or would that enhance the training?

I learned about your program from the August 2005 issue of *Runner's World* and now have your Web site bookmarked. I am very excited about starting your program, and I've already determined my various paces. I knew

STRENGTH TRAINING FOR RUNNERS: THE ESSENTIALS

- Strengthening the core muscles is important for maintaining good running form.
- Strengthening the muscles that stabilize the hips and knees is very important for injury prevention.

you guys would not think my question too strange since you are runners yourselves.

Thank you,

Runner
San Antonio, Texas

FIRST Comments:

The anonymous letter writer's schedule is hectic. FIRST urged him to examine the thinking behind doing lower body strength training only once a week. During a taper phase, once a week may be sufficient. During a base or build phase, twice a week is recommended.

The runner did not say what lower body strength exercises he did. We recommended that he select effective lower body strength exercises *for runners.* There are myriad exercises often suggested for runners, and they can be great for variety, but they may make selection of the right combination confusing. In fact, many books suggest very complex sequences of exercises. Consistent with our goal of optimizing training time, we have selected five Key Strength Training Exercises for runners. You can complete the set of five exercises in 15 minutes.

Weight training, resistance training, strength training: They are all the same. Since this chapter focuses on training that will work the musculoskeletal system and will frequently use body weight as the resistance, we generally use the term *strength training,* rather than *weight* or *resistance* training. There is no consensus regarding the optimal scheduling of weight training for runners.

- Muscular imbalances are often associated with running-specific injuries.
- Strengthening a weak muscle can eliminate imbalances between opposing muscle groups.
- Many runners avoid or neglect strength training.

STRENGTH TRAINING FOR RUNNERS: Q&A

Q. ***What are the primary benefits of strength training for runners?***

A. The goal of strength training for runners is not necessarily adding muscle mass. More important are:

- Improving muscular strength
- Improving local muscular endurance
- Maintaining current muscle mass
- Prehabilitation, or "prehab," for injury prevention
- Post-injury rehabilitation
- Being a "fit" runner

When you become fatigued, your form deteriorates (poor running economy). The deterioration comes not only from tired legs but also from tired arms, a tired back, and tired abdominal muscles. Having a strong torso helps hold your form together in the latter stages of a workout or a race.

Strength training improves running economy (one of the key determinants of running performance), permitting faster running over the same distance with less consumption of oxygen. Improved running economy means you can run for a longer time before exhaustion sets in.

Q. ***What are the potential liabilities associated with strength training? What should a runner avoid in his or her strength training program?***

A. Liabilities include:

- Injury due to poor form
- Additional bulk (muscle and weight gain) following an unnecessarily extensive strength training program

Our advice is to train the muscle groups that will be of greatest benefit in running. If you follow a body builder's strength training routine, you will probably find minimal, if any improvement, in your running performance. In fact, it is possible that a "standard" strength training routine would result in diminished running performances.

Q. ***Why don't runners strength train?***

A. Some of the reasons why runners do not strength train are:

- They do not know what to do.
- They do not have the time or energy.
- They do not want to bulk up or gain weight.
- They are afraid that strength training will hurt their running performance.

Q. ***What exercises should be included in strength training for runners?***

A. There is no single method of strength training that has been shown to be unequivocally superior for runners. Many of our recommended exercises are core exercises and multijoint exercises. Core exercises and multijoint exercises tend to be more specific to normal body movement. With the FIRST strength training exercises, you won't isolate a single muscle group, the typical approach of many strength training routines.

The American College of Sports Medicine (ACSM) recommends 8 to 10 exercises that work the major muscle groups. While we endorse the ACSM position statement, we have selected five Key Strength Training Exercises that will enhance running performance. These strength training recommendations are designed so that a runner can do them in a timely manner with minimal equipment.

Q. ***Do I really need to do lower body strength exercises?***

A. Many runners think, *I don't need to work my legs because I use them all the time running.* During running, your legs are being worked, but primarily, they are being trained solely for endurance, not strength. Strength training will help improve your leg strength, so that you can generate more force with each stride. Strength training will also help balance the fitness of all of the major muscles of your lower body and help you avoid injury.

Q. ***How often should I do strength training? How many sets and repetitions are ideal?***

A. The ACSM recommends that strength training be performed two or three times per week. Aim for three, but make sure that you get in at least two strength training workouts a week. During a taper phase, once a week is okay.

Since time and energy to train always seem limited, do one set of each exercise. For your strength training program to promote both muscular strength and muscular endurance, complete 10 to 15 repetitions per exercise and aim to reach near-fatigue on the last few repetitions.

Q. ***In what order should I do my exercises?***

A. Typically, you should train the larger and stronger muscle groups first and then progress to the smaller muscle groups. Why? Your smaller muscles act as supporting muscles when you train the larger muscle groups. If you fatigue the smaller muscle groups first, they won't help much as you stress the larger muscle groups. This puts you at an increased risk for injury. We have listed our strength training exercises in the order we think they should be performed.

Q. *How should I breathe when doing strength training exercises?*

A. Avoid the temptation to hold your breath when strength training. Even veteran athletes fail to breathe when exerting effort and are often unaware of it. You should breathe continuously. Exhale on the exertion or lifting movement and inhale on the return or lowering movement.

Q. *Should I strength train year-round?*

A. Varying your routine periodically is important to stimulate adaptation. FIRST believes that year-round strength training is fine as long as you reduce your strength training program during the final 2 weeks before a key race.

STRENGTH TRAINING FOR RUNNERS: THE SCIENCE

Most adults lose about ½ pound of muscle each year after the age of 20. Muscle mass is associated with metabolism. Muscle burns calories at a higher rate than fat, so the more muscle you have, the more efficient you are (and the more you need to eat). Strength training builds muscle to prevent or reduce muscle loss and help improve metabolism—a key to maintaining your weight.

Studies have shown that as few as 6 weeks of proper strength training can significantly reduce or completely relieve kneecap pain or "runner's knee." Strength training also reduces the recurrence of many other common injuries, including hip and lower back pain. By strengthening muscle, as well as bone and connective tissue (ligaments attach bone to bone, and tendons attach muscle to bone), strength training not only helps to prevent injury but also helps to reduce the severity of injury when it does occur. Running injuries are a runner's worst nightmare!

In addition to injury prevention, weight training improves performance. Studies show that with as little as 10 weeks of strength training, 10-K times decrease by an average of 2 to 3 percent. The research has also shown that running economy improves as a result of strength training.

Standing Wall Slide

This exercise is a squat that improves strength and stability. It emphasizes your hamstrings, quadriceps, and glutes.

- Stand with your back, shoulders, and head against a wall, and look straight ahead. Your feet should be shoulder-width apart, flat on the floor, and about 12 inches away from the wall.
- Keeping your head against the wall and your shoulders relaxed, slide down the wall by slowly bending your knees. Lower your back and butt toward the floor until your thighs are almost parallel to the floor.
- Make sure your knees do not extend beyond your toes. (If they do, walk your feet out a little farther in front of you.)
- Hold this position for a count of five. Slowly straighten your legs and return to the starting position, keeping your head and torso in contact with the wall.
- Perform 10 to 15 repetitions.

Because this exercise strengthens the quadriceps, hamstrings, and glutes, it may be helpful for patellofemoral syndrome or patellar tendinitis.

To make this exercise more challenging . . .

- Hold 10-, 12-, or 15-pound dumbbells by your sides as you perform the wall slides.
- Use a stability ball between the wall and your back (position the ball at hip height).
- To work your glutes more, put your feet and knees together as you perform the standing wall slide.

Single Leg Squat

This exercise is a squat using only one leg. It improves your strength and stability and emphasizes the hamstrings and the glutes. This is a demanding exercise. Don't give up; after a few workouts of this exercise, you will get better.

- Tighten your abs for core stability and balance.
- Bend one leg at the knee, lifting the foot behind you and with your lower leg roughly parallel to the ground. Your knees should be aligned with each other.
- NOTE: You can stand next to a wall and place your hand on the wall to help with balance, if necessary.
- Squat down (bending the knee of the weight-bearing leg) to "drop" your butt toward the floor on the one leg until your fingers are able to touch the floor.
- Squat down using the weight-bearing leg. Bend only slightly at the waist.

- NOTE: To avoid bending too much at the waist, look forward rather than down.
- Flex (straighten) your knees and hips to return to an upright (standing) position.
- Perform the single leg squat in a controlled fashion.
- NOTE: Try to make sure you do this squat with your leg rather than bending forward at the hip.
- Perform 10 to 15 single leg squats with one leg, then switch to the other leg.

Variation: As your leg strength improves, you can begin to hold dumbbells in your hands.

FIRST Success

I had been thinking about running a marathon but was unsure about a training program. I was running a few days a week (my runs were usually 3 to 10 miles) and lifting weight 3 days a week. After reading about the FIRST program in *Runner's World*, I felt the program would work for me.

The workouts were great. I did not miss a single one. The days I did not run, I rode a stationary bike and lifted weights. I like the structure of the program and felt confident going into the marathon.

I ran the Philadelphia Marathon, my first marathon, and I ran a 3:17, thanks to the FIRST program. It was tough between miles 21 and 25, but this would be the case with many programs. I felt really great. I had a person tell me during the marathon that I look more like a triathlete than a marathoner. I felt that the strength program I incorporated with the running allowed me to be in this condition.

I would recommend this program to anyone who is interested in a structured and easy-to-follow program. It offers a lot of variety, and the results speak for themselves if one trains properly.

Thank you,

Erik Hawk
TEACHER
BLOOMSBURY, NEW JERSEY

Key Strength Training Exercise #2

Walking Lunge

This exercise improves functional strength of the leg, works the glutes and quads, and helps to keep your hip flexors flexible. You will need a clear path at least 4 feet wide and 10 yards long for this exercise.

- Stand with your hands by your side, your feet shoulder-width apart, and facing straight ahead.
- Step forward with your right foot, landing on the heel and rolling onto the forefoot.
- Lower your body by flexing your right knee and hip. Your left heel will come up off the floor, and your left knee should bend close to 90 degrees, until it is almost in contact with floor.
- Once your right knee reaches 90 degrees, press upward through your heel and midfoot, and bring your left leg forward.
- As you return to an upright position, lift your left knee up, and now lunge forward with your left leg.
- NOTE: Your left leg should avoid touching the floor until it is the forward or leading leg. In other words, walk continuously without bringing your feet together.
- Keep your torso upright during the lunges, and repeat by alternating lunges with opposite legs.
- Perform the walking lunge in a controlled manner and avoid bouncing.
- Take a total of 10 steps, then turn around and return to the start.

Variation: As you get stronger, you can hold weights in your hands at your sides.

Key Strength Training Exercise #3

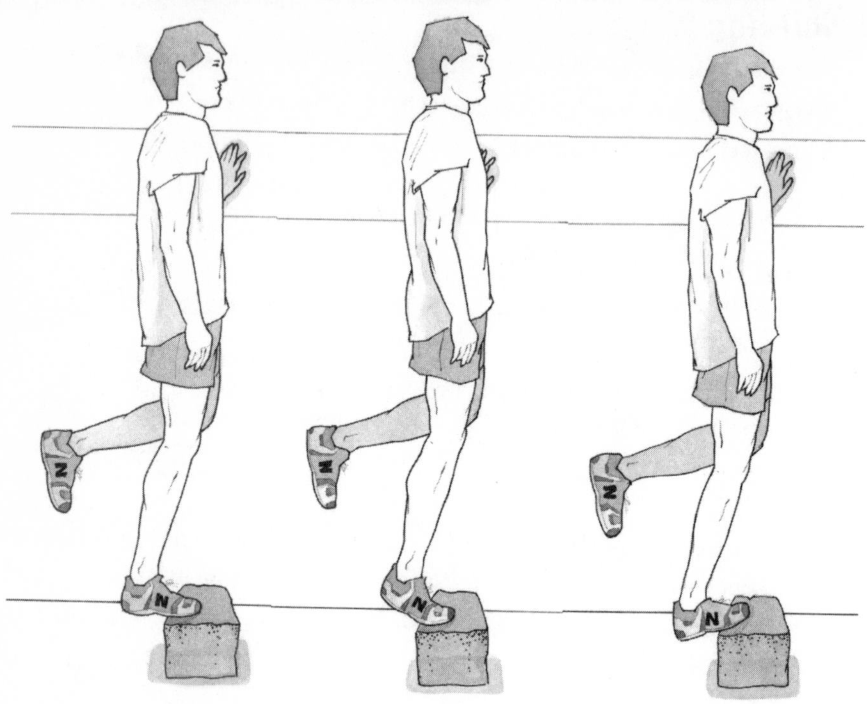

Calf Raise

This single leg calf raise exercise strengthens your gastrocnemius and soleus muscles.

- Place the balls of both feet on the edge of a raised surface, such as a step or curb, letting your heels and arches extend off the edge of the surface.
- Place your hands on a wall or other support to assist with balance while keeping your legs and back straight and your head up.
- Bend one leg at the knee, lifting the foot behind you, with your lower leg roughly parallel to the ground. Your knees should be aligned with each other.
- Rise up on your toes as high as possible and hold for a second.
- Lower your heel as low as possible until your calf is stretched.
- Focus on rising up as high as possible every time you perform a repetition—don't let the height decrease.
- Complete 10 to 12 repetitions with each leg, then repeat with opposite leg.
- NOTE: Avoid bending at the knees. Keep your weight-bearing knee and leg straight throughout the exercise.
- NOTE: Avoid letting your hips move backward or forward; focus on keeping your movement vertical.

Variations: As your leg strength improves, try holding a dumbbell in one hand (on the same side as the calf being worked), hanging down at your side.

As an alternative, you may do a seated calf raise instead.

Sit comfortably with the balls of your feet on the edge of a block or platform approximately 4 inches high. With your feet parallel to each other, place your feet shoulder-width apart. With your forearms resting on your thighs, hold dumbbells just beyond your knees (or rest a barbell on your thighs, just above your knees).

Lower your heels by bending your ankles until your calves are stretched. Raise your heels by extending your ankles as high as possible. Lift and lower your heels with all the weight on the balls of your feet. Repeat 12 to 20 times.

Pushup on a Stability Ball

A stability pushup requires a stability or physioball, and it is much more difficult than a standard pushup. This is a great exercise for chest, triceps, and shoulder stabilization, and it challenges your core stability as well.

- Lie with your chest on the stability ball and place your hands on the ball at the sides of your chest.
- Place your toes on the floor with your legs straight.
- Your head, shoulders, hips, knees, and ankles should all be in a straight line.
- Keep your torso straight (avoid bending at the hips) as you push your body up, until your arms are almost straight (do not lock your elbows).
- Keep your head, shoulders, hips, knees, and ankles all in a straight line.
- At the "up" position, hold and balance for a second.
- Slowly and with good body control, lower yourself to the starting position (until you feel the ball on your chest).
- Control the stability ball and maintain your straight body position.
- NOTE: Both your upper and lower body must remain straight throughout the movement.
- Perform the stability ball pushup in a controlled manner, and avoid bouncing. Focus on controlling the ball; don't let the ball control you. Work up to 15 to 25 pushups.

Variations: You can place your feet shoulder-width apart to aid in balance and stability. You can place your feet closer together to increase difficulty.

Single Arm Bent-Over Row with Dumbbell

This exercise works the major muscles of the upper back.

- Tighten your abs for core stability.
- Grasp a dumbbell with one hand and stand with your feet in a staggered stance (the heel of one foot should be about 12 inches in front of the rear foot).
- NOTE: Your forward foot/leg should be on the opposite side of your body as the arm that is holding the dumbbell.
- Bend both knees slightly (to reduce stress on your lower back) and bend forward at the waist.
- Pull your elbow up and back, bringing the dumbbell toward your chest.
- Slowly lower the dumbbell until your arm is extended and your shoulder is stretched forward.
- Perform 10 to 15 bent-over rows with one arm, then switch to the other arm.

13

Flexibility and Form

I avoided stretching for a long time because it is difficult for me. Several years ago, after injuries that were serious enough to prevent me from running, I learned from a physical therapist who specializes in the biomechanics of running that I have ankles with tightly spaced bones and connective tissue that hinder flexibility. The leg is a kinetic chain, and tightness in one joint will cause unnatural forces on other muscles and joints.

It was only through the guidance of the physical therapist in modifying my biomechanics that I could return to running. Much of that therapy included stretching. In particular, if I don't stretch my lower calves and work on my ankle flexibility, I incur knots in my calves. If I don't stretch my hip flexors, I develop hamstring problems because they improperly bear stress that should be put on the gluteal muscles.

Individual differences in flexibility are every bit as great as differences in cardiorespiratory attributes. My brother and I have similar measures of aerobic endurance and running résumés, but our degree of flexibility is considerably different. I have less flexibility and always have, since we were young boys. When we were kids, he could put a toe in his mouth

(continued on page 200)

The Runner Writes:

Dear FIRST:

Thank you for providing the FIRST lecture and training clinic for runners on form and flexibility last week. It was helpful for me to see your slides demonstrating proper running form. Participating in the drills as a group after the lecture has made me more comfortable doing them on my own. By doing the stretches we learned in the clinic, I feel that I have improved my form as well.

Because of your instructions, I think I'm running more relaxed. On my long run last weekend, I noticed that I didn't have the shoulder and arm tightness that I usually experience after a 2-hour run. By concentrating on my turnover rate, I feel lighter on my feet, and I believe that I have eliminated the overstriding that I was guilty of before. In addition, I had none of the hamstring tightness that I normally experience.

Thanks again for the handouts and demonstrations.

James Mac Millan, DO
Physician
Travelers Rest, South Carolina

FIRST Replies:

There is a lot of disagreement about when to stretch and whether or not it's even valuable. Part of the reason for the disagreement is that it is difficult to design research to determine the effects of stretching. Relying on survey data for stretching is questionable.

Those who have been injured will begin stretching to cure a problem. Those who have never been injured see no reason to begin stretching. If you survey runners, the results will show that those who stretch have injuries, and those who don't stretch are injury-free. You can see how this leads to a false conclusion about the efficacy of stretching.

Maybe there are not strong data to support a specific recommendation, but it is well-recognized by sports scientists and athletes that flexibility is important to athletic performance. For runners in particular, ankle, hamstring, and hip flexor flexibility affects form and performance. A lack of flexibility often leads to strained muscles or connective tissue. We have definitely found that running form and flexibility affect performance. Proper form will improve efficiency and, thus, economy, and it also helps runners avoid injuries.

Jim Mac Millan attended one of our free public lectures and clinics that focused on proper running flexibility and form. That session, conducted by FIRST coach Mickey McCauley, focused on helping runners attain efficient running form. Mickey, a former sub-1:50 800-meter collegiate runner, whose own exemplary running form provides a good model for runners, has a critical eye for recognizing flaws in a runner's form. At our running clinics, Mickey is able to provide feedback, suggest drills, and give runners tips for developing a more efficient running style.

Good form requires practice and good flexibility. Runners need to monitor their form to make sure that they stay relaxed and aren't losing efficiency due to needless muscular tension. Fatigue often causes runners to tighten their upper bodies, which reduces efficiency. Going through a mental checklist periodically while training and racing can help remind you that your hands, arms, neck, etc. need to be relaxed. In particular, runners tend to lean forward and push their hips back when fatigued, a body position not conducive to economical and effective running.

We recommend that you take time to incorporate two **Key Drills** and four **Key Stretches** into your training. These drills and stretches can be completed in a short amount of time, but they will pay big dividends. The drills can be combined with your warmup stride running. In keeping with our approach of developing a program that is realistic and also effective, we have not provided a comprehensive set of stretches or drills. Our experience is that most runners don't have the time to devote to extensive stretching and drilling, as do collegiate teams and elite runners. (They often devote several hours per day to training.) We strive to assist runners who have limited time to attain optimal results. Incorporating the two drills and four stretches along with strides doesn't take much time, but the benefits are considerable.

Gait Analysis: A Scientific Approach

Coauthor Ray Moss, PhD, has developed a gait analysis lab, in addition to metabolic and body composition assessment systems, at our Human Performance Laboratory at Furman University. This sophisticated, high-speed, multiple-camera digital capturing system captures a runner's form in minute detail. It is then digitized and analyzed with computer software. Ray can show runners flaws in their form and suggest how they can eliminate extraneous movements. In particular, this detailed, biomechanical analysis provides injured runners with recommendations for modifications in their running form that can address the source of the injury.

while I struggled to get mine half as close. He could sit in a squat with his heels on the ground, and I would topple over trying.

Scientific studies may not definitively confirm that stretching helps. However, I believe it's possible that stretching is necessary for some people and not for others. I rely on the case study of two brothers to support my assumption. With my limited ankle flexibility and tight hamstrings, I must stretch in order to continue running; my brother has never stretched and has never been injured. The lesson? Know your needs and limitations.

The letter on page 198 from a local physician who attended one of our clinics illustrates the value of spending time on form and flexibility.

FLEXIBILITY: THE ESSENTIALS

- Stretching is done by most runners only after they have become injured.
- Inflexible runners don't like to stretch because it is difficult for them.
- There are no definitive studies showing the benefits of stretching for injury prevention or performance enhancement.
- Most runners develop tight hamstring and calf muscles;

FIRST Success

I just completed a marathon using your FIRST program and am extremely pleased with the results. I ran two marathons last year at 3:51 (Boston and Omaha) under another training program. FIRST was more interesting because of the cross-training and intensity, but it didn't waste my time. I finished with a 3:33:41 at the Olathe (Kansas) Marathon this past weekend and felt incredible. You've done an incredible service for those runners like myself who felt they could have reached a plateau.

Thanks,

David P. Rondeau
OMAHA, NEBRASKA

stretching can improve flexibility and maintain the elasticity of those muscle groups.

- Tight hamstring and calf muscles can reduce stride length.
- Stretching can reduce muscular stiffness.
- It is important to stretch properly; stretching should not be uncomfortable or painful.
- Expect improvement in flexibility only after weeks or months of regular stretching; be faithful to stretching regularly and consistently.
- Assume each stretch slowly and hold it for approximately 30 seconds.

FLEXIBILITY AND FORM: Q&A

Q. *What is good running form?*

A. Good running form includes the following:

- Keep your trunk erect.
- Keep your head level, with your gaze fixed on the horizon ahead of you.

- Keep your upper body relaxed, with your shoulders down.
- Keep your hips tall.
- Keep arms and fists relaxed.
- Keep elbow angles from 60 to 140 degrees.
- Imitate leg action with the arms.
- Don't let your arms cross the vertical midline of your body.
- Move your legs forward, not up and down.
- Avoid exaggerated knee lifts.
- Try to be quick and light on your feet.
- Don't overstride. Your leading foot should not land too far beyond your center of gravity.

Q. ***What is flexibility and what are the benefits associated with it?***

A. *Flexibility* is typically defined as the ability of a joint to move freely through its full range of motion. Flexibility is joint-specific and is not a general trait. What a cyclist needs to do for flexibility may be very different from what a runner needs to do.

Stretching for flexibility improves range of motion and can promote relaxation. It can also improve performance (although the jury is still out on this one) and decrease the risk of musculoskeletal injury and muscular tension. Though stretching does not reduce soreness, it can, in some cases, improve body alignment and help stabilize joints.

Q. ***What factors influence flexibility?***

A. Many factors influence a joint's flexibility, and people vary greatly in their flexibility. You should not try to compete with your training partner when it comes to flexibility or stretching. Factors that influence flexibility include:

- Joint structure
- Muscle elasticity and length
- Connective tissue
- Nervous system activity

- Physical activity level
- Skin
- Body fat composition
- Tissue injury
- Body temperature
- Age
- Sex

Q. ***What are the potential problems associated with limited flexibility?***

A. According to the adage "you are only as strong as your weakest link," limited flexibility may have a detrimental impact on one's running. Some running-related problems associated with limited flexibility include:

- Lower back dysfunction
- Postural problems
- Shortened stride
- Muscular strains ("pulled hamstring")

Q. ***How can I improve my flexibility?***

A. To improve the flexibility of a joint, several fitness principles come into play; in particular, muscle elongation is required (the overload principle). In other words, you must stretch your muscles beyond their normal range of motion.

Q. ***When should a runner stretch?***

A. For flexibility and running preparation, follow this sequence:

- Warm up with 10 to 20 minutes of easy jogging.
- Perform two Key Drills (see pages 205 and 206).
- Perform a Key Run Workout.
- Do a cooldown recovery run.
- Perform four Key Stretches after the workout.

Q. ***What are the two Key Drills recommended as part of the FIRST training program?***

A. Dynamic mobility exercises raise your body temperature, increase bloodflow to your muscles, activate your nervous system, and prepare you for running, a mobility activity. Perform the two **Key Drills**, dynamic mobility exercises, after a brief 10- to 20-minute warmup and prior to the planned workout.

Two Key Drills Can Help Your Running Form and Efficiency

Strides are runs of 80 to 100 meters, fast but relaxed. You should accelerate gradually over the first three-quarters of the distance and then decelerate to the end. Use strides to practice good form and relaxed running. Strides work fast-twitch fibers in a non-stressful way. Complete recovery should occur between repetitions. Twenty seconds is usually enough recovery time for 100 meters. Strides can be included as part of a warmup or after an easy run. Performing strides on a grass field or flat area will help flush out legs made sluggish from slow running.

Running drills emphasize good running form. They also help strengthen the muscles needed for strong, efficient running. The hips and ankles are exercised through a greater range of motion during these drills than during normal runs. While there are many running drills, we include two drills to be used during your strides. Doing strides with "butt kicks" and "high knee lifts" can also enhance your running form.

Begin your stride warmup by doing the "butt kicks" for 20 meters and then striding for 80 meters, gradually accelerating for 60 meters and then decelerating for 20 meters. After recovery, turn around and do the high knee lifts for 20 meters, and then stride for 80 meters, gradually accelerating for 60 meters and then decelerating for 20 meters.

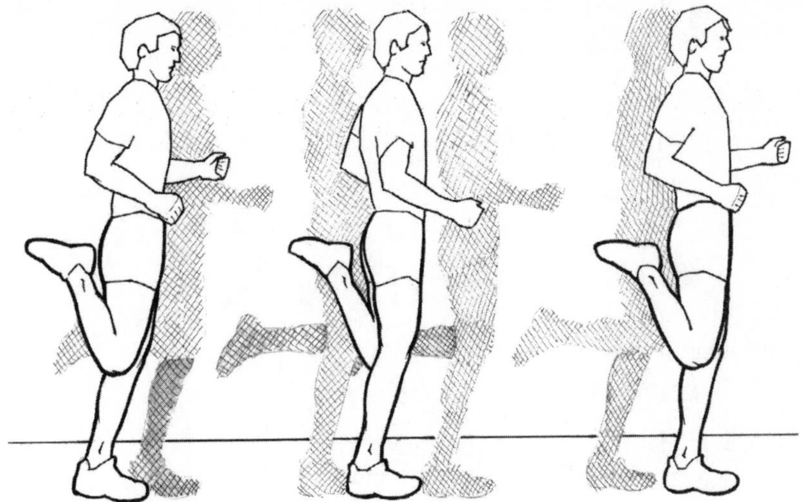

Key Drill #1: **Butt Kicks**

Primarily a hamstring drill, butt kicks involve trying to kick your own butt with each step. Angle your body slightly forward, take short steps, and kick your heels back and up as high as you can. Stay on the balls of your feet and keep your thighs perpendicular to the ground.

Butt kicks improve leg turnover and heel recovery. Heel recovery is the part of the running motion where your leg rises up and coils for the next forward stride. Since one aim of this drill is to increase leg turnover, not stride length, your steps should be quick. Focus on a smooth, but quick, action.

Perform butt kicks for 20 meters, then gradually stride/accelerate for 60 meters before decelerating for the last 20 meters of the stride.

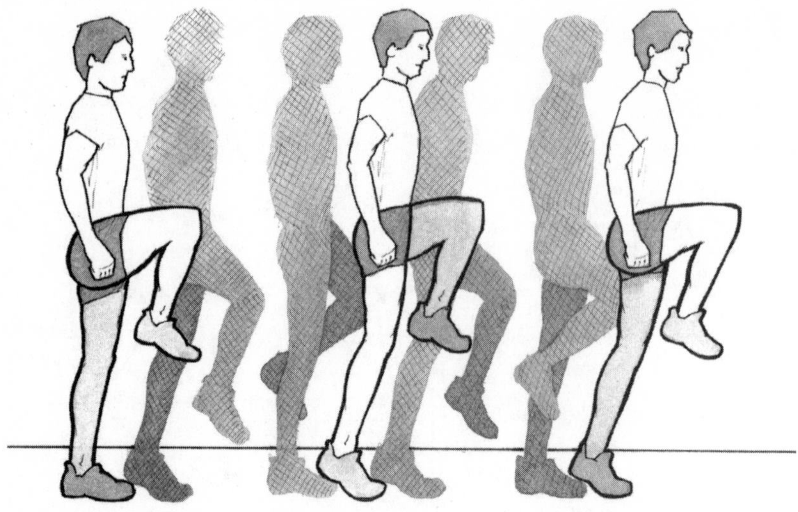

Key Drill #2: High Knee Lifts

The aim of high knees is to increase leg turnover and improve your knee lift. This drill strengthens the calves and hip flexors, and it emphasizes proper running posture and the liftoff phase of running.

High knee lifts involve taking short steps and lifting your knees up as high as they can go. Think of yourself as performing an exaggerated march or as "proud running" with very slight forward lean. The idea is to stay "tall" while rapidly lifting and driving down the knees. You should be bringing your legs up in front of you and maintaining a nice upright posture.

Turnover is rapid, so you take as many steps as possible over 20 meters. The aim is not to move forward quickly but to take quick/rapid steps while lifting your knees high. As with butt kicks, this drill is about leg turnover, not stride length.

You will feel this one in the front of your hips and thighs (hip flexors) as they will be working hard to lift your legs up high in front of you.

Perform this drill for 20 meters and then gradually stride/accelerate for 60 meters before decelerating for the last 20 meters of the stride.

Four Key Stretches to Enhance Flexibility for Running

Q. *What stretches should I do?*

A. After a workout (run or cross-training) and cooldown, static stretching is recommended. Do the four **Key Stretches** after the workout or later that day.

Key Stretch #1: Standing Calf Stretch

Starting Position

Facing a wall, stand slightly more than arm's length away. Lean forward and place both hands on the wall with your arms straight. Have one leg forward with the knee bent, and the other leg extended back with the knee straight.

Your body weight should be supported by your rear leg and your arms. The forward leg should not provide any body support.

Doing the Stretch

Push the heel of your rear foot down on the floor and push your hips forward and toward the wall.

After holding this stretch for 30 to 45 seconds, bend the back knee down slightly toward the ground, and hold for another 30 to 45 seconds.

Repeat with the opposite leg.

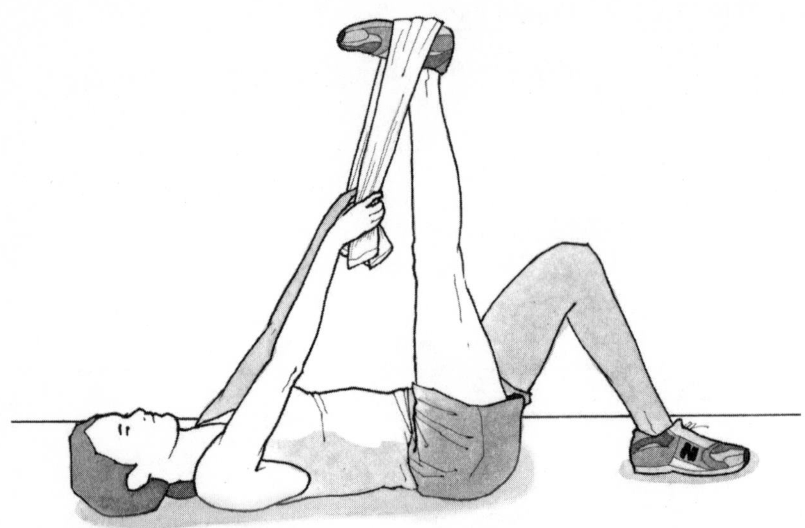

Key Stretch #2: Lying Hamstring Stretch

Starting Position

Sit down on a mat or the floor with both of your knees bent. Put a towel or stretch cord under the middle of one foot. Grasp the ends of the towel with your hands. As you lie down on your back, continue gripping the towel with both hands, and raise the foot with the towel, keeping that leg straight.

If you don't have a towel or stretch cord on hand, grab behind your straight leg just above the knee with both hands. Pull that knee toward your chest.

Doing the Stretch

Keep your leg straight and pull your straight leg toward your chest/head. Keep the other leg bent, with your foot on the floor, and rest your head on the floor.

Hold the stretch for 30 to 45 seconds. Repeat with the opposite leg.

Key Stretch #3: Quadriceps Lunge Stretch

Starting Position

Lunge forward with your right foot forward and your left leg extended back. Balance yourself by placing both hands on your right knee. Your left rear knee should be slightly bent but should not touch the floor. Your body weight should be supported by both legs/feet.

Your feet should be far enough apart that your right knee does not extend beyond your right toes.

Doing the Stretch

Keep your body upright (close to vertical) and push your hips forward. Your forward (right) foot should remain flat on the floor, and your rear (left) foot should point forward. You should be up on the ball of that foot.

You may also feel the stretch in the calf (soleus) of your rear (left) leg.

Hold the stretch for 30 to 45 seconds, then repeat with your left leg forward.

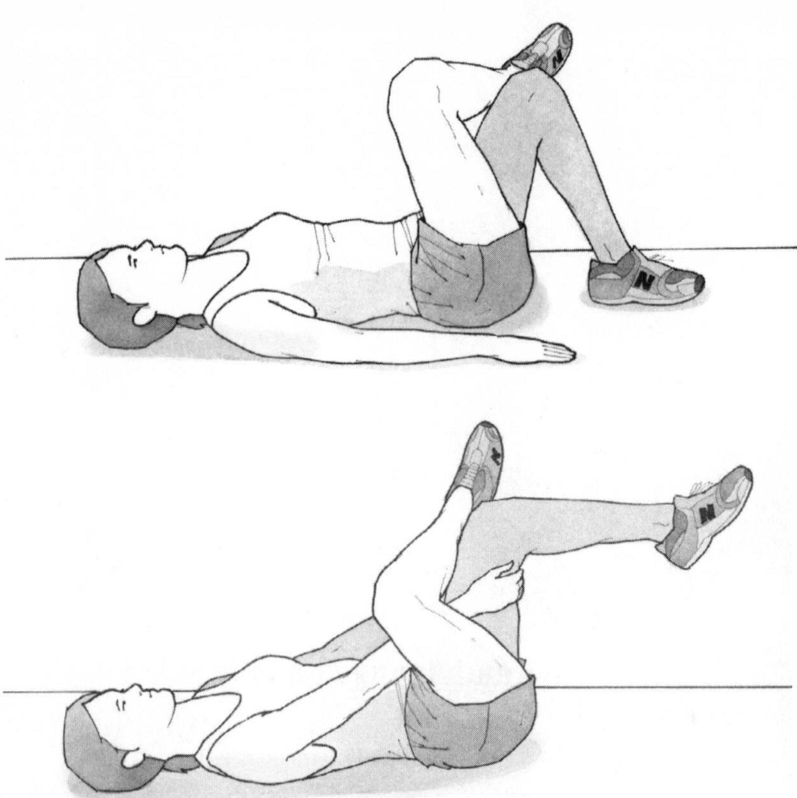

Key Stretch #4: Glute/Piriformis Stretch

Starting Position

Lie on your back. Bend both of your knees, with your feet flat on the floor (the heels of your feet will be 12 to 18 inches from your buttocks). Cross one leg over the thigh of your other leg, with the ankle just above the knee. Then grasp with both hands behind the knee/thigh of your bent lower leg.

Doing the Stretch

Pull your leg toward your torso, rest your head on the floor, and hold this stretch for 30 to 60 seconds. Repeat with the opposite leg.

FINAL COMMENTS ON FLEXIBILITY AND FORM

Stretching is important for healthy flexibility, and it should not be overlooked. Poor technique can also result in ineffective stretching. Common mistakes made when stretching include:

- Stretching prior to warmup
- Overstretching to the point of pain
- Performing stretches incorrectly (a local fitness specialist can assist you in person with the correct technique)

It's important to have someone with a trained eye correct inefficient and potentially injurious form. Find a running coach who will either watch or videotape your running and stretching. You must practice good form just as you practice running faster and farther.

There are hundreds of movements that can improve flexibility. A flexibility program should include exercises and movements that work all the major joints of the body.

FIRST Success

Just a note to let you know that I used the FIRST training program as my "program of choice" to prepare for this year's Flying Pig Marathon in Cincinnati. I had completed the "Pig" in 2003 in 5:02 and in 2005 in 5:00.

After completing both of those, I was completely wiped out for a couple of days, walking down steps backward, not being able to drive for 2 days because I couldn't push in the clutch, etc.

After following the FIRST training for this year's marathon, I completed the race in 4:33—a minute per mile faster. I also worked in the yard that afternoon. I believe in your program. My running partner and I are planning to use it again and even run a second marathon this fall.

Thanks for helping me set a PR and enjoy a great race.

Sincerely,

Carl Kappes
CONSTRUCTION SERVICES, SALES
CINCINNATI, OHIO

REAL RUNNER REPORT

I thought that you and your staff would appreciate an update with my use of the FIRST program. I used the program for Boston Marathon 2006 along with your suggestions for hill workouts. Simply put, my results have been phenomenal. During the Boston training, I did two half-marathon tuneups and did consecutive PRs. I beat my previous half-marathon PR by 3 minutes. I was confident going into Boston, even though I did far fewer total miles than last year, and my 51-year-old body felt strong.

Boston 2006 was fantastic. My time last year was 3:58, but this year I did 3:27, about 30 minutes better. To top it off, my Boston 2006 time was a marathon PR by 1 minute. I set a marathon PR at Chicago last year using your program.

I have really been pleased with your program and have passed on your information to many runners and triathletes. It works!

Thanks again for your help.

Tim Kabot

ORAL AND MAXILLOFACIAL SURGEON

LIBERTYVILLE, ILLINOIS

BONUS SECTION

Getting to Boston

14

The Reality of Boston: How to Qualify

High school state championships, NCAA regional tournaments, and AAU national championships: As a basketball player, I competed in all of these exciting events, but none treated every competitor as a hero like the Boston Marathon does. Running through a corridor of adoring fans for 26.2 miles is an exhilarating experience.

I can easily understand why we receive many messages from runners asking whether we can help them qualify for Boston. Because of that intense desire to meet the Boston qualifying standard, we have included a chapter devoted to assisting runners who seek to earn their Boston bib. First, runners need to know whether they are fit enough to attempt a Boston qualifier, and second, they need to have a training plan that will prepare them for the qualifying standard. In this chapter, you will find both. We have identified racing performances at shorter races and training times that tell you whether you are fit enough to meet the qualifying time. For each of the 16 different Boston qualifying standards, there is a 16-week training plan to prepare you for earning your ticket to Beantown.

(continued on page 218)

The Runner Writes:

Dear FIRST:

Gentlemen, not long ago, a good friend called me and suggested that I check out a program he read about on the *Runner's World* magazine Web site. He knows I'm the type of person who looks for unique training programs to try out, and at 35, I know I will never see the Olympics, so I have that option. The program was the Less-Is-More Marathon Plan from the Furman Institute of Running. When I read it, I was a bit skeptical, but thought, *why not?* Being a veteran triathlete with a couple of Ironman races under my belt, I came from the theory every other athlete comes from: run more, run fast. The only problem was, I was continually injured. My IT (iliotibial) bands were shot, and I truly thought my running days were over. I started the FIRST program several months ago, and what I found was that not only did I feel better but I was also running faster, and my IT bands actually started feeling better. I made a commitment to the FIRST program, I would run exactly what you prescribed in the magazine article.

As I used your program, I decided to set up a couple of races to give me a gauge on my progress. I chose two races, a 15-K and a half-marathon. You must also realize that my other training partners were also watching to see if the program worked as well as you stated in the article. I didn't run the 15-K to see how fast I could run as much as to see where my fitness level was. The 15-K race was . . . well . . . the fastest I had ever run for that distance. When the race finished, I wanted to see where I had placed and realized I won my age division. Several more weeks of training and it was time for the half-marathon. Again, I was there only to check my fitness level, and let's not forget, I was in the middle of the program, so I knew this was just a training run. The race finished, and I took third in my age group.

I would like to change the subject for a second and take you back a few years ago. I had just finished the Great Floridian Ironman distance triathlon when I decided to travel to Jacksonville and run their marathon. My goal: qualify for Boston. I was in the best shape of my life and knew there wouldn't be a better chance for me than 7 weeks after an Ironman. I finished that race and missed qualifying by 57 seconds. It was only my third marathon but my most disappointing: to get so close and falter at the end. I ran two more marathons after that, and the last one was a disaster, everything that could go wrong did. This was right about the time I had to take some serious time off due to ITBS in both legs. Everyone thought I was done racing, including myself. My friends asked every week to train, and week after week, I turned them down. It had been a year and a half since my last race, and that 57-second debacle wouldn't leave me alone. This is where the FIRST program comes in.

Gentlemen, I could go on and on about what your program did for me. I am pleased to say thank you. My wife, 8 months pregnant with our first child, watched me yesterday morning cross the finish line at the Miami Marathon and *qualify* for Boston.

I thank you for helping me accomplish a dream come true.

Sincerely,

James DeVriendt
Boston qualifier and soon-to-be dad
Sales/Marketing
Melbourne, Florida

FIRST Comments:

Mr. DeVriendt's message is typical of the many messages received by FIRST from appreciative Boston qualifiers. Many of our inquiries from runners request help for Boston Marathon qualification. Qualifying for Boston requires meeting the time standard specific to your age and sex in a certified marathon.

Trying to qualify for Boston probably causes more poor marathon performances than any other factor. Attempting to qualify for Boston when the qualifying time is unrealistic can cause you to get injured by training for a too-ambitious finish time or running too fast at the beginning of the race. Invariably, you'll suffer through the last half of the race, slowing considerably, and finish in a time slower than what your training predicted.

However, we believe that there is not a more thrilling experience in the sport of running than running the Boston Marathon. For that reason, we understand why runners are willing to risk a poor marathon qualifying attempt and even injury to qualify. For those reasons, below you'll find a program that lets you know whether Boston is realistic and that lays out a training program that will lead to a Boston bib to be worn on Patriot's Day.

(continued)

The Runner Writes *(continued)*

How do marathoners know whether their Boston qualifying times are realistic goals? Meeting the time standard, like meeting your personal goal time in any marathon, requires being properly trained for the 26.2 mile distance and having a lot of factors—personal and external—favorable on race day. Fortunately, there are some criteria that marathoners can use to determine whether they are ready for a qualifying attempt.

Judge your readiness by using our criteria for every Boston qualifying time. Take your finish times from 5-K, 10-K, and half-marathon races and see whether you meet the criteria for your qualifying time. Another method that FIRST provides for determining whether you are ready is to run all three specified workouts for the first week in the schedule for your target time for Boston in the same week. If you can complete the three workouts successfully, then you are ready to begin the training program provided for your specific qualifying time.

Below are 16 sets of criteria and 16 training programs, one to match each Boston qualifying time. Young and old, male and female, there's a program for you. Meet the criteria, follow the program, and look for us in Hopkinton!

For Men 35 and Younger, You Must Run 3:10 to BQ (Boston Qualify)

Qualifying for Boston is realistic:

If you can:

Run a 5-K in 19:30

Run a 10-K in 40:50

Run a half-marathon in 1:30:25 (Note: The half-marathon is the best predictor.)

If you can complete one of each of these three Key Run Workouts in the *same* week:

Key Run Workout #1: Track Repeats (complete one of the workouts listed below)

6 × 800m at 2:52-per-800m pace with a 400m recovery jog between intervals

5 × 1000m at 3:37-per-1000m pace with a 400m recovery jog between intervals

4 × 1200m at 4:24-per-1200m pace with a 400m recovery jog between intervals

3 × 1600m at 6:01-per-1600m pace with a 400m recovery jog between intervals

Key Run Workout #2: Tempo Run (complete one of the tempo runs)

After a 1-mile warmup, complete a 3-mile training run in 19:45 minutes.

After a 1-mile warmup, complete a 5-mile training run in 34:10.

After a 1-mile warmup, complete an 8-mile training run in 56:30.

Key Run Workout #3: Long Run

Complete a 15- to 20-mile run at 7:40-per-mile pace.

If you can complete one of each Key Run Workout and meet the target paces, then we feel that you are ready to start training with this program.

FIRST "3PLUS2" MARATHON TRAINING PROGRAM SAMPLE WEEK

DAY 1	DAY 2	DAY 3	DAY 4	DAY 5	DAY 6	DAY 7
Cross-Train (XT#1)	Key Run Workout #1	Cross-Train (XT#2)	Key Run Workout #2	Off	Key Run Workout #3	Optional Cross-Train or Rest

See Chapter 5 for cross-training workouts.

BOSTON MARATHON QUALIFYING TRAINING PROGRAM FOR MEN 35 AND YOUNGER (3:10)

WEEK	KEY RUN WORKOUT #1	KEY RUN WORKOUT #2	KEY RUN WORKOUT #3
16	10–20 min warmup 3 × 1600m @ 6:01 (1 min RI) 10 min cooldown	6 mile run: 2 miles easy, 2 miles @ 6:34/mile, 2 miles easy	13 miles @ 7:45/mile
15	1 mile warmup 4 × 800m @ 2:52 (2 min RI) 10 min cooldown	7 mile run: 1 mile easy, 5 miles @ 7:15/mile, 1 mile easy	15 miles @ 8:00/mile
14	10–20 min warmup 1200m @ 4:24, 1000m @ 3:37, 800m @ 2:52, 600m @ 2:08, 400m @ 1:24 (all with 200m RI) 10 min cooldown	7 mile run: 1 mile easy, 5 miles @ 7:04/mile, 1 mile easy	17 miles @ 8:00/mile
13	10–20 min warmup 5 × 1000m @ 3:37 (400m RI) 10 min cooldown	6 mile run: 1 mile easy, 4 miles @ 6:49/mile, 1 mile easy	20 miles @ 8:15/mile
12	10–20 min warmup 3 × 1600m @ 6:01 (1 min RI) 10 min cooldown	6 mile run: 2 miles easy, 3 miles @ 6:34/mile, 1 mile easy	18 miles @ 8:00/mile
11	10–20 min warmup 2 × 1200m @ 4:24 (2 min RI), 4 × 800m @ 2:52 (2 min RI) 10 min cooldown	6 mile run: 1 mile easy, 5 miles @ 6:49/mile	20 miles @ 8:00/mile
10	10–20 min warmup 6 × 800m @ 2:52 (1:30 RI) 10 min cooldown	8 mile run: 1 mile easy, 6 miles @ 7:04/mile, 1 mile easy	13 miles @ 7:30/mile
9	10–20 min warmup 2 × (6 × 400m @ 1:24) (1:30 RI) (2:30 RI between sets) 10 min cooldown	6 mile run: 2 miles easy, 3 miles @ 6:34/mile, 1 mile easy	18 miles @ 7:45/mile

WEEK	KEY RUN WORKOUT #1	KEY RUN WORKOUT #2	KEY RUN WORKOUT #3
8	10–20 min warmup 1600m @ 6:01 (400m RI), 3200m @ 12:22 (800m RI), 2 × 800m @ 2:52 (400m RI) 10 min cooldown	6 mile run: 1 mile easy, 4 miles @ 6:49/mile, 1 mile easy	20 miles @ 7:45/mile
7	10–20 min warmup 3 × (2 × 1200m @ 4:24) (2 min RI) (4 min between sets) 10 min cooldown	11 mile run: 1 mile easy, 10 miles @ 7:15/mile	15 miles @ 7:35/mile
6	10–20 min warmup 1000m @ 3:37, 2000m @ 7:36, 1000m @ 3:37, 1000m @ 3:37 (all with 400m RI) 10 min cooldown	6 mile run: 1 mile easy, 5 miles @ 6:49/mile	20 miles @ 7:45/mile
5	10–20 min warmup 3 × 1600m @ 6:01 (400m RI) 10 min cooldown	11 mile run: 1 mile easy, 10 miles @ 7:15/mile	15 miles @ 7:25/mile
4	10–20 min warmup 10 × 400m @ 1:24 (400m RI) 10 min cooldown	8 mile run: 1 mile easy, 7 miles @ 7:15/mile	20 miles @ 7:30/mile
3	10–20 min warmup 8 × 800m @ 2:52 (1:30 RI) 10 min cooldown	6 mile run: 1 mile easy, 5 miles @ 6:49/mile	13 miles @ 7:15/mile
2	10–20 min warmup 5 × 1000m @ 3:37 (400m RI) 10 min cooldown	6 mile run: 2 miles easy, 3 miles @ 6:34/mile, 1 mile easy	10 miles @ 7:15/mile
1	10–20 min warmup 6 × 400m @ 1:24 (400m RI) 10 min cooldown	3 mile run: 1 mile easy, 2 miles @ 7:15/mile	**MARATHON DAY** 26.2 miles @ 7:15/mile

RI = Rest interval, which may be a timed rest/recovery interval or a distance that you walk/jog after each track repeat.

For Men 35 to 39, You Must Run 3:15 to BQ

Qualifying for Boston is realistic:

If you can:

Run a 5-K in 20:05

Run a 10-K in 42:00

Run a half-marathon in 1:33:30 (*Note:* The half-marathon is the best predictor.)

If you can complete one of each of these three Key Run Workouts in the *same* week:

Key Run Workout #1: Track Repeats (complete one of the workouts listed below)

6 × 800m at 2:58-per-800m pace with a 400m recovery jog between intervals

5 × 1000m at 3:44-per-1000m pace with a 400m recovery jog between intervals

4 × 1200m at 4:33-per-1200m pace with a 400m recovery jog between intervals

3 × 1600m at 6:12-per-1600m pace with a 400m recovery jog between intervals

Key Run Workout #2: Tempo Run (complete one of the tempo runs)

After a 1-mile warmup, complete a 3-mile training run in 20:15.

After a 1-mile warmup, complete a 5-mile training run in 35:00.

After a 1-mile warmup, complete an 8-mile training run in 58:00.

Key Run Workout #3: Long Run

Complete a 15- to 20-mile run at 7:50-per-mile pace.

If you can complete one of each Key Run Workout and meet the target paces, then we feel that you are ready to start training with this program.

BOSTON MARATHON QUALIFYING TRAINING PROGRAM FOR MEN 35 TO 39 (3:15)

WEEK	KEY RUN WORKOUT #1	KEY RUN WORKOUT #2	KEY RUN WORKOUT #3
16	10–20 min warmup 3 × 1600m @ 6:12 (1 min RI) 10 min cooldown	6 mile run: 2 miles easy, 2 miles @ 6:45/mile, 2 miles easy	13 miles @ 7:56/mile
15	1 mile warmup 4 × 800m @ 2:58 (2 min RI) 10 min cooldown	7 mile run: 1 mile easy, 5 miles @ 7:26/mile, 1 mile easy	15 miles @ 8:11/mile
14	10–20 min warmup 1200m @ 4:33, 1000m @ 3:44, 800m @ 2:58, 600m @ 2:13, 400m @ 1:27 (all with 200m RI) 10 min cooldown	7 mile run: 1 mile easy, 5 miles @ 7:15/mile, 1 mile easy	17 miles @ 8:11/mile
13	10–20 min warmup 5 × 1000m @ 3:44 (400m RI) 10 min cooldown	6 mile run: 1 mile easy, 4 miles @ 7:00/mile, 1 mile easy	20 miles @ 8:26/mile
12	10–20 min warmup 3 × 1600m @ 6:12 (1 min RI) 10 min cooldown	6 mile run: 2 miles easy, 3 miles @ 6:45/mile, 1 mile easy	18 miles @ 8:11/mile
11	10–20 min warmup 2 × 1200m @ 4:33 (2 min RI), 4 × 800m @ 2:58 (2 min RI) 10 min cooldown	6 mile run: 1 mile easy, 5 miles @ 7:00/mile	20 miles @ 8:11/mile
10	10–20 min warmup 6 × 800m @ 2:58 (1:30 RI) 10 min cooldown	8 mile run: 1 mile easy, 6 miles @ 7:00/mile, 1 mile easy	13 miles @ 7:41/mile
9	10–20 min warmup 2 × (6 × 400m @ 1:27) (1:30 RI) (2:30 RI between sets) 10 min cooldown	6 mile run: 2 miles easy, 3 miles @ 6:45/mile, 1 mile easy	18 miles @ 7:56/mile

BOSTON MARATHON QUALIFYING TRAINING PROGRAM FOR MEN 35 TO 39 (3:15) (*continued*)

WEEK	KEY RUN WORKOUT #1	KEY RUN WORKOUT #2	KEY RUN WORKOUT #3
8	10–20 min warmup 1600m @ 6:12 (400m RI), 3200m @ 12:40 (800m RI), 2 × 800m @ 2:58 (400m RI) 10 min cooldown	6 mile run: 1 mile easy, 4 miles @ 7:00/mile, 1 mile easy	20 miles @ 7:56/mile
7	10–20 min warmup 3 × (2 × 1200m @ 4:33) (2 min RI) (4 min RI between sets) 10 min cooldown	11 mile run: 1 mile easy, 10 miles @ 7:26/mile	15 miles @ 7:46/mile
6	10–20 min warmup 1000m @ 3:44, 2000m @ 7:50, 1000m @ 3:44, 1000m @ 3:44 (all with 400m RI) 10 min cooldown	6 mile run: 1 mile easy, 5 miles @ 7:00/mile	20 miles @ 7:56/mile
5	10–20 min warmup 3 × 1600m @ 6:12 (400m RI) 10 min cooldown	11 mile run: 1 mile easy, 10 miles @ 7:26/mile	15 miles @ 7:36/mile
4	10–20 min warmup 10 × 400m @ 1:27 (400m RI) 10 min cooldown	8 mile run 1 mile easy, 7 miles @ 7:26/mile	20 miles @ 7:41/mile
3	10–20 min warmup 8 × 800m @ 2:58 (1:30 RI) 10 min cooldown	6 mile run: 1 mile easy, 5 miles @ 7:00/mile	13 miles @ 7:26/mile
2	10–20 min warmup 5 × 1000m @ 3:44 (400m RI) 10 min cooldown	6 mile run: 2 miles easy, 3 miles @ 6:45/mile, 1 mile easy	10 miles @ 7:26/mile
1	10–20 min warmup 6 × 400m @ 1:27 (400m RI) 10 min cooldown	3 mile run: 1 mile easy, 2 miles @ 7:26/mile	**MARATHON DAY** 26.2 miles @ 7:26/mile

RI = Rest interval, which may be a timed rest/recovery interval or a distance that you walk/jog after each track repeat.

For Men 40 to 44, You Must Run 3:20 to BQ

Qualifying for Boston is realistic:

If you can:

Run a 5-K in 20:35

Run a 10-K in 43:00

Run a half-marathon in 1:35:30 (*Note:* The half-marathon is the best predictor.)

If you can complete one of each of these three Key Run Workouts in the *same* week:

Key Run Workout #1: Track Repeats (complete one of the workouts listed below)

6 × 800m at 3:03-per-800m pace with a 400m recovery jog between intervals

5 × 1000m at 3:50-per-1000m pace with a 400m recovery jog between intervals

4 × 1200m at 4:40-per-1200m pace with a 400m recovery jog between intervals

3 × 1600m at 6:22-per-1600m pace with a 400m recovery jog between intervals

Key Run Workout #2: Tempo run (complete one of the tempo runs)

After a 1-mile warmup, complete a 3-mile training run in 20:42.

After a 1-mile warmup, complete a 5-mile training run in 35:45.

After a 1-mile warmup, complete an 8-mile training run in 59:12.

Key Run Workout #3: Long run

Complete a 15- to 20-mile run at 8:03-per-mile pace.

If you can complete one of each Key Run Workout and meet the target paces, then we feel that you are ready to start training with this program.

BOSTON MARATHON QUALIFYING TRAINING PROGRAM FOR MEN 40 TO 44 (3:20)

WEEK	KEY RUN WORKOUT #1	KEY RUN WORKOUT #2	KEY RUN WORKOUT #3
16	10–20 min warmup 3 × 1600m @ 6:22 (1 min RI) 10 min cooldown	6 mile run: 2 miles easy, 2 miles @ 6:54/mile, 2 miles easy	13 miles @ 8:08/mile
15	1 mile warmup 4 × 800m @ 3:03 (2 min RI) 10 min cooldown	7 mile run: 1 mile easy, 5 miles @ 7:38/mile, 1 mile easy	15 miles @ 8:23/mile
14	10–20 min warmup 1200m @ 4:40, 1000m @ 3:50, 800m @ 3:03, 600m @ 2:16, 400m @ 1:30 (all with 200m RI) 10 min cooldown	7 mile run: 1 mile easy, 5 miles @ 7:24/mile, 1 mile easy	17 miles @ 8:23/mile
13	10–20 min warmup 5 × 1000m @ 3:50 (400m RI) 10 min cooldown	6 mile run: 1 mile easy, 4 miles @ 7:09/mile, 1 mile easy	20 miles @ 8:38/mile
12	10–20 min warmup 3 × 1600m @ 6:22 (1 min RI) 10 min cooldown	6 mile run: 2 miles easy, 3 miles @ 6:54/mile, 1 mile easy	18 miles @ 8:23/mile
11	10–20 min warmup 2 × 1200m @ 4:40 (2 min RI), 4 × 800m @ 3:03 (2 min RI) 10 min cooldown	6 mile run: 1 mile easy, 5 miles @ 7:09/mile	20 miles @ 8:23/mile
10	10–20 min warmup 6 × 800m @ 3:03 (1:30 RI) 10 min cooldown	8 mile run: 1 mile easy, 6 miles @ 7:24/mile, 1 mile easy	13 miles @ 7:53/mile
9	10–20 min warmup 2 × (6 × 400m @ 1:30) (1:30 RI) (2:30 RI between sets) 10 min cooldown	6 mile run: 2 miles easy, 3 miles @ 6:54/mile, 1 mile easy	18 miles @ 8:08/mile

WEEK	KEY RUN WORKOUT #1	KEY RUN WORKOUT #2	KEY RUN WORKOUT #3
8	10–20 min warmup 1600m @ 6:22 (400m RI), 3200m @ 13:04 (800m RI), 2 × 800m @ 3:03 (400m RI) 10 min cooldown	6 mile run: 1 mile easy, 4 miles @ 7:09/mile, 1 mile easy	20 miles @ 8:08/mile
7	10–20 min warmup 3 × (2 × 1200m @ 4:40) (2 min RI) (4 min between sets) 10 min cooldown	11 mile run: 1 mile easy, 10 miles @ 7:38/mile	15 miles @ 7:58/mile
6	10–20 min warmup 1000m @ 3:50, 2000m @ 8:02, 1000m @ 3:50, 1000m @ 3:50 (all with 400m RI) 10 min cooldown	6 mile run: 1 mile easy, 5 miles @ 7:09/mile	20 miles @ 8:08/mile
5	10–20 min warmup 3 × 1600m @ 6:22 (400m RI) 10 min cooldown	11 mile run: 1 mile easy, 10 miles @ 7:38/mile	15 miles @ 7:48/mile
4	10–20 min warmup 10 × 400m @ 1:30 (400m RI) 10 min cooldown	8 mile run: 1 mile easy, 7 miles @ 7:38/mile	20 miles @ 7:53/mile
3	10–20 min warmup 8 × 800m @ 3:03 (1:30 RI) 10 min cooldown	6 mile run: 1 mile easy, 5 miles @ 7:09/mile	13 miles @ 7:38/mile
2	10–20 min warmup 5 × 1000m @ 3:50 (400m RI) 10 min cooldown	6 mile run: 2 miles easy, 3 miles @ 6:54/mile, 1 mile easy	10 miles @ 7:38/mile
1	10–20 min warmup 6 × 400m @ 1:30 (400m RI) 10 min cooldown	3 mile run: 1 mile easy, 2 miles @ 7:38/mile	**MARATHON DAY** 26.2 miles @ 7:38/mile

RI = Rest interval, which may be a timed rest/recovery interval or a distance that you walk/jog after each track repeat.

For Men 45 to 49, You Must Run 3:30 to BQ

Qualifying for Boston is realistic:

If you can:

Run a 5-K in 21:35

Run a 10-K in 45:10

Run a half-marathon in 1:40 (*Note:* The half-marathon is the best predictor.)

If you can complete one of each of these three Key Run Workouts in the *same* week:

Key Run Workout #1: Track Repeats (complete one of the workouts listed below)

6 × 800m at 3:13-per-800m pace with a 400m recovery jog between intervals

5 × 1000m at 4:03-per-1000m pace with a 400m recovery jog between intervals

4 × 1200m at 4:55-per-1200m pace with a 400m recovery jog between intervals

3 × 1600m at 6:41-per-1600m pace with a 400m recovery jog between intervals

Key Run Workout #2: Tempo Run (complete one of the tempo runs)

After a 1-mile warmup, complete a 3-mile training run in 21:42.

After a 1-mile warmup, complete a 5-mile training run in 37:30.

After a 1-mile warmup, complete an 8-mile training run in 62:00.

Key Run Workout #3: Long Run

Complete a 15- to 20-mile run at 8:25-per-mile pace.

If you can complete one of each Key Run Workout and meet the target paces, then we feel that you are ready to start training with this program.

BOSTON MARATHON QUALIFYING TRAINING PROGRAM FOR MEN 45 TO 49 (3:30)

WEEK	KEY RUN WORKOUT #1	KEY RUN WORKOUT #2	KEY RUN WORKOUT #3
16	10–20 min warmup 3 × 1600m @ 6:41 (1 min RI) 10 min cooldown	6 mile run: 2 miles easy, 2 miles @ 7:14/mile, 2 miles easy	13 miles @ 8:30/mile
15	1 mile warmup 4 × 800m @ 3:13 (2 min RI) 10 min cooldown	7 mile run: 1 mile easy, 5 miles @ 8:00/mile, 1 mile easy	15 miles @ 8:45/mile
14	10–20 min warmup 1200m @ 4:55, 1000m @ 4:03, 800m @ 3:13, 600m @ 2:24, 400m @ 1:35 (all with 200m RI) 10 min cooldown	7 mile run: 1 mile easy, 5 miles @ 7:44/mile, 1 mile easy	17 miles @ 8:45/mile
13	10–20 min warmup 5 × 1000m @ 4:03 (400m RI) 10 min cooldown	6 mile run: 1 mile easy, 4 miles @ 7:29/mile, 1 mile easy	20 miles @ 9:00/mile
12	10–20 min warmup 3 × 1600m @ 6:41 (1 min RI) 10 min cooldown	6 mile run: 2 miles easy, 3 miles @ 7:14/mile, 1 mile easy	18 miles @ 8:45/mile
11	10–20 min warmup 2 × 1200m @ 4:55 (2 min RI) 4 × 800m @ 3:13 (2 min RI) 10 min cooldown	6 mile run: 1 mile easy, 5 miles @ 7:29/mile	20 miles @ 8:45/mile
10	10–20 min warmup 6 × 800m @ 3:13 (1:30 RI) 10 min cooldown	8 mile run: 1 mile easy, 6 miles @ 7:44/mile, 1 mile easy	13 miles @ 8:15/mile
9	10–20 min warmup 2 × (6 × 400m @ 1:35) (1:30 RI) (2:30 RI between sets) 10 min cooldown	6 mile run: 2 miles easy, 3 miles @ 7:14/mile, 1 mile easy	18 miles @ 8:30/mile

BOSTON MARATHON QUALIFYING TRAINING PROGRAM FOR MEN 45 TO 49 (3:30) (*continued*)

WEEK	KEY RUN WORKOUT #1	KEY RUN WORKOUT #2	KEY RUN WORKOUT #3
8	10–20 min warmup 1600m @ 6:41 (400m RI), 3200m @ 13:42 (800m RI), 2 × 800m @ 3:13 (400m RI) 10 min cooldown	6 mile run: 1 mile easy, 4 miles @ 7:29/mile, 1 mile easy	20 miles @ 8:30/mile
7	10–20 min warmup 3 × (2 × 1200m @ 4:55) (2 min RI) (4 min between sets) 10 min cooldown	11 mile run: 1 mile easy, 10 miles @ 8:00/mile	15 miles @ 8:20/mile
6	10–20 min warmup 1000m @ 4:03, 2000m @ 8:26, 1000m @ 4:03, 1000m @ 4:03 (all with 400m RI) 10 min cooldown	6 mile run: 1 mile easy, 5 miles @ 7:29/mile	20 miles @ 8:30/mile
5	10–20 min warmup 3 × 1600m @ 6:41 (400m RI) 10 min cooldown	11 mile run: 1 mile easy, 10 miles @ 8:00/mile	15 miles @ 8:10/mile
4	10–20 min warmup 10 × 400m @ 1:35 (400m RI) 10 min cooldown	8 mile run: 1 mile easy, 7 miles @ 8:00/mile	20 miles @ 8:15/mile
3	10–20 min warmup 8 × 800m @ 3:13 (1:30 RI) 10 min cooldown	6 mile run: 1 mile easy, 5 miles @ 7:29/mile	13 miles @ 8:00/mile
2	10–20 min warmup 5 × 1000m @ 4:03 (400m RI) 10 min cooldown	6 mile run: 2 miles easy, 3 miles @ 7:14/mile, 1 mile easy	10 miles @ 8:00/mile
1	10–20 min warmup 6 × 400m @ 1:35 (400m RI) 10 min cooldown	3 mile run: 1 mile easy, 2 miles @ 8:00/mile	**MARATHON DAY** 26.2 miles @ 8:00/mile

RI = Rest interval, which may be a timed rest/recovery interval or a distance that you walk/jog after each track repeat.

For Men 50 to 54, You Must Run 3:35 to BQ

Qualifying for Boston is realistic:

If you can:

Run a 5-K in 22:05

Run a 10-K in 46:10

Run a half-marathon in 1:42:20 (*Note:* The half-marathon is the best predictor.)

If you can complete one of each of these three Key Run Workouts in the *same* week:

Key Run Workout #1: Track Repeats (complete one of the workouts listed below)

6 × 800m at 3:17-per-800m pace with a 400m recovery jog between intervals

5 × 1000m at 4:09-per-1000m pace with a 400m recovery jog between intervals

4 × 1200m at 5:02-per-1200m pace with a 400m recovery jog between intervals

3 × 1600m at 6:51-per-1600m pace with a 400m recovery jog between intervals

Key Run Workout #2: Tempo Run (complete one of the tempo runs)

After a 1-mile warmup, complete a 3-mile training run in 22:09.

After a 1-mile warmup, complete a 5-mile training run in 38:10.

After a 1-mile warmup, complete an 8-mile training run in 63:04.

Key Run Workout #3: Long run

Complete a 15- to 20-mile run at 8:37-per-mile pace.

If you can complete one of each Key Run Workout and meet the target paces, then we feel that you are ready to start training with this program.

BOSTON MARATHON QUALIFYING TRAINING PROGRAM FOR MEN 50 TO 54 (3:35)

WEEK	KEY RUN WORKOUT #1	KEY RUN WORKOUT #2	KEY RUN WORKOUT #3
16	10–20 min warmup 3 × 1600m @ 6:51 (1 min RI) 10 min cooldown	6 mile run: 2 miles easy, 2 miles @ 7:23/mile, 2 miles easy	13 miles @ 8:42/mile
15	1 mile warmup 4 × 800m @ 3:17 (2 min RI) 10 min cooldown	7 mile run: 1 mile easy, 5 miles @ 8:12/mile, 1 mile easy	15 miles @ 8:57/mile
14	10–20 min warmup 1200m @ 5:02, 1000m @ 4:09, 800m @ 3:17, 600m @ 2:27, 400m @ 1:37 (all with 200m RI) 10 min cooldown	7 mile run: 1 mile easy, 5 miles @ 7:53/mile, 1 mile easy	17 miles @ 8:57/mile
13	10–20 min warmup 5 × 1000m @ 4:09 (400m RI) 10 min cooldown	6 mile run: 1 mile easy, 4 miles @ 7:38/mile, 1 mile easy	20 miles @ 9:12/mile
12	10–20 min warmup 3 × 1600m @ 6:51 (1 min RI) 10 min cooldown	6 mile run: 2 miles easy, 3 miles @ 7:23/mile, 1 mile easy	18 miles @ 8:57/mile
11	10–20 min warmup 2 × 1200m @ 5:02 (2 min RI), 4 × 800m @ 3:17 (2 min RI) 10 min cooldown	6 mile run: 1 mile easy, 5 miles @ 7:38/mile	20 miles @ 8:57/mile
10	10–20 min warmup 6 × 800m @ 3:17 (1:30 RI) 10 min cooldown	8 mile run: 1 mile easy, 6 miles @ 7:53/mile, 1 mile easy	13 miles @ 8:27/mile
9	10–20 min warmup 2 × (6 × 400m @ 1:37) (1:30 RI) (2:30 RI between sets) 10 min cooldown	6 mile run: 2 miles easy, 3 miles @ 7:23/mile, 1 mile easy	18 miles @ 8:42/mile

WEEK	KEY RUN WORKOUT #1	KEY RUN WORKOUT #2	KEY RUN WORKOUT #3
8	10–20 min warmup 1600m @ 6:51 (400m RI), 3200m @ 14:02 (800m RI), 2 × 800m @ 3:17 (400m RI) 10 min cooldown	6 mile run: 1 mile easy, 4 miles @ 7:38/mile, 1 mile easy	20 miles @ 8:42/mile
7	10–20 min warmup 3 × (2 × 1200m @ 5:02) (2 min RI) (4 min between sets) 10 min cooldown	11 mile run: 1 mile easy, 10 miles @ 8:12/mile	15 miles @ 8:32/mile
6	10–20 min warmup 1000m @ 4:09, 2000m @ 8:38, 1000m @ 4:09, 1000m @ 4:09 (all with 400m RI) 10 min cooldown	6 mile run: 1 mile easy, 5 miles @ 7:38/mile	20 miles @ 8:42/mile
5	10–20 min warmup 3 × 1600m @ 6:51 (400m RI) 10 min cooldown	11 mile run: 1 mile easy, 10 miles @ 8:12/mile	15 miles @ 8:22/mile
4	10–20 min warmup 10 × 400m @ 1:37 (400m RI) 10 min cooldown	8 mile run: 1 mile easy, 7 miles @ 8:12/mile	20 miles @ 8:27/mile
3	10–20 min warmup 8 × 800m @ 3:17 (1:30 RI) 10 min cooldown	6 mile run: 1 mile easy, 5 miles @ 7:38/mile	13 miles @ 8:12/mile
2	10–20 min warmup 5 × 1000m @ 4:09 (400m RI) 10 min cooldown	6 mile run: 2 miles easy, 3 miles @ 7:23/mile, 1 mile easy	10 miles @ 8:12/mile
1	10–20 min warmup 6 × 400m @ 1:37 (400m RI) 10 min cooldown	3 mile run: 1 mile easy, 2 miles @ 8:12/mile	**MARATHON DAY** 26.2 miles @ 8:12/mile

RI = Rest interval, which may be a timed rest/recovery interval or a distance that you walk/jog after each track repeat.

For Women 18 to 34, You Must Run 3:40 to BQ

Qualifying for Boston is realistic:

If you can:

Run a 5-K in 22:40

Run a 10-K in 47:25

Run a half-marathon in 1:45:00 (*Note:* The half-marathon is the best predictor.)

If you can complete one of each of these three Key Run Workouts in the *same* week:

Key Run Workout #1: Track Repeats (complete one of the workouts listed below)

6 × 800m at 3:23-per-800m pace with a 400m recovery jog between intervals

5 × 1000m at 4:16-per-1000m pace with a 400m recovery jog between intervals

4 × 1200m at 5:10-per-1200m pace with a 400m recovery jog between intervals

3 × 1600m at 7:02-per-1600m pace with a 400m recovery jog between intervals

Key Run Workout #2: Tempo Run (complete one of the tempo runs)

After a 1-mile warmup, complete a 3-mile training run in 22:45.

After a 1-mile warmup, complete a 5-mile training run in 39:10.

After a 1-mile warmup, complete an 8-mile training run in 64:40.

Key Run Workout #3: Long Run

Complete a 15- to 20-mile run at 8:48-per-mile pace.

If you can complete one of each Key Run Workout and meet the target paces, then we feel that you are ready to start training with this program.

BOSTON MARATHON QUALIFYING TRAINING PROGRAM FOR WOMEN 18 TO 34 (3:40)

WEEK	KEY RUN WORKOUT #1	KEY RUN WORKOUT #2	KEY RUN WORKOUT #3
16	10–20 min warmup 3 × 1600m @ 7:02 (1 min RI) 10 min cooldown	6 mile run: 2 miles easy, 2 miles @ 7:35/mile, 2 miles easy	13 miles @ 8:53/mile
15	1 mile warmup 4 × 800m @ 3:23 (2 min RI) 10 min cooldown	7 mile run: 1 mile easy, 5 miles @ 8:23/mile, 1 mile easy	15 miles @ 9:08/mile
14	10–20 min warmup 1200m @ 5:10, 1000m @ 4:16, 800m @ 3:23, 600m @ 2:31, 400m @ 1:39 (all with 200m RI) 10 min cooldown	7 mile run: 1 mile easy, 5 miles @ 8:05/mile, 1 mile easy	17 miles @ 9:08/mile
13	10–20 min warmup 5 × 1000m @ 4:16 (400m RI) 10 min cooldown	6 mile run: 1 mile easy, 4 miles @ 7:50/mile, 1 mile easy	20 miles @ 9:23/mile
12	10–20 min warmup 3 × 1600m @ 7:02 (1 min RI) 10 min cooldown	6 mile run: 2 miles easy, 3 miles @ 7:35/mile, 1 mile easy	18 miles @ 9:08/mile
11	10–20 min warmup 2 × 1200m @ 5:10 (2 min RI), 4 × 800m @ 3:23 (2 min RI) 10 min cooldown	6 mile run: 1 mile easy, 5 miles @ 7:50/mile	20 miles @ 9:08/mile
10	10–20 min warmup 6 × 800m @ 3:23 (1:30 RI) 10 min cooldown	8 mile run: 1 mile easy, 6 miles @ 8:05/mile, 1 mile easy	13 miles @ 8:38/mile
9	10–20 min warmup 2 × (6 × 400m @ 1:39) (1:30 RI) (2:30 RI between sets) 10 min cooldown	6 mile run: 2 miles easy, 3 miles @ 7:35/mile, 1 mile easy	18 miles @ 8:53/mile

BOSTON MARATHON QUALIFYING TRAINING PROGRAM FOR WOMEN 18 TO 34 (3:40) (*continued*)

WEEK	KEY RUN WORKOUT #1	KEY RUN WORKOUT #2	KEY RUN WORKOUT #3
8	10–20 min warmup 1600m @ 7:02 (400m RI), 3200m @ 14:24 (800m RI), 2 × 800m @ 3:23 (400m RI) 10 min cooldown	6 mile run: 1 mile easy, 4 miles @ 7:50/mile, 1 mile easy	20 miles @ 8:53/mile
7	10–20 min warmup 3 × (2 × 1200m @ 5:10) (2 min RI) (4 min between sets) 10 min cooldown	11 mile run: 1 mile easy, 10 miles @ 8:23/mile	15 miles @ 8:43/mile
6	10–20 min warmup 1000m @ 4:16, 2000m @ 8:52, 1000m @ 4:16, 1000m @ 4:16 (all with 400m RI) 10 min cooldown	6 mile run: 1 mile easy, 5 miles @ 7:50/mile	20 miles @ 8:53/mile
5	10–20 min warmup 3 × 1600m @ 7:02 (400m RI) 10 min cooldown	11 mile run: 1 mile easy, 10 miles @ 8:23/mile	15 miles @ 8:33/mile
4	10–20 min warmup 10 × 400m @ 1:39 (400m RI) 10 min cooldown	8 mile run: 1 mile easy, 7 miles @ 8:23/mile	20 miles @ 8:38/mile
3	10–20 min warmup 8 × 800m @ 3:23 (1:30 RI) 10 min cooldown	6 mile run: 1 mile easy, 5 miles @ 7:50/mile	13 miles @ 8:23/mile
2	10–20 min warmup 5 × 1000m @ 4:16 (400m RI) 10 min cooldown	6 mile run: 2 miles easy, 3 miles @ 7:35/mile, 1 mile easy	10 miles @ 8:23/mile
1	10–20 min warmup 6 × 400m @ 1:39 (400m RI) 10 min cooldown	3 mile run: 1 mile easy, 2 miles @ 8:23/mile	**MARATHON DAY** 26.2 miles @ 8:23/mile

RI = Rest interval, which may be a timed rest/recovery interval or a distance that you walk/jog after each track repeat.

For Men 55 to 59 and Women 35 to 39, You Must Run 3:45 to BQ

Qualifying for Boston is realistic:

If you can:

Run a 5-K in 23:10

Run a 10-K in 48:30

Run a half-marathon in 1:47:25 (*Note*: The half-marathon is the best predictor.)

If you can complete one of each of these three Key Run Workouts in the *same* week:

Key Run Workout #1: Track Repeats (complete one of the workouts listed below)

6 × 800m at 3:28-per-800m pace with a 400m recovery jog between intervals

5 × 1000m at 4:22-per-1000m pace with a 400m recovery jog between intervals

4 × 1200m at 5:18-per-1200m pace with a 400m recovery jog between intervals

3 × 1600m at 7:11-per-1600m pace with a 400m recovery jog between intervals

Key Run Workout #2: Tempo Run (complete one of the tempo runs)

After a 1-mile warmup, complete a 3-mile training run in 23:15.

After a 1-mile warmup, complete a 5-mile training run in 40:00.

After a 1-mile warmup, complete an 8-mile training run in 66:00.

Key Run Workout #3: Long run

Complete a 15- to 20-mile run at 9:00-per-mile pace.

If you can complete one of each Key Run Workout and meet the target paces, then we feel that you are ready to start training with this program.

BOSTON MARATHON QUALIFYING TRAINING PROGRAM FOR MEN 55 TO 59 AND WOMEN 35 TO 39 (3:45)

WEEK	KEY RUN WORKOUT #1	KEY RUN WORKOUT #2	KEY RUN WORKOUT #3
16	10–20 min warmup 3 × 1600m @ 7:11 (1 min RI) 10 min cooldown	6 mile run: 2 miles easy, 2 miles @ 7:44/mile, 2 miles easy	13 miles @ 9:05/mile
15	1 mile warmup 4 × 800m @ 3:28 (2 min RI) 10 min cooldown	7 mile run: 1 mile easy, 5 miles @ 8:35/mile, 1 mile easy	15 miles @ 9:20/mile
14	10–20 min warmup 1200m @ 5:18, 1000m @ 4:22, 800m @ 3:28, 600m @ 2:35, 400m @ 1:42 (all with 200m RI) 10 min cooldown	7 mile run: 1 mile easy, 5 miles @ 8:14/mile, 1 mile easy	17 miles @ 9:20/mile
13	10–20 min warmup 5 × 1000m @ 4:22 (400m RI) 10 min cooldown	6 mile run: 1 mile easy, 4 miles @ 7:59/mile, 1 mile easy	20 miles @ 9:35/mile
12	10–20 min warmup 3 × 1600m @ 7:11 (1 min RI) 10 min cooldown	6 mile run: 2 miles easy, 3 miles @ 7:44/mile, 1 mile easy	18 miles @ 9:20/mile
11	10–20 min warmup 2 × 1200m @ 5:18 (2 min RI), 4 × 800m @ 3:28 (2 min RI) 10 min cooldown	6 mile run: 1 mile easy, 5 miles @ 7:59/mile	20 miles @ 9:20/mile
10	10–20 min warmup 6 × 800m @ 3:28 (1:30 RI) 10 min cooldown	8 mile run: 1 mile easy, 6 miles @ 8:14/mile, 1 mile easy	13 miles @ 8:50/mile
9	10–20 min warmup 2 × (6 × 400m @ 1:42) (1:30 RI) (2:30 RI between sets) 10 min cooldown	6 mile run: 2 miles easy, 3 miles @ 7:44/mile, 1 mile easy	18 miles @ 9:05/mile

WEEK	KEY RUN WORKOUT #1	KEY RUN WORKOUT #2	KEY RUN WORKOUT #3
8	10–20 min warmup 1600m @ 7:11 (400m RI), 3200m @ 14:42 (800m RI), 2 × 800m @ 3:28 (400m RI) 10 min cooldown	6 mile run: 1 mile easy, 4 miles @ 7:59/mile, 1 mile easy	20 miles @ 9:05/mile
7	10–20 min warmup 3 × (2 × 1200m @ 5:18) (2 min RI) (4 min between sets) 10 min cooldown	11 mile run: 1 mile easy, 10 miles @ 8:35/mile	15 miles @ 8:55/mile
6	10–20 min warmup 1000m @ 4:22, 2000m @ 9:04, 1000m @ 4:22, 1000m @ 4:22 (all with 400m RI) 10 min cooldown	6 mile run: 1 mile easy, 5 miles @ 7:59/mile	20 miles @ 9:05/mile
5	10–20 min warmup 3 × 1600m @ 7:11 (400m RI) 10 min cooldown	11 mile run: 1 mile easy, 10 miles @ 8:35/mile	15 miles @ 8:45/mile
4	10–20 min warmup 10 × 400m @ 1:42 (400m RI) 10 min cooldown	8 mile run: 1 mile easy, 7 miles @ 8:35/mile	20 miles @ 8:50/mile
3	10–20 min warmup 8 × 800m @ 3:28 (1:30 RI) 10 min cooldown	6 mile run: 1 mile easy, 5 miles @ 7:59/mile	13 miles @ 8:35/mile
2	10–20 min warmup 5 × 1000m @ 4:22 (400m RI) 10 min cooldown	6 mile run: 2 miles easy, 3 miles @ 7:44/mile, 1 mile easy	10 miles @ 8:35/mile
1	10–20 min warmup 6 × 400m @ 1:42 (400m RI) 10 min cooldown	3 mile run: 1 mile easy, 2 miles @ 8:35/mile	**MARATHON DAY** 26.2 miles @ 8:35/mile

RI = Rest interval, which may be a timed rest/recovery interval or a distance that you walk/jog after each track repeat.

For Women 40 to 44, You Must Run 3:50 to BQ

Qualifying for Boston is realistic:

If you can:

Run a 5-K in 23:40

Run a 10-K in 49:31

Run a half-marathon in 1:49:42 (*Note:* The half-marathon is the best predictor.)

If you can complete one of each of these three Key Run Workouts in the *same* week:

Key Run Workout #1: Track Repeats (complete one of the workouts listed below)

6 × 800m at 3:33-per-800m pace with a 400m recovery jog between intervals

5 × 1000m at 4:28-per-1000m pace with a 400m recovery jog between intervals

4 × 1200m at 5:25-per-1200m pace with a 400m recovery jog between intervals

3 × 1600m at 7:21-per-1600m pace with a 400m recovery jog between intervals

Key Run Workout #2: Tempo run (complete one of the tempo runs)

After a 1-mile warmup, complete a 3-mile training run in 23:12.

After a 1-mile warmup, complete a 5-mile training run in 40:45.

After a 1-mile warmup, complete an 8-mile training run in 67:12.

Key Run Workout #3: Long run

Complete a 15- to 20-mile run at 9:11-per-mile pace.

If you can complete one of each Key Run Workout and meet the target paces, then we feel that you are ready to start training with this program.

BOSTON MARATHON QUALIFYING TRAINING PROGRAM FOR WOMEN 40 TO 44 (3:50)

WEEK	KEY RUN WORKOUT #1	KEY RUN WORKOUT #2	KEY RUN WORKOUT #3
16	10–20 min warmup 3 × 1600m @ 7:21 (1 min RI) 10 min cooldown	6 mile run: 2 miles easy, 2 miles @ 7:54/mile, 2 miles easy	13 miles @ 9:16/mile
15	1 mile warmup 4 × 800m @ 3:33 (2 min RI) 10 min cooldown	7 mile run: 1 mile easy, 5 miles @ 8:46/mile, 1 mile easy	15 miles @ 9:31/mile
14	10–20 min warmup 1200m @ 5:25, 1000m @ 4:28, 800m @ 3:33, 600m @ 2:38, 400m @ 1:44 (all with 200m RI) 10 min cooldown	7 mile run: 1 mile easy, 5 miles @ 8:24/mile, 1 mile easy	17 miles @ 9:31/mile
13	10–20 min warmup 5 × 1000m @ 4:28 (400m RI) 10 min cooldown	6 mile run: 1 mile easy, 4 miles @ 8:09/mile, 1 mile easy	20 miles @ 9:46/mile
12	10–20 min warmup 3 × 1600m @ 7:21 (1 min RI) 10 min cooldown	6 mile run: 2 miles easy, 3 miles @ 7:54/mile, 1 mile easy	18 miles @ 9:31/mile
11	10–20 min warmup 2 × 1200m @ 5:25 (2 min RI), 4 × 800m @ 3:33 (2 min RI) 10 min cooldown	6 mile run: 1 mile easy, 5 miles @ 8:09/mile	20 miles @ 9:31/mile
10	10–20 min warmup 6 × 800m @ 3:33 (1:30 RI) 10 min cooldown	8 mile run: 1 mile easy, 6 miles @ 8:24/mile, 1 mile easy	13 miles @ 9:01/mile
9	10–20 min warmup 2 × (6 × 400m @ 1:44) (1:30 RI) (2:30 RI between sets) 10 min cooldown	6 mile run: 2 miles easy, 3 miles @ 7:54/mile, 1 mile easy	18 miles @ 9:16/mile

BOSTON MARATHON QUALIFYING TRAINING PROGRAM FOR WOMEN 40 TO 44 (3:50) (*continued*)

WEEK	KEY RUN WORKOUT #1	KEY RUN WORKOUT #2	KEY RUN WORKOUT #3
8	10–20 min warmup 1600m @ 7:21 (400m RI), 3200m @ 15:02 (800m RI), 2 × 800m @ 3:33 (400m RI) 10 min cooldown	6 mile run: 1 mile easy, 4 miles @ 8:09/mile, 1 mile easy	20 miles @ 9:16/mile
7	10–20 min warmup 3 × (2 × 1200m @ 5:25) (2 min RI) (4 min between sets) 10 min cooldown	11 mile run: 1 mile easy, 10 miles @ 8:46/mile	15 miles @ 9:06/mile
6	10–20 min warmup 1000m @ 4:28, 2000m @ 9:16, 1000m @ 4:28, 1000m @ 4:28 (all with 400m RI) 10 min cooldown	6 mile run: 1 mile easy, 5 miles @ 8:09/mile	20 miles @ 9:16/mile
5	10–20 min warmup 3 × 1600m @ 7:21 (400m RI) 10 min cooldown	11 mile run: 1 mile easy, 10 miles @ 8:46/mile	15 miles @ 8:56/mile
4	10–20 min warmup 10 × 400m @ 1:44 (400m RI) 10 min cooldown	8 mile run: 1 mile easy, 7 miles @ 8:46/mile	20 miles @ 9:01/mile
3	10–20 min warmup 8 × 800m @ 3:33 (1:30 RI) 10 min cooldown	6 mile run: 1 mile easy, 5 miles @ 8:09/mile	13 miles @ 8:46/mile
2	10–20 min warmup 5 × 1000m @ 4:28 (400m RI) 10 min cooldown	6 mile run: 2 miles easy, 3 miles @ 7:54/mile, 1 mile easy	10 miles @ 8:46/mile
1	10–20 min warmup 6 × 400m @ 1:44 (400m RI) 10 min cooldown	3 mile run: 1 mile easy, 2 miles @ 8:46/mile	**MARATHON DAY** 26.2 miles @ 8:46/mile

RI = Rest interval, which may be a timed rest/recovery interval or a distance that you walk/jog after each track repeat.

For Men 60 to 64 and Women 45 to 49, You Must Run 4:00 to BQ

Qualifying for Boston is realistic:

If you can:

Run a 5-K in 24:40

Run a 10-K in 51:36

Run a half-marathon in 1:54:20 (*Note:* The half-marathon is the best predictor.)

If you can complete one of each of these three Key Run Workouts in the *same* week:

Key Run Workout #1: Track Repeats (complete one of the workouts listed below)

6 × 800m at 3:42-per-800m pace with a 400m recovery jog between intervals

5 × 1000m at 4:40-per-1000m pace with a 400m recovery jog between intervals

4 × 1200m at 5:39-per-1200m pace with a 400m recovery jog between intervals

3 × 1600m at 7:40-per-1600m pace with a 400m recovery jog between intervals

Key Run Workout #2: Tempo Run (complete one of the tempo runs)

After a 1-mile warmup, complete a 3-mile training run in 24:39.

After a 1-mile warmup, complete a 5-mile training run in 42:20.

After a 1-mile warmup, complete an 8-mile training run in 69:34.

Key Run Workout #3: Long Run

Complete a 15- to 20-mile run at 9:34-per-mile pace.

If you can complete one of each Key Run Workout and meet the target paces, then we feel that you are ready to start training with this program.

BOSTON MARATHON QUALIFYING TRAINING PROGRAM FOR MEN 60 TO 64 AND WOMEN 45 TO 49 (4:00)

WEEK	KEY RUN WORKOUT #1	KEY RUN WORKOUT #2	KEY RUN WORKOUT #3
16	10–20 min warmup 3 × 1600m @ 7:40 (1 min RI) 10 min cooldown	6 mile run: 2 miles easy, 2 miles @ 8:13/mile, 2 miles easy	13 miles @ 9:39/mile
15	1 mile warmup 4 × 800m @ 3:42 (2 min RI) 10 min cooldown	7 mile run: 1 mile easy, 5 miles @ 9:09/mile, 1 mile easy	15 miles @ 9:54/mile
14	10–20 min warmup 1200m @ 5:39, 1000m @ 4:40, 800m @ 3:42, 600m @ 2:46, 400m @ 1:49 (all with 200m RI) 10 min cooldown	7 mile run: 1 mile easy, 5 miles @ 8:43/mile, 1 mile easy	17 miles @ 9:54/mile
13	10–20 min warmup 5 × 1000m @ 4:40 (400m RI) 10 min cooldown	6 mile run: 1 mile easy, 4 miles @ 8:28/mile, 1 mile easy	20 miles @ 10:09/mile
12	10–20 min warmup 3 × 1600m @ 7:40 (1 min RI) 10 min cooldown	6 mile run: 2 miles easy, 3 miles @ 8:13/mile, 1 mile easy	18 miles @ 9:54/mile
11	10–20 min warmup 2 × 1200m @ 5:39 (2 min RI), 4 × 800m @ 3:42 (2 min RI) 10 min cooldown	6 mile run: 1 mile easy, 5 miles @ 8:28/mile	20 miles @ 9:54/mile
10	10–20 min warmup 6 × 800m @ 3:42 (1:30 RI) 10 min cooldown	8 mile run: 1 mile easy, 6 miles @ 8:43/mile, 1 mile easy	13 miles @ 9:24/mile
9	10–20 min warmup 2 × (6 × 400m @ 1:49) (1:30 RI) (2:30 RI between sets) 10 min cooldown	6 mile run: 2 miles easy, 3 miles @ 8:13/mile, 1 mile easy	18 miles @ 9:39/mile

WEEK	KEY RUN WORKOUT #1	KEY RUN WORKOUT #2	KEY RUN WORKOUT #3
8	10–20 min warmup 1600m @ 7:40 (400m RI), 3200m @ 15:40 (800m RI), 2 × 800m @ 3:42 (400m RI) 10 min cooldown	6 mile run: 1 mile easy, 4 miles @ 8:28/mile, 1 mile easy	20 miles @ 9:39/mile
7	10–20 min warmup 3 × (2 × 1200m @ 5:39) (2 min RI) (4 min between sets) 10 min cooldown	11 mile run: 1 mile easy, 10 miles @ 9:09/mile	15 miles @ 9:29/mile
6	10–20 min warmup 1000m @ 4:40, 2000m @ 9:40, 1000m @ 4:40, 1000m @ 4:40 (all with 400m RI) 10 min cooldown	6 mile run: 1 mile easy, 5 miles @ 8:28/mile	20 miles @ 9:39/mile
5	10–20 min warmup 3 × 1600m @ 7:40 (400m RI) 10 min cooldown	11 mile run: 1 mile easy, 10 miles @ 9:09/mile	15 miles @ 9:19/mile
4	10–20 min warmup 10 × 400m @ 1:49 (400m RI) 10 min cooldown	8 mile run: 1 mile easy, 7 miles @ 9:09/mile	20 miles @ 9:24/mile
3	10–20 min warmup 8 × 800m @ 3:42 (1:30 RI) 10 min cooldown	6 mile run: 1 mile easy, 5 miles @ 8:28/mile	13 miles @ 9:09/mile
2	10–20 min warmup 5 × 1000m @ 4:40 (400m RI) 10 min cooldown	6 mile run: 2 miles easy, 3 miles @ 8:13/mile, 1 mile easy	10 miles @ 9:09/mile
1	10–20 min warmup 6 × 400m @ 1:49 (400m RI) 10 min cooldown	3 mile run: 1 mile easy, 2 miles @ 9:09/mile	**MARATHON DAY** 26.2 miles @ 9:09/mile

RI = Rest interval, which may be a timed rest/recovery interval or a distance that you walk/jog after each track repeat.

For Women 50 to 54, You Must Run 4:05 to BQ

Qualifying for Boston is realistic:

If you can:

Run a 5-K in 25:10

Run a 10-K in 52:39

Run a half-marathon in 1:56:39 (*Note:* The half-marathon is the best predictor.)

If you can complete one of each of these three Key Run Workouts in the *same* week:

Key Run Workout #1: Track Repeats (complete one of the workouts listed below)

6 × 800m at 3:47-per-800m pace with a 400m recovery jog between intervals

5 × 1000m at 4:46-per-1000m pace with a 400m recovery jog between intervals

4 × 1200m at 5:46-per-1200m pace with a 400m recovery jog between intervals

3 × 1600m at 7:50-per-1600m pace with a 400m recovery jog between intervals

Key Run Workout #2: Tempo Run (complete one of the tempo runs)

After a 1-mile warmup, complete a 3-mile training run in 25:09.

After a 1-mile warmup, complete a 5-mile training run in 43:10.

After a 1-mile warmup, complete an 8-mile training run in 71:04.

Key Run Workout #3: Long Run

Complete a 15- to 20-mile run at 9:46-per-mile pace.

If you can complete one of each Key Run Workout and meet the target paces, then we feel that you are ready to start training with this program.

BOSTON MARATHON QUALIFYING TRAINING PROGRAM FOR WOMEN 50 TO 54 (4:05)

WEEK	KEY RUN WORKOUT #1	KEY RUN WORKOUT #2	KEY RUN WORKOUT #3
16	10–20 min warmup 3 × 1600m @ 7:50 (1 min RI) 10 min cooldown	6 mile run: 2 miles easy, 2 miles @ 8:23/mile, 2 miles easy	13 miles @ 9:51/mile
15	1 mile warmup 4 × 800m @ 3:47 (2 min RI) 10 min cooldown	7 mile run: 1 mile easy, 5 miles @ 9:21/mile, 1 mile easy	15 miles @ 10:06/mile
14	10–20 min warmup 1200m @ 5:46, 1000m @ 4:46, 800m @ 3:47, 600m @ 2:49, 400m @ 1:51 (all with 200m RI) 10 min cooldown	7 mile run: 1 mile easy, 5 miles @ 8:53/mile, 1 mile easy	17 miles @ 10:06/mile
13	10–20 min warmup 5 × 1000m @ 4:46 (400m RI) 10 min cooldown	6 mile run: 1 mile easy, 4 miles @ 8:38/mile, 1 mile easy	20 miles @ 10:21/mile
12	10–20 min warmup 3 × 1600m @ 7:50 (1 min RI) 10 min cooldown	6 mile run: 2 miles easy, 3 miles @ 8:23/mile, 1 mile easy	18 miles @ 10:06/mile
11	10–20 min warmup 2 × 1200m @ 5:46 (2 min RI), 4 × 800m @ 3:47 (2 min RI) 10 min cooldown	6 mile run: 1 mile easy, 5 miles @ 8:38/mile	20 miles @ 10:06/mile
10	10–20 min warmup 6 × 800m @ 3:47 (1:30 RI) 10 min cooldown	8 mile run: 1 mile easy, 6 miles @ 8:53/mile, 1 mile easy	13 miles @ 9:36/mile
9	10–20 min warmup 2 × (6 × 400m @ 1:51) (1:30 RI) (2:30 RI between sets) 10 min cooldown	6 mile run: 2 miles easy, 3 miles @ 8:23/mile, 1 mile easy	18 miles @ 9:51/mile

BOSTON MARATHON QUALIFYING TRAINING PROGRAM FOR WOMEN 50 TO 54 (4:05) (*continued*)

WEEK	KEY RUN WORKOUT #1	KEY RUN WORKOUT #2	KEY RUN WORKOUT #3
8	10–20 min warmup 1600m @ 7:50 (400m RI), 3200m @ 16:00 (800m RI), 2 × 800m @ 3:47 (400m RI) 10 min cooldown	6 mile run: 1 mile easy, 4 miles @ 8:38/mile, 1 mile easy	20 miles @ 9:51/mile
7	10–20 min warmup 3 × (2 × 1200m @ 5:46) (2 min RI) (4 min between sets) 10 min cooldown	11 mile run: 1 mile easy, 10 miles @ 9:21/mile	15 miles @ 9:41/mile
6	10–20 min warmup 1000m @ 4:46, 2000m @ 9:52, 1000m @ 4:46, 1000m @ 4:46 (all with 400m RI) 10 min cooldown	6 mile run: 1 mile easy, 5 miles @ 8:38/mile	20 miles @ 9:51/mile
5	10–20 min warmup 3 × 1600m @ 7:50 (400m RI) 10 min cooldown	11 mile run: 1 mile easy, 10 miles @ 9:21/mile	15 miles @ 9:31/mile
4	10–20 min warmup 10 × 400m @ 1:51 (400m RI) 10 min cooldown	8 mile run: 1 mile easy, 7 miles @ 9:21/mile	20 miles @ 9:36/mile
3	10–20 min warmup 8 × 800m @ 3:47 (1:30 RI) 10 min cooldown	6 mile run: 1 mile easy, 5 miles @ 8:38/mile	13 miles @ 9:21/mile
2	10–20 min warmup 5 × 1000m @ 4:46 (400m RI) 10 min cooldown	6 mile run: 2 miles easy, 3 miles @ 8:23/mile, 1 mile easy	10 miles @ 9:21/mile
1	10–20 min warmup 6 × 400m @ 1:51 (400m RI) 10 min cooldown	3 mile run: 1 mile easy, 2 miles @ 9:21/mile	**MARATHON DAY** 26.2 miles @ 9:21/mile

RI = Rest interval, which may be a timed rest/recovery interval or a distance that you walk/jog after each track repeat.

For Men 65 to 69 and Women 55 to 59, You Must Run 4:15 to BQ

Qualifying for Boston is realistic:

If you can:

Run a 5-K in 26:15

Run a 10-K in 54:55

Run a half-marathon in 2:01:40 (*Note:* The half-marathon is the best predictor.)

If you can complete one of each of these three Key Run Workouts in the *same* week:

Key Run Workout #1: Track Repeats (complete one of the workouts listed below)

6 × 800m at 3:58-per-800m pace with a 400m recovery jog between intervals

5 × 1000m at 4:59-per-1000m pace with a 400m recovery jog between intervals

4 × 1200m at 6:02-per-1200m pace with a 400m recovery jog between intervals

3 × 1600m at 8:11-per-1600m pace with a 400m recovery jog between intervals

Key Run Workout #2: Tempo Run (complete one of the tempo runs)

After a 1-mile warmup, complete a 3-mile training run in 26:12.

After a 1-mile warmup, complete a 5-mile training run in 44:55.

After a 1-mile warmup, complete an 8-mile training run in 73:52.

Key Run Workout #3: Long Run

Complete a 15- to 20-mile run at 10:09-per-mile pace.

If you can complete one of each Key Run Workout and meet the target paces, then we feel that you are ready to start training with this program.

BOSTON MARATHON QUALIFYING TRAINING PROGRAM FOR MEN 65 TO 69 AND WOMEN 55 TO 59 (4:15)

WEEK	KEY RUN WORKOUT #1	KEY RUN WORKOUT #2	KEY RUN WORKOUT #3
16	10–20 min warmup 3 × 1600m @ 8:11 (1 min RI) 10 min cooldown	6 mile run: 2 miles easy, 2 miles @ 8:44/mile, 2 miles easy	13 miles @ 10:14/mile
15	1 mile warmup 4 × 800m @ 3:58 (2 min RI) 10 min cooldown	7 mile run: 1 mile easy, 5 miles @ 9:44/mile, 1 mile easy	15 miles @ 10:29/mile
14	10–20 min warmup 1200m @ 6:02, 1000m @ 4:59, 800m @ 3:58, 600m @ 2:57, 400m @ 1:57 (all with 200m RI) 10 min cooldown	7 mile run: 1 mile easy, 5 miles @ 9:14/mile, 1 mile easy	17 miles @ 10:29/mile
13	10–20 min warmup 5 × 1000m @ 4:59 (400m RI) 10 min cooldown	6 mile run: 1 mile easy, 4 miles @ 8:59/mile, 1 mile easy	20 miles @ 10:44/mile
12	10–20 min warmup 3 × 1600m @ 8:11 (1 min RI) 10 min cooldown	6 mile run: 2 miles easy, 3 miles @ 8:44/mile, 1 mile easy	18 miles @ 10:29/mile
11	10–20 min warmup 2 × 1200m @ 6:02 (2 min RI), 4 × 800m @ 3:58 (2 min RI) 10 min cooldown	6 mile run: 1 mile easy, 5 miles @ 8:59/mile	20 miles @ 10:29/mile
10	10–20 min warmup 6 × 800m @ 3:58 (1:30 RI) 10 min cooldown	8 mile run: 1 mile easy, 6 miles @ 9:14/mile, 1 mile easy	13 miles @ 9:59/mile
9	10–20 min warmup 2 × (6 × 400m @ 1:57) (1:30 RI) (2:30 RI between sets) 10 min cooldown	6 mile run: 2 miles easy, 3 miles @ 8:44/mile, 1 mile easy	18 miles @ 10:14/mile

WEEK	KEY RUN WORKOUT #1	KEY RUN WORKOUT #2	KEY RUN WORKOUT #3
8	10–20 min warmup 1600m @ 8:11 (400m RI), 3200m @ 16:42 (800m RI), 2 × 800m @ 3:58 (400m RI) 10 min cooldown	6 mile run: 1 mile easy, 4 miles @ 8:59/mile, 1 mile easy	20 miles @ 10:14/mile
7	10–20 min warmup 3 × (2 × 1200m @ 6:02) (2 min RI) (4 min between sets) 10 min cooldown	11 mile run: 1 mile easy, 10 miles @ 9:44/mile	15 miles @ 10:04/mile
6	10–20 min warmup 1000m @ 4:59, 2000m @ 10:19, 1000m @ 4:59, 1000m @ 4:59 (all with 400m RI) 10 min cooldown	6 mile run: 1 mile easy, 5 miles @ 8:59/mile	20 miles @ 10:14/mile
5	10–20 min warmup 3 × 1600m @ 8:11 (400m RI) 10 min cooldown	11 mile run: 1 mile easy, 10 miles @ 9:44/mile	15 miles @ 9:54/mile
4	10–20 min warmup 10 × 400m @ 1:57 (400m RI) 10 min cooldown	8 mile run: 1 mile easy, 7 miles @ 9:44/mile	20 miles @ 9:59/mile
3	10–20 min warmup 8 × 800m @ 3:58 (1:30 RI) 10 min cooldown	6 mile run: 1 mile easy, 5 miles @ 8:59/mile	13 miles @ 9:44/mile
2	10–20 min warmup 5 × 1000m @ 4:59 (400m RI) 10 min cooldown	6 mile run: 2 miles easy, 3 miles @ 8:44/mile, 1 mile easy	10 miles @ 9:44/mile
1	10–20 min warmup 6 × 400m @ 1:57 (400m RI) 10 min cooldown	3 mile run: 1 mile easy, 2 miles @ 9:44/mile	**MARATHON DAY** 26.2 miles @ 9:44/mile

RI = Rest interval, which may be a timed rest/recovery interval or a distance that you walk/jog after each track repeat.

For Men 70 to 74 and Women 60 to 64, You Must Run 4:30 to BQ

Qualifying for Boston is realistic:

If you can:

Run a 5-K in 27:45

Run a 10-K in 58:05

Run a half-marathon in 2:08:35 (*Note:* The half-marathon is the best predictor.)

If you can complete one of each of these three Key Run Workouts in the *same* week:

Key Run Workout #1: Track Repeats (complete one of the workouts listed below)

6 × 800m at 4:12-per-800m pace with a 400m recovery jog between intervals

5 × 1000m at 5:17-per-1000m pace with a 400m recovery jog between intervals

4 × 1200m at 6:24-per-1200m pace with a 400m recovery jog between intervals

3 × 1600m at 8:40-per-1600m pace with a 400m recovery jog between intervals

Key Run Workout #2: Tempo Run (complete one of the tempo runs)

After a 1-mile warmup, complete a 3-mile training run in 27:39.

After a 1-mile warmup, complete a 5-mile training run in 47:20.

After a 1-mile warmup, complete an 8-mile training run in 77:44.

Key Run Workout #3: Long Run

Complete a 15- to 20-mile run at 10:43-per-mile pace.

If you can complete one of each Key Run Workout and meet the target paces, then we feel that you are ready to start training with this program.

BOSTON MARATHON QUALIFYING TRAINING PROGRAM FOR MEN 70 TO 74 AND WOMEN 60 TO 64 (4:30)

WEEK	KEY RUN WORKOUT #1	KEY RUN WORKOUT #2	KEY RUN WORKOUT #3
16	10–20 min warmup 3 × 1600m @ 8:40 (1 min RI) 10 min cooldown	6 mile run: 2 miles easy, 2 miles @ 9:13/mile, 2 miles easy	13 miles @ 10:48/mile
15	1 mile warmup 4 × 800m @ 4:12 (2 min RI) 10 min cooldown	7 mile run: 1 mile easy, 5 miles @ 10:18/mile, 1 mile easy	15 miles @ 11:03/mile
14	10–20 min warmup 1200m @ 6:24, 1000m @ 5:17, 800m @ 4:12, 600m @ 3:08, 400m @ 2:04 (all with 200m RI) 10 min cooldown	7 mile run: 1 mile easy, 5 miles @ 9:43/mile, 1 mile easy	17 miles @ 11:03/mile
13	10–20 min warmup 5 × 1000m @ 5:17 (400m RI) 10 min cooldown	6 mile run: 1 mile easy, 4 miles @ 9:28/mile, 1 mile easy	20 miles @ 11:18/mile
12	10–20 min warmup 3 × 1600m @ 8:40 (1 min RI) 10 min cooldown	6 mile run: 2 miles easy, 3 miles @ 9:13/mile, 1 mile easy	18 miles @ 11:03/mile
11	10–20 min warmup 2 × 1200m @ 6:24 (2 min RI), 4 × 800m @ 4:12 (2 min RI) 10 min cooldown	6 mile run: 1 mile easy, 5 miles @ 9:28/mile	20 miles @ 11:03/mile
10	10–20 min warmup 6 × 800m @ 4:12 (1:30 RI) 10 min cooldown	8 mile run: 1 mile easy, 6 miles @ 9:43/mile, 1 mile easy	13 miles @ 10:33/mile
9	10–20 min warmup 2 × (6 × 400m @ 2:04) (1:30 RI) (2:30 RI between sets) 10 min cooldown	6 mile run: 2 miles easy, 3 miles @ 9:13/mile, 1 mile easy	18 miles @ 10:48/mile

BOSTON MARATHON QUALIFYING TRAINING PROGRAM FOR MEN 70 TO 74 AND WOMEN 60 TO 64 (4:30) (*continued*)

WEEK	KEY RUN WORKOUT #1	KEY RUN WORKOUT #2	KEY RUN WORKOUT #3
8	10–20 min warmup 1600m @ 8:40 (400m RI), 3200m @ 17:40 (800m RI), 2 × 800m @ 4:12 (400m RI) 10 min cooldown	6 mile run: 1 mile easy, 4 miles @ 9:28/mile, 1 mile easy	20 miles @ 10:48/mile
7	10–20 min warmup 3 × (2 × 1200m @ 6:24) (2 min RI) (4 min between sets) 10 min cooldown	11 mile run: 1 mile easy, 10 miles @ 10:18/mile	15 miles @ 10:38/mile
6	10–20 min warmup 1000m @ 5:17, 2000m @ 10:55, 1000m @ 5:17, 1000m @ 5:17 (all with 400m RI) 10 min cooldown	6 mile run: 1 mile easy, 5 miles @ 9:28/mile	20 miles @ 10:48/mile
5	10–20 min warmup 3 × 1600m @ 8:40 (400m RI) 10 min cooldown	11 mile run: 1 mile easy, 10 miles @ 10:18/mile	15 miles @ 10:28/mile
4	10–20 min warmup 10 × 400m @ 2:04 (400m RI) 10 min cooldown	8 mile run: 1 mile easy, 7 miles @ 10:18/mile	20 miles @ 10:33/mile
3	10–20 min warmup 8 × 800m @ 4:12 (1:30 RI) 10 min cooldown	6 mile run: 1 mile easy, 5 miles @ 9:28/mile	13 miles @ 10:18/mile
2	10–20 min warmup 5 × 1000m @ 5:17 (400m RI) 10 min cooldown	6 mile run: 2 miles easy, 3 miles @ 9:13/mile, 1 mile easy	10 miles @ 10:18/mile
1	10–20 min warmup 6 × 400m @ 2:04 (400m RI) 10 min cooldown	3 mile run: 1 mile easy, 2 miles @ 10:18/mile	**MARATHON DAY** 26.2 miles @ 10:18/mile

RI = Rest interval, which may be a timed rest/recovery interval or a distance that you walk/jog after each track repeat.

For Men 75 to 79 and Women 65 to 69, You Must Run 4:45 to BQ

Qualifying for Boston is realistic:

If you can:

Run a 5-K in 29:15

Run a 10-K in 1:01:10

Run a half-marathon in 2:15:35 (*Note:* The half-marathon is the best predictor.)

If you can complete one of each of these three Key Run Workouts in the *same* week:

Key Run Workout #1: Track Repeats (complete one of the workouts listed below)

6 × 800m at 4:26-per-800m pace with a 400m recovery jog between intervals

5 × 1000m at 5:35-per-1000m pace with a 400m recovery jog between intervals

4 × 1200m at 6:46-per-1200m pace with a 400m recovery jog between intervals

3 × 1600m at 9:08-per-1600m pace with a 400m recovery jog between intervals

Key Run Workout #2: Tempo Run (complete one of the tempo runs)

After a 1-mile warmup, complete a 3-mile training run in 29:06.

After a 1-mile warmup, complete a 5-mile training run in 49:45.

After a 1-mile warmup, complete an 8-mile training run in 81:36.

Key Run Workout #3: Long Run

Complete a 15- to 20-mile run at 11:17-per-mile pace.

If you can complete one of each Key Run Workout and meet the target paces, then we feel that you are ready to start training with this program.

BOSTON MARATHON QUALIFYING TRAINING PROGRAM FOR MEN 75 TO 79 AND WOMEN 65 TO 69 (4:45)

WEEK	KEY RUN WORKOUT #1	KEY RUN WORKOUT #2	KEY RUN WORKOUT #3
16	10–20 min warmup 3 × 1600m @ 9:09 (1 min RI) 10 min cooldown	6 mile run: 2 miles easy, 2 miles @ 9:42/mile, 2 miles easy	13 miles @ 11:22/mile
15	1 mile warmup 4 × 800m @ 4:26 (2 min RI) 10 min cooldown	7 mile run: 1 mile easy, 5 miles @ 10:52/mile, 1 mile easy	15 miles @ 11:37/mile
14	10–20 min warmup 1200m @ 6:46, 1000m @ 5:35, 800m @ 4:26, 600m @ 3:18, 400m @ 2:11 (all with 200m RI) 10 min cooldown	7 mile run: 1 mile easy, 5 miles @ 10:12/mile, 1 mile easy	17 miles @ 11:37/mile
13	10–20 min warmup 5 × 1000m @ 5:35 (400m RI) 10 min cooldown	6 mile run: 1 mile easy, 4 miles @ 9:57/mile, 1 mile easy	20 miles @ 11:52/mile
12	10–20 min warmup 3 × 1600m @ 9:09 (1 min RI) 10 min cooldown	6 mile run: 2 miles easy, 3 miles @ 9:42/mile, 1 mile easy	18 miles @ 11:37/mile
11	10–20 min warmup 2 × 1200m @ 6:46 (2 min RI), 4 × 800m @ 4:26 (2 min RI) 10 min cooldown	6 mile run: 1 mile easy, 5 miles @ 9:57/mile	20 miles @ 11:37/mile
10	10–20 min warmup 6 × 800m @ 4:26 (1:30 RI) 10 min cooldown	8 mile run: 1 mile easy, 6 miles @ 10:12/mile, 1 mile easy	13 miles @ 11:07/mile
9	10–20 min warmup 2 × (6 × 400m @ 2:11) (1:30 RI) (2:30 RI between sets) 10 min cooldown	6 mile run: 2 miles easy, 3 miles @ 9:42/mile, 1 mile easy	18 miles @ 11:22/mile

WEEK	KEY RUN WORKOUT #1	KEY RUN WORKOUT #2	KEY RUN WORKOUT #3
8	10–20 min warmup 1600m @ 9:09 (400m RI), 3200m @ 18:38 (800m RI), 2 × 800m @ 4:26 (400m RI) 10 min cooldown	6 mile run: 1 mile easy, 4 miles @ 9:57/mile, 1 mile easy	20 miles @ 11:22/mile
7	10–20 min warmup 3 × (2 × 1200m @ 6:46) (2 min RI) (4 min between sets) 10 min cooldown	11 mile run: 1 mile easy, 10 miles @ 10:52/mile	15 miles @ 11:12/mile
6	10–20 min warmup 1000m @ 5:35, 2000m @ 11:31, 1000m @ 5:35, 1000m @ 5:35 (all with 400m RI) 10 min cooldown	6 mile run: 1 mile easy, 5 miles @ 9:57/mile	20 miles @ 11:22/mile
5	10–20 min warmup 3 × 1600m @ 9:09 (400m RI) 10 min cooldown	11 mile run: 1 mile easy, 10 miles @ 10:52/mile	15 miles @ 11:02/mile
4	10–20 min warmup 10 × 400m @ 2:11 (400m RI) 10 min cooldown	8 mile run: 1 mile easy, 7 miles @ 10:52/mile	20 miles @ 11:07/mile
3	10–20 min warmup 8 × 800m @ 4:26 (1:30 RI) 10 min cooldown	6 mile run: 1 mile easy, 5 miles @ 9:57/mile	13 miles @ 10:52/mile
2	10–20 min warmup 5 × 1000m @ 5:35 (400m RI) 10 min cooldown	6 mile run: 2 miles easy, 3 miles @ 9:42/mile, 1 mile easy	10 miles @ 10:52/mile
1	10–20 min warmup 6 × 400m @ 2:11 (400m RI) 10 min cooldown	3 mile run: 1 mile easy, 2 miles @ 10:52/mile	**MARATHON DAY** 26.2 miles @ 10:52/mile

RI = Rest interval, which may be a timed rest/recovery interval or a distance that you walk/jog after each track repeat.

For Men 80 and Older and Women 70 to 74, You Must Run 5:00 to BQ

Qualifying for Boston is realistic:

If you can:

Run a 5-K in 30:50

Run a 10-K in 1:04:31

Run a half-marathon in 2:22:55 (*Note:* The half-marathon is the best predictor.)

If you can complete one of each of these three Key Run Workouts in the *same* week:

Key Run Workout #1: Track Repeats (complete one of the workouts listed below)

6 × 800m at 4:42-per-800m pace with a 400m recovery jog between intervals

5 × 1000m at 5:54-per-1000m pace with a 400m recovery jog between intervals

4 × 1200m at 7:09-per-1200m pace with a 400m recovery jog between intervals

3 × 1600m at 9:39-per-1600m pace with a 400m recovery jog between intervals

Key Run Workout #2: Tempo Run (complete one of the tempo runs)

After a 1-mile warmup, complete a 3-mile training run in 30:36.

After a 1-mile warmup, complete a 5-mile training run in 52:15.

After a 1-mile warmup, complete an 8-mile training run in 83:28.

Key Run Workout #3: Long Run

Complete a 15- to 20-mile run at 11:51-per-mile pace.

If you can complete one of each Key Run Workout and meet the target paces, then we feel that you are ready to start training with this program.

BOSTON MARATHON QUALIFYING TRAINING PROGRAM FOR MEN 80 AND OLDER AND WOMEN 70 TO 74 (5:00)

WEEK	KEY RUN WORKOUT #1	KEY RUN WORKOUT #2	KEY RUN WORKOUT #3
16	10–20 min warmup 3 × 1600m @ 9:39 (1 min RI) 10 min cooldown	6 mile run: 2 miles easy, 2 miles @ 10:12/mile, 2 miles easy	13 miles @ 11:56/mile
15	1 mile warmup 4 × 800m @ 4:42 (2 min RI) 10 min cooldown	7 mile run: 1 mile easy, 5 miles @ 11:26/mile, 1 mile easy	15 miles @ 12:11/mile
14	10–20 min warmup 1200m @ 7:09, 1000m @ 5:54, 800m @ 4:42, 600m @ 3:30, 400m @ 2:19 (all with 200m RI) 10 min cooldown	7 mile run: 1 mile easy, 5 miles @ 10:42/mile, 1 mile easy	17 miles @ 12:11/mile
13	10–20 min warmup 5 × 1000m @ 5:54 (400m RI) 10 min cooldown	6 mile run: 1 mile easy, 4 miles @ 10:27/mile, 1 mile easy	20 miles @ 12:26/mile
12	10–20 min warmup 3 × 1600m @ 9:39 (1 min RI) 10 min cooldown	6 mile run: 2 miles easy, 3 miles @ 10:12/mile, 1 mile easy	18 miles @ 12:11/mile
11	10–20 min warmup 2 × 1200m @ 7:09 (2 min RI), 4 × 800m @ 4:42 (2 min RI) 10 min cooldown	6 mile run: 1 mile easy, 5 miles @ 10:27/mile	20 miles @ 12:11/mile
10	10–20 min warmup 6 × 800m @ 4:42 (1:30 RI) 10 min cooldown	8 mile run: 1 mile easy, 6 miles @ 10:42/mile, 1 mile easy	13 miles @ 11:41/mile
9	10–20 min warmup 2 × (6 × 400m @ 2:19) (1:30 RI) (2:30 RI between sets) 10 min cooldown	6 mile run: 2 miles easy, 3 miles @ 10:12/mile, 1 mile easy	18 miles @ 11:56/mile

BOSTON MARATHON QUALIFYING TRAINING PROGRAM FOR MEN 80 AND OLDER AND WOMEN 70 TO 74 (5:00) (*continued*)

WEEK	KEY RUN WORKOUT #1	KEY RUN WORKOUT #2	KEY RUN WORKOUT #3
8	10–20 min warmup 1600m @ 9:39 (400m RI), 3200m @ 19:38 (800m RI), 2 × 800m @ 4:42 (400m RI) 10 min cooldown	6 mile run: 1 mile easy, 4 miles @ 10:27/mile, 1 mile easy	20 miles @ 11:56/mile
7	10–20 min warmup 3 × (2 × 1200m @ 7:09) (2 min RI) (4 min between sets) 10 min cooldown	11 mile run: 1 mile easy, 10 miles @ 11:26/mile	15 miles @ 11:46/mile
6	10–20 min warmup 1000m @ 5:54, 2000m @ 12:09, 1000m @ 5:54, 1000m @ 5:54 (all with 400m RI) 10 min cooldown	6 mile run: 1 mile easy, 5 miles @ 10:27/mile	20 miles @ 11:56/mile
5	10–20 min warmup 3 × 1600m @ 9:39 (400m RI) 10 min cooldown	11 mile run: 1 mile easy, 10 miles @ 11:26/mile	15 miles @ 11:36/mile
4	10–20 min warmup 10 × 400m @ 2:19 (400m RI) 10 min cooldown	8 mile run: 1 mile easy, 7 miles @ 11:26/mile	20 miles @ 11:41/mile
3	10–20 min warmup 8 × 800m @ 4:42 (1:30 RI) 10 min cooldown	6 mile run: 1 mile easy, 5 miles @ 10:27/mile	13 miles @ 11:26/mile
2	10–20 min warmup 5 × 1000m @ 5:54 (400m RI) 10 min cooldown	6 mile run: 2 miles easy, 3 miles @ 10:12/mile, 1 mile easy	10 miles @ 11:26/mile
1	10–20 min warmup 6 × 400m @ 2:19 (400m RI) 10 min cooldown	3 mile run: 1 mile easy, 2 miles @ 11:26/mile	**MARATHON DAY** 26.2 miles @ 11:26/mile

RI = Rest interval, which may be a timed rest/recovery interval or a distance that you walk/jog after each track repeat.

Appendix A: Pace Table

The following pace table gives your finish time for the 5-K, 10-K, half-marathon, and marathon based on your race pace per mile. For example, if you ran a 6:00-per-mile pace for the entire race, your 5-K race finish time would be 18:39; your 10-K race finish time would be 37:18; your half-marathon time would be 1:18:39; and your marathon time would be 2:37:19. The pace table can be used to find the pace needed for a specific race finish time. The pace time is given in minutes and seconds per mile (mm:ss/mile).

RACE DISTANCE

PACE (MM:SS/MILE)	5-K	10-K	HALF-MARATHON	MARATHON
0:05:00	0:15:33	0:31:05	1:05:33	2:11:06
0:05:01	0:15:36	0:31:11	1:05:46	2:11:32
0:05:02	0:15:39	0:31:17	1:05:59	2:11:58
0:05:03	0:15:42	0:31:24	1:06:12	2:12:24
0:05:04	0:15:45	0:31:30	1:06:25	2:12:51
0:05:05	0:15:48	0:31:36	1:06:38	2:13:17
0:05:06	0:15:51	0:31:42	1:06:51	2:13:43
0:05:07	0:15:54	0:31:49	1:07:05	2:14:09
0:05:08	0:15:57	0:31:55	1:07:18	2:14:35
0:05:09	0:16:00	0:32:01	1:07:31	2:15:02
0:05:10	0:16:04	0:32:07	1:07:44	2:15:28
0:05:11	0:16:07	0:32:13	1:07:57	2:15:54
0:05:12	0:16:10	0:32:20	1:08:10	2:16:20
0:05:13	0:16:13	0:32:26	1:08:23	2:16:46
0:05:14	0:16:16	0:32:32	1:08:36	2:17:13
0:05:15	0:16:19	0:32:38	1:08:49	2:17:39
0:05:16	0:16:22	0:32:45	1:09:03	2:18:05
0:05:17	0:16:25	0:32:51	1:09:16	2:18:31
0:05:18	0:16:28	0:32:57	1:09:29	2:18:58
0:05:19	0:16:32	0:33:03	1:09:42	2:19:24
0:05:20	0:16:35	0:33:09	1:09:55	2:19:50
0:05:21	0:16:38	0:33:16	1:10:08	2:20:16
0:05:22	0:16:41	0:33:22	1:10:21	2:20:42
0:05:23	0:16:44	0:33:28	1:10:34	2:21:09
0:05:24	0:16:47	0:33:34	1:10:47	2:21:35
0:05:25	0:16:50	0:33:40	1:11:01	2:22:01
0:05:26	0:16:53	0:33:47	1:11:14	2:22:27
0:05:27	0:16:56	0:33:53	1:11:27	2:22:54
0:05:28	0:17:00	0:33:59	1:11:40	2:23:20
0:05:29	0:17:03	0:34:05	1:11:53	2:23:46
0:05:30	0:17:06	0:34:12	1:12:06	2:24:12
0:05:31	0:17:09	0:34:18	1:12:19	2:24:38
0:05:32	0:17:12	0:34:24	1:12:32	2:25:05
0:05:33	0:17:15	0:34:30	1:12:45	2:25:31
0:05:34	0:17:18	0:34:36	1:12:59	2:25:57
0:05:35	0:17:21	0:34:43	1:13:12	2:26:23
0:05:36	0:17:24	0:34:49	1:13:25	2:26:50
0:05:37	0:17:28	0:34:55	1:13:38	2:27:16
0:05:38	0:17:31	0:35:01	1:13:51	2:27:42
0:05:39	0:17:34	0:35:07	1:14:04	2:28:08

PACE (MM:SS/MILE)	5-K	10-K	HALF-MARATHON	MARATHON
0:05:40	0:17:37	0:35:14	1:14:17	2:28:34
0:05:41	0:17:40	0:35:20	1:14:30	2:29:01
0:05:42	0:17:43	0:35:26	1:14:43	2:29:27
0:05:43	0:17:46	0:35:32	1:14:57	2:29:53
0:05:44	0:17:49	0:35:39	1:15:10	2:30:19
0:05:45	0:17:52	0:35:45	1:15:23	2:30:45
0:05:46	0:17:56	0:35:51	1:15:36	2:31:12
0:05:47	0:17:59	0:35:57	1:15:49	2:31:38
0:05:48	0:18:02	0:36:03	1:16:02	2:32:04
0:05:49	0:18:05	0:36:10	1:16:15	2:32:30
0:05:50	0:18:08	0:36:16	1:16:28	2:32:57
0:05:51	0:18:11	0:36:22	1:16:41	2:33:23
0:05:52	0:18:14	0:36:28	1:16:55	2:33:49
0:05:53	0:18:17	0:36:35	1:17:08	2:34:15
0:05:54	0:18:20	0:36:41	1:17:21	2:34:41
0:05:55	0:18:23	0:36:47	1:17:34	2:35:08
0:05:56	0:18:27	0:36:53	1:17:47	2:35:34
0:05:57	0:18:30	0:36:59	1:18:00	2:36:00
0:05:58	0:18:33	0:37:06	1:18:13	2:36:26
0:05:59	0:18:36	0:37:12	1:18:26	2:36:53
0:06:00	0:18:39	0:37:18	1:18:39	2:37:19
0:06:01	0:18:42	0:37:24	1:18:52	2:37:45
0:06:02	0:18:45	0:37:30	1:19:06	2:38:11
0:06:03	0:18:48	0:37:37	1:19:19	2:38:37
0:06:04	0:18:51	0:37:43	1:19:32	2:39:04
0:06:05	0:18:55	0:37:49	1:19:45	2:39:30
0:06:06	0:18:58	0:37:55	1:19:58	2:39:56
0:06:07	0:19:01	0:38:02	1:20:11	2:40:22
0:06:08	0:19:04	0:38:08	1:20:24	2:40:49
0:06:09	0:19:07	0:38:14	1:20:37	2:41:15
0:06:10	0:19:10	0:38:20	1:20:50	2:41:41
0:06:11	0:19:13	0:38:26	1:21:04	2:42:07
0:06:12	0:19:16	0:38:33	1:21:17	2:42:33
0:06:13	0:19:19	0:38:39	1:21:30	2:43:00
0:06:14	0:19:23	0:38:45	1:21:43	2:43:26
0:06:15	0:19:26	0:38:51	1:21:56	2:43:52
0:06:16	0:19:29	0:38:58	1:22:09	2:44:18
0:06:17	0:19:32	0:39:04	1:22:22	2:44:44
0:06:18	0:19:35	0:39:10	1:22:35	2:45:11
0:06:19	0:19:38	0:39:16	1:22:48	2:45:37
0:06:20	0:19:41	0:39:22	1:23:02	2:46:03

PACE (MM:SS/MILE)	5-K	10-K	HALF-MARATHON	MARATHON
0:06:21	0:19:44	0:39:29	1:23:15	2:46:29
0:06:22	0:19:47	0:39:35	1:23:28	2:46:56
0:06:23	0:19:51	0:39:41	1:23:41	2:47:22
0:06:24	0:19:54	0:39:47	1:23:54	2:47:48
0:06:25	0:19:57	0:39:53	1:24:07	2:48:14
0:06:26	0:20:00	0:40:00	1:24:20	2:48:40
0:06:27	0:20:03	0:40:06	1:24:33	2:49:07
0:06:28	0:20:06	0:40:12	1:24:46	2:49:33
0:06:29	0:20:09	0:40:18	1:25:00	2:49:59
0:06:30	0:20:12	0:40:25	1:25:13	2:50:25
0:06:31	0:20:15	0:40:31	1:25:26	2:50:52
0:06:32	0:20:18	0:40:37	1:25:39	2:51:18
0:06:33	0:20:22	0:40:43	1:25:52	2:51:44
0:06:34	0:20:25	0:40:49	1:26:05	2:52:10
0:06:35	0:20:28	0:40:56	1:26:18	2:52:36
0:06:36	0:20:31	0:41:02	1:26:31	2:53:03
0:06:37	0:20:34	0:41:08	1:26:44	2:53:29
0:06:38	0:20:37	0:41:14	1:26:58	2:53:55
0:06:39	0:20:40	0:41:21	1:27:11	2:54:21
0:06:40	0:20:43	0:41:27	1:27:24	2:54:48
0:06:41	0:20:46	0:41:33	1:27:37	2:55:14
0:06:42	0:20:50	0:41:39	1:27:50	2:55:40
0:06:43	0:20:53	0:41:45	1:28:03	2:56:06
0:06:44	0:20:56	0:41:52	1:28:16	2:56:32
0:06:45	0:20:59	0:41:58	1:28:29	2:56:59
0:06:46	0:21:02	0:42:04	1:28:42	2:57:25
0:06:47	0:21:05	0:42:10	1:28:56	2:57:51
0:06:48	0:21:08	0:42:16	1:29:09	2:58:17
0:06:49	0:21:11	0:42:23	1:29:22	2:58:43
0:06:50	0:21:14	0:42:29	1:29:35	2:59:10
0:06:51	0:21:18	0:42:35	1:29:48	2:59:36
0:06:52	0:21:21	0:42:41	1:30:01	3:00:02
0:06:53	0:21:24	0:42:48	1:30:14	3:00:28
0:06:54	0:21:27	0:42:54	1:30:27	3:00:55
0:06:55	0:21:30	0:43:00	1:30:40	3:01:21
0:06:56	0:21:33	0:43:06	1:30:54	3:01:47
0:06:57	0:21:36	0:43:12	1:31:07	3:02:13
0:06:58	0:21:39	0:43:19	1:31:20	3:02:39
0:06:59	0:21:42	0:43:25	1:31:33	3:03:06
0:07:00	0:21:46	0:43:31	1:31:46	3:03:32
0:07:01	0:21:49	0:43:37	1:31:59	3:03:58

PACE (MM:SS/MILE)	5-K	10-K	HALF-MARATHON	MARATHON
0:07:02	0:21:52	0:43:43	1:32:12	3:04:24
0:07:03	0:21:55	0:43:50	1:32:25	3:04:51
0:07:04	0:21:58	0:43:56	1:32:38	3:05:17
0:07:05	0:22:01	0:44:02	1:32:51	3:05:43
0:07:06	0:22:04	0:44:08	1:33:05	3:06:09
0:07:07	0:22:07	0:44:15	1:33:18	3:06:35
0:07:08	0:22:10	0:44:21	1:33:31	3:07:02
0:07:09	0:22:14	0:44:27	1:33:44	3:07:28
0:07:10	0:22:17	0:44:33	1:33:57	3:07:54
0:07:11	0:22:20	0:44:39	1:34:10	3:08:20
0:07:12	0:22:23	0:44:46	1:34:23	3:08:47
0:07:13	0:22:26	0:44:52	1:34:36	3:09:13
0:07:14	0:22:29	0:44:58	1:34:49	3:09:39
0:07:15	0:22:32	0:45:04	1:35:03	3:10:05
0:07:16	0:22:35	0:45:11	1:35:16	3:10:31
0:07:17	0:22:38	0:45:17	1:35:29	3:10:58
0:07:18	0:22:41	0:45:23	1:35:42	3:11:24
0:07:19	0:22:45	0:45:29	1:35:55	3:11:50
0:07:20	0:22:48	0:45:35	1:36:08	3:12:16
0:07:21	0:22:51	0:45:42	1:36:21	3:12:42
0:07:22	0:22:54	0:45:48	1:36:34	3:13:09
0:07:23	0:22:57	0:45:54	1:36:47	3:13:35
0:07:24	0:23:00	0:46:00	1:37:01	3:14:01
0:07:25	0:23:03	0:46:06	1:37:14	3:14:27
0:07:26	0:23:06	0:46:13	1:37:27	3:14:54
0:07:27	0:23:09	0:46:19	1:37:40	3:15:20
0:07:28	0:23:13	0:46:25	1:37:53	3:15:46
0:07:29	0:23:16	0:46:31	1:38:06	3:16:12
0:07:30	0:23:19	0:46:38	1:38:19	3:16:38
0:07:31	0:23:22	0:46:44	1:38:32	3:17:05
0:07:32	0:23:25	0:46:50	1:38:45	3:17:31
0:07:33	0:23:28	0:46:56	1:38:59	3:17:57
0:07:34	0:23:31	0:47:02	1:39:12	3:18:23
0:07:35	0:23:34	0:47:09	1:39:25	3:18:50
0:07:36	0:23:37	0:47:15	1:39:38	3:19:16
0:07:37	0:23:41	0:47:21	1:39:51	3:19:42
0:07:38	0:23:44	0:47:27	1:40:04	3:20:08
0:07:39	0:23:47	0:47:34	1:40:17	3:20:34
0:07:40	0:23:50	0:47:40	1:40:30	3:21:01
0:07:41	0:23:53	0:47:46	1:40:43	3:21:27
0:07:42	0:23:56	0:47:52	1:40:57	3:21:53

PACE (MM:SS/MILE)	5-K	10-K	HALF-MARATHON	MARATHON
0:07:43	0:23:59	0:47:58	1:41:10	3:22:19
0:07:44	0:24:02	0:48:05	1:41:23	3:22:46
0:07:45	0:24:05	0:48:11	1:41:36	3:23:12
0:07:46	0:24:09	0:48:17	1:41:49	3:23:38
0:07:47	0:24:12	0:48:23	1:42:02	3:24:04
0:07:48	0:24:15	0:48:29	1:42:15	3:24:30
0:07:49	0:24:18	0:48:36	1:42:28	3:24:57
0:07:50	0:24:21	0:48:42	1:42:41	3:25:23
0:07:51	0:24:24	0:48:48	1:42:55	3:25:49
0:07:52	0:24:27	0:48:54	1:43:08	3:26:15
0:07:53	0:24:30	0:49:01	1:43:21	3:26:41
0:07:54	0:24:33	0:49:07	1:43:34	3:27:08
0:07:55	0:24:36	0:49:13	1:43:47	3:27:34
0:07:56	0:24:40	0:49:19	1:44:00	3:28:00
0:07:57	0:24:43	0:49:25	1:44:13	3:28:26
0:07:58	0:24:46	0:49:32	1:44:26	3:28:53
0:07:59	0:24:49	0:49:38	1:44:39	3:29:19
0:08:00	0:24:52	0:49:44	1:44:53	3:29:45
0:08:01	0:24:55	0:49:50	1:45:06	3:30:11
0:08:02	0:24:58	0:49:56	1:45:19	3:30:37
0:08:03	0:25:01	0:50:03	1:45:32	3:31:04
0:08:04	0:25:04	0:50:09	1:45:45	3:31:30
0:08:05	0:25:08	0:50:15	1:45:58	3:31:56
0:08:06	0:25:11	0:50:21	1:46:11	3:32:22
0:08:07	0:25:14	0:50:28	1:46:24	3:32:49
0:08:08	0:25:17	0:50:34	1:46:37	3:33:15
0:08:09	0:25:20	0:50:40	1:46:50	3:33:41
0:08:10	0:25:23	0:50:46	1:47:04	3:34:07
0:08:11	0:25:26	0:50:52	1:47:17	3:34:33
0:08:12	0:25:29	0:50:59	1:47:30	3:35:00
0:08:13	0:25:32	0:51:05	1:47:43	3:35:26
0:08:14	0:25:36	0:51:11	1:47:56	3:35:52
0:08:15	0:25:39	0:51:17	1:48:09	3:36:18
0:08:16	0:25:42	0:51:24	1:48:22	3:36:45
0:08:17	0:25:45	0:51:30	1:48:35	3:37:11
0:08:18	0:25:48	0:51:36	1:48:48	3:37:37
0:08:19	0:25:51	0:51:42	1:49:02	3:38:03
0:08:20	0:25:54	0:51:48	1:49:15	3:38:29
0:08:21	0:25:57	0:51:55	1:49:28	3:38:56
0:08:22	0:26:00	0:52:01	1:49:41	3:39:22
0:08:23	0:26:04	0:52:07	1:49:54	3:39:48

PACE (MM:SS/MILE)	5-K	10-K	HALF-MARATHON	MARATHON
0:08:24	0:26:07	0:52:13	1:50:07	3:40:14
0:08:25	0:26:10	0:52:19	1:50:20	3:40:40
0:08:26	0:26:13	0:52:26	1:50:33	3:41:07
0:08:27	0:26:16	0:52:32	1:50:46	3:41:33
0:08:28	0:26:19	0:52:38	1:51:00	3:41:59
0:08:29	0:26:22	0:52:44	1:51:13	3:42:25
0:08:30	0:26:25	0:52:51	1:51:26	3:42:52
0:08:31	0:26:28	0:52:57	1:51:39	3:43:18
0:08:32	0:26:32	0:53:03	1:51:52	3:43:44
0:08:33	0:26:35	0:53:09	1:52:05	3:44:10
0:08:34	0:26:38	0:53:15	1:52:18	3:44:36
0:08:35	0:26:41	0:53:22	1:52:31	3:45:03
0:08:36	0:26:44	0:53:28	1:52:44	3:45:29
0:08:37	0:26:47	0:53:34	1:52:58	3:45:55
0:08:38	0:26:50	0:53:40	1:53:11	3:46:21
0:08:39	0:26:53	0:53:47	1:53:24	3:46:48
0:08:40	0:26:56	0:53:53	1:53:37	3:47:14
0:08:41	0:26:59	0:53:59	1:53:50	3:47:40
0:08:42	0:27:03	0:54:05	1:54:03	3:48:06
0:08:43	0:27:06	0:54:11	1:54:16	3:48:32
0:08:44	0:27:09	0:54:18	1:54:29	3:48:59
0:08:45	0:27:12	0:54:24	1:54:42	3:49:25
0:08:46	0:27:15	0:54:30	1:54:56	3:49:51
0:08:47	0:27:18	0:54:36	1:55:09	3:50:17
0:08:48	0:27:21	0:54:42	1:55:22	3:50:44
0:08:49	0:27:24	0:54:49	1:55:35	3:51:10
0:08:50	0:27:27	0:54:55	1:55:48	3:51:36
0:08:51	0:27:31	0:55:01	1:56:01	3:52:02
0:08:52	0:27:34	0:55:07	1:56:14	3:52:28
0:08:53	0:27:37	0:55:14	1:56:27	3:52:55
0:08:54	0:27:40	0:55:20	1:56:40	3:53:21
0:08:55	0:27:43	0:55:26	1:56:54	3:53:47
0:08:56	0:27:46	0:55:32	1:57:07	3:54:13
0:08:57	0:27:49	0:55:38	1:57:20	3:54:39
0:08:58	0:27:52	0:55:45	1:57:33	3:55:06
0:08:59	0:27:55	0:55:51	1:57:46	3:55:32
0:09:00	0:27:59	0:55:57	1:57:59	3:55:58
0:09:01	0:28:02	0:56:03	1:58:12	3:56:24
0:09:02	0:28:05	0:56:10	1:58:25	3:56:51
0:09:03	0:28:08	0:56:16	1:58:38	3:57:17
0:09:04	0:28:11	0:56:22	1:58:52	3:57:43

PACE (MM:SS/MILE)	5-K	10-K	HALF-MARATHON	MARATHON
0:09:05	0:28:14	0:56:28	1:59:05	3:58:09
0:09:06	0:28:17	0:56:34	1:59:18	3:58:35
0:09:07	0:28:20	0:56:41	1:59:31	3:59:02
0:09:08	0:28:23	0:56:47	1:59:44	3:59:28
0:09:09	0:28:27	0:56:53	1:59:57	3:59:54
0:09:10	0:28:30	0:56:59	2:00:10	4:00:20
0:09:11	0:28:33	0:57:05	2:00:23	4:00:47
0:09:12	0:28:36	0:57:12	2:00:36	4:01:13
0:09:13	0:28:39	0:57:18	2:00:49	4:01:39
0:09:14	0:28:42	0:57:24	2:01:03	4:02:05
0:09:15	0:28:45	0:57:30	2:01:16	4:02:31
0:09:16	0:28:48	0:57:37	2:01:29	4:02:58
0:09:17	0:28:51	0:57:43	2:01:42	4:03:24
0:09:18	0:28:54	0:57:49	2:01:55	4:03:50
0:09:19	0:28:58	0:57:55	2:02:08	4:04:16
0:09:20	0:29:01	0:58:01	2:02:21	4:04:43
0:09:21	0:29:04	0:58:08	2:02:34	4:05:09
0:09:22	0:29:07	0:58:14	2:02:47	4:05:35
0:09:23	0:29:10	0:58:20	2:03:01	4:06:01
0:09:24	0:29:13	0:58:26	2:03:14	4:06:27
0:09:25	0:29:16	0:58:32	2:03:27	4:06:54
0:09:26	0:29:19	0:58:39	2:03:40	4:07:20
0:09:27	0:29:22	0:58:45	2:03:53	4:07:46
0:09:28	0:29:26	0:58:51	2:04:06	4:08:12
0:09:29	0:29:29	0:58:57	2:04:19	4:08:38
0:09:30	0:29:32	0:59:04	2:04:32	4:09:05
0:09:31	0:29:35	0:59:10	2:04:45	4:09:31
0:09:32	0:29:38	0:59:16	2:04:59	4:09:57
0:09:33	0:29:41	0:59:22	2:05:12	4:10:23
0:09:34	0:29:44	0:59:28	2:05:25	4:10:50
0:09:35	0:29:47	0:59:35	2:05:38	4:11:16
0:09:36	0:29:50	0:59:41	2:05:51	4:11:42
0:09:37	0:29:54	0:59:47	2:06:04	4:12:08
0:09:38	0:29:57	0:59:53	2:06:17	4:12:34
0:09:39	0:30:00	1:00:00	2:06:30	4:13:01
0:09:40	0:30:03	1:00:06	2:06:43	4:13:27
0:09:41	0:30:06	1:00:12	2:06:57	4:13:53
0:09:42	0:30:09	1:00:18	2:07:10	4:14:19
0:09:43	0:30:12	1:00:24	2:07:23	4:14:46
0:09:44	0:30:15	1:00:31	2:07:36	4:15:12
0:09:45	0:30:18	1:00:37	2:07:49	4:15:38

PACE (MM:SS/MILE)	5-K	10-K	HALF-MARATHON	MARATHON
0:09:46	0:30:22	1:00:43	2:08:02	4:16:04
0:09:47	0:30:25	1:00:49	2:08:15	4:16:30
0:09:48	0:30:28	1:00:55	2:08:28	4:16:57
0:09:49	0:30:31	1:01:02	2:08:41	4:17:23
0:09:50	0:30:34	1:01:08	2:08:55	4:17:49
0:09:51	0:30:37	1:01:14	2:09:08	4:18:15
0:09:52	0:30:40	1:01:20	2:09:21	4:18:42
0:09:53	0:30:43	1:01:27	2:09:34	4:19:08
0:09:54	0:30:46	1:01:33	2:09:47	4:19:34
0:09:55	0:30:49	1:01:39	2:10:00	4:20:00
0:09:56	0:30:53	1:01:45	2:10:13	4:20:26
0:09:57	0:30:56	1:01:51	2:10:26	4:20:53
0:09:58	0:30:59	1:01:58	2:10:39	4:21:19
0:09:59	0:31:02	1:02:04	2:10:53	4:21:45
0:10:00	0:31:05	1:02:10	2:11:06	4:22:11
0:10:01	0:31:08	1:02:16	2:11:19	4:22:37
0:10:02	0:31:11	1:02:23	2:11:32	4:23:04
0:10:03	0:31:14	1:02:29	2:11:45	4:23:30
0:10:04	0:31:17	1:02:35	2:11:58	4:23:56
0:10:05	0:31:21	1:02:41	2:12:11	4:24:22
0:10:06	0:31:24	1:02:47	2:12:24	4:24:49
0:10:07	0:31:27	1:02:54	2:12:37	4:25:15
0:10:08	0:31:30	1:03:00	2:12:51	4:25:41
0:10:09	0:31:33	1:03:06	2:13:04	4:26:07
0:10:10	0:31:36	1:03:12	2:13:17	4:26:33
0:10:11	0:31:39	1:03:18	2:13:30	4:27:00
0:10:12	0:31:42	1:03:25	2:13:43	4:27:26
0:10:13	0:31:45	1:03:31	2:13:56	4:27:52
0:10:14	0:31:49	1:03:37	2:14:09	4:28:18
0:10:15	0:31:52	1:03:43	2:14:22	4:28:45
0:10:16	0:31:55	1:03:50	2:14:35	4:29:11
0:10:17	0:31:58	1:03:56	2:14:48	4:29:37
0:10:18	0:32:01	1:04:02	2:15:02	4:30:03
0:10:19	0:32:04	1:04:08	2:15:15	4:30:29
0:10:20	0:32:07	1:04:14	2:15:28	4:30:56
0:10:21	0:32:10	1:04:21	2:15:41	4:31:22
0:10:22	0:32:13	1:04:27	2:15:54	4:31:48
0:10:23	0:32:17	1:04:33	2:16:07	4:32:14
0:10:24	0:32:20	1:04:39	2:16:20	4:32:41
0:10:25	0:32:23	1:04:46	2:16:33	4:33:07
0:10:26	0:32:26	1:04:52	2:16:46	4:33:33

PACE (MM:SS/MILE)	5-K	10-K	HALF-MARATHON	MARATHON
0:10:27	0:32:29	1:04:58	2:17:00	4:33:59
0:10:28	0:32:32	1:05:04	2:17:13	4:34:25
0:10:29	0:32:35	1:05:10	2:17:26	4:34:52
0:10:30	0:32:38	1:05:17	2:17:39	4:35:18
0:10:31	0:32:41	1:05:23	2:17:52	4:35:44
0:10:32	0:32:45	1:05:29	2:18:05	4:36:10
0:10:33	0:32:48	1:05:35	2:18:18	4:36:37
0:10:34	0:32:51	1:05:41	2:18:31	4:37:03
0:10:35	0:32:54	1:05:48	2:18:44	4:37:29
0:10:36	0:32:57	1:05:54	2:18:58	4:37:55
0:10:37	0:33:00	1:06:00	2:19:11	4:38:21
0:10:38	0:33:03	1:06:06	2:19:24	4:38:48
0:10:39	0:33:06	1:06:13	2:19:37	4:39:14
0:10:40	0:33:09	1:06:19	2:19:50	4:39:40
0:10:41	0:33:12	1:06:25	2:20:03	4:40:06
0:10:42	0:33:16	1:06:31	2:20:16	4:40:32
0:10:43	0:33:19	1:06:37	2:20:29	4:40:59
0:10:44	0:33:22	1:06:44	2:20:42	4:41:25
0:10:45	0:33:25	1:06:50	2:20:56	4:41:51
0:10:46	0:33:28	1:06:56	2:21:09	4:42:17
0:10:47	0:33:31	1:07:02	2:21:22	4:42:44
0:10:48	0:33:34	1:07:08	2:21:35	4:43:10
0:10:49	0:33:37	1:07:15	2:21:48	4:43:36
0:10:50	0:33:40	1:07:21	2:22:01	4:44:02
0:10:51	0:33:44	1:07:27	2:22:14	4:44:28
0:10:52	0:33:47	1:07:33	2:22:27	4:44:55
0:10:53	0:33:50	1:07:40	2:22:40	4:45:21
0:10:54	0:33:53	1:07:46	2:22:54	4:45:47
0:10:55	0:33:56	1:07:52	2:23:07	4:46:13
0:10:56	0:33:59	1:07:58	2:23:20	4:46:40
0:10:57	0:34:02	1:08:04	2:23:33	4:47:06
0:10:58	0:34:05	1:08:11	2:23:46	4:47:32
0:10:59	0:34:08	1:08:17	2:23:59	4:47:58
0:11:00	0:34:12	1:08:23	2:24:12	4:48:24
0:11:01	0:34:15	1:08:29	2:24:25	4:48:51
0:11:02	0:34:18	1:08:36	2:24:38	4:49:17
0:11:03	0:34:21	1:08:42	2:24:52	4:49:43
0:11:04	0:34:24	1:08:48	2:25:05	4:50:09
0:11:05	0:34:27	1:08:54	2:25:18	4:50:36
0:11:06	0:34:30	1:09:00	2:25:31	4:51:02
0:11:07	0:34:33	1:09:07	2:25:44	4:51:28

PACE (MM:SS/MILE)	5-K	10-K	HALF-MARATHON	MARATHON
0:11:08	0:34:36	1:09:13	2:25:57	4:51:54
0:11:09	0:34:40	1:09:19	2:26:10	4:52:20
0:11:10	0:34:43	1:09:25	2:26:23	4:52:47
0:11:11	0:34:46	1:09:31	2:26:36	4:53:13
0:11:12	0:34:49	1:09:38	2:26:50	4:53:39
0:11:13	0:34:52	1:09:44	2:27:03	4:54:05
0:11:14	0:34:55	1:09:50	2:27:16	4:54:31
0:11:15	0:34:58	1:09:56	2:27:29	4:54:58
0:11:16	0:35:01	1:10:03	2:27:42	4:55:24
0:11:17	0:35:04	1:10:09	2:27:55	4:55:50
0:11:18	0:35:07	1:10:15	2:28:08	4:56:16
0:11:19	0:35:11	1:10:21	2:28:21	4:56:43
0:11:20	0:35:14	1:10:27	2:28:34	4:57:09
0:11:21	0:35:17	1:10:34	2:28:48	4:57:35
0:11:22	0:35:20	1:10:40	2:29:01	4:58:01
0:11:23	0:35:23	1:10:46	2:29:14	4:58:27
0:11:24	0:35:26	1:10:52	2:29:27	4:58:54
0:11:25	0:35:29	1:10:59	2:29:40	4:59:20
0:11:26	0:35:32	1:11:05	2:29:53	4:59:46
0:11:27	0:35:35	1:11:11	2:30:06	5:00:12
0:11:28	0:35:39	1:11:17	2:30:19	5:00:39
0:11:29	0:35:42	1:11:23	2:30:32	5:01:05
0:11:30	0:35:45	1:11:30	2:30:45	5:01:31
0:11:31	0:35:48	1:11:36	2:30:59	5:01:57
0:11:32	0:35:51	1:11:42	2:31:12	5:02:23
0:11:33	0:35:54	1:11:48	2:31:25	5:02:50
0:11:34	0:35:57	1:11:54	2:31:38	5:03:16
0:11:35	0:36:00	1:12:01	2:31:51	5:03:42
0:11:36	0:36:03	1:12:07	2:32:04	5:04:08
0:11:37	0:36:07	1:12:13	2:32:17	5:04:35
0:11:38	0:36:10	1:12:19	2:32:30	5:05:01
0:11:39	0:36:13	1:12:26	2:32:43	5:05:27
0:11:40	0:36:16	1:12:32	2:32:57	5:05:53
0:11:41	0:36:19	1:12:38	2:33:10	5:06:19
0:11:42	0:36:22	1:12:44	2:33:23	5:06:46
0:11:43	0:36:25	1:12:50	2:33:36	5:07:12
0:11:44	0:36:28	1:12:57	2:33:49	5:07:38
0:11:45	0:36:31	1:13:03	2:34:02	5:08:04
0:11:46	0:36:35	1:13:09	2:34:15	5:08:30
0:11:47	0:36:38	1:13:15	2:34:28	5:08:57
0:11:48	0:36:41	1:13:21	2:34:41	5:09:23

PACE (MM:SS/MILE)	5-K	10-K	HALF-MARATHON	MARATHON
0:11:49	0:36:44	1:13:28	2:34:55	5:09:49
0:11:50	0:36:47	1:13:34	2:35:08	5:10:15
0:11:51	0:36:50	1:13:40	2:35:21	5:10:42
0:11:52	0:36:53	1:13:46	2:35:34	5:11:08
0:11:53	0:36:56	1:13:53	2:35:47	5:11:34
0:11:54	0:36:59	1:13:59	2:36:00	5:12:00
0:11:55	0:37:03	1:14:05	2:36:13	5:12:26
0:11:56	0:37:06	1:14:11	2:36:26	5:12:53
0:11:57	0:37:09	1:14:17	2:36:39	5:13:19
0:11:58	0:37:12	1:14:24	2:36:53	5:13:45
0:11:59	0:37:15	1:14:30	2:37:06	5:14:11
0:12:00	0:37:18	1:14:36	2:37:19	5:14:38
0:12:01	0:37:21	1:14:42	2:37:32	5:15:04
0:12:02	0:37:24	1:14:49	2:37:45	5:15:30
0:12:03	0:37:27	1:14:55	2:37:58	5:15:56
0:12:04	0:37:30	1:15:01	2:38:11	5:16:22
0:12:05	0:37:34	1:15:07	2:38:24	5:16:49
0:12:06	0:37:37	1:15:13	2:38:37	5:17:15
0:12:07	0:37:40	1:15:20	2:38:51	5:17:41
0:12:08	0:37:43	1:15:26	2:39:04	5:18:07
0:12:09	0:37:46	1:15:32	2:39:17	5:18:34
0:12:10	0:37:49	1:15:38	2:39:30	5:19:00
0:12:11	0:37:52	1:15:44	2:39:43	5:19:26
0:12:12	0:37:55	1:15:51	2:39:56	5:19:52
0:12:13	0:37:58	1:15:57	2:40:09	5:20:18
0:12:14	0:38:02	1:16:03	2:40:22	5:20:45
0:12:15	0:38:05	1:16:09	2:40:35	5:21:11
0:12:16	0:38:08	1:16:16	2:40:49	5:21:37
0:12:17	0:38:11	1:16:22	2:41:02	5:22:03
0:12:18	0:38:14	1:16:28	2:41:15	5:22:29
0:12:19	0:38:17	1:16:34	2:41:28	5:22:56
0:12:20	0:38:20	1:16:40	2:41:41	5:23:22
0:12:21	0:38:23	1:16:47	2:41:54	5:23:48
0:12:22	0:38:26	1:16:53	2:42:07	5:24:14
0:12:23	0:38:30	1:16:59	2:42:20	5:24:41
0:12:24	0:38:33	1:17:05	2:42:33	5:25:07
0:12:25	0:38:36	1:17:12	2:42:47	5:25:33
0:12:26	0:38:39	1:17:18	2:43:00	5:25:59
0:12:27	0:38:42	1:17:24	2:43:13	5:26:25
0:12:28	0:38:45	1:17:30	2:43:26	5:26:52

Appendix B: How to Calculate Paces

Runners' lives are complicated by the intersection of metric and English race distances and a Babylonian-era base-60 time system. Use these methods to simplify calculating your average race pace.

For calculating pace in minutes and seconds per mile:

1. Take your race time and convert it to total seconds. How? Multiply the number of hours (if any) by 3600. Multiply minutes by 60. Add these two figures and then add the race time seconds to that total. *Examples*: A marathon run in 3:47:23 converts to 10800 (3 × 3600) + 2820 (47 × 60) + 23 = 13643 seconds. A 5-mile race run in 33:15 converts to 1980 (33 × 60) + 15 = 1995 seconds.
2. Divide the total number of seconds by the distance for the race in miles. If the race is a metric distance, you must find the mile equivalent for the distance. (See the chart on the next page.) *Examples from above*: Marathon pace: 13643 seconds ÷ 26.22 miles = 520.3 seconds per mile. A 5-mile pace: 1995 seconds ÷ 5 miles = 399 seconds per mile.

3. Convert the seconds per mile to minutes and seconds per mile by dividing by 60 and noting the remainder seconds. For the marathon pace: 520.3 seconds per mile ÷ 60 = 8 minutes 40.3 seconds per mile. For the 5-mile pace: 399 seconds per mile ÷ 60 = 6 minutes 39 seconds per mile.

For calculating pace in minutes and seconds per kilometer:

1. Take your race time and convert it to total seconds. That is, multiply the number of hours (if any) by 3600. Multiply minutes by 60. Add these two figures and then add the race time seconds to that total. *Examples:* A marathon run in 3:47:23 converts to 10800 (3 × 3600) + 2820 (47 × 60) + 23 = 13643 seconds. An 8-K race run in 33:15 converts to 1980 (33 × 60) + 15 = 1995 seconds.
2. Divide the total number of seconds by the distance for the race in kilometers. If the race is an English distance, you must find the metric equivalent for the distance. (See the chart below.) *Examples from above:* Marathon pace: 13643 seconds ÷ 42.2 kilometers = 323.3 seconds per kilometer. An 8-K pace: 1995 seconds ÷ 8 kilometers = 249.4 seconds per kilometer.
3. Convert the seconds per kilometer to minutes and seconds per kilometer by dividing by 60 and noting the remainder seconds. For the marathon pace: 323.3 seconds per kilometer ÷ 60 = 5 minutes 23.3 seconds per kilometer. For the 8-K pace: 249.4 seconds per kilometer ÷ 60 = 4 minutes 9.4 seconds per kilometer.

DISTANCE EQUIVALENTS FOR COMMON RACE DISTANCES

MILES	KILOMETERS	KILOMETERS	MILES
1	1.609	1	0.6214
5	8.045	5	3.107
8	12.872	8	4.971
10	16.090	10	6.214
13.109 (half-marathon)	21.095	21.095 (half-marathon)	13.109
15	24.135	15	9.321
20	32.180	20	12.427
26.219 (marathon)	42.190	42.190 (marathon)	26.219

Acknowledgments

I begin these acknowledgments with a public expression of my sincere appreciation for the close and congenial association of more than 20 years with my coauthors. Our brotherly relationship has made our work enjoyable. Because of a deep respect for each other, our spirited debates enabled us to question every detail of our program without anyone being offended. That questioning led to the refinement of the FIRST training programs that runners have favorably embraced.

The countless hours that Scott Murr and I have spent discussing training approaches and then testing them on the roads and track laid the foundation for the development of FIRST and the "**3plus2**" training program. Scott has challenged Ray and me to think creatively about FIRST, our laboratory methods, and our training programs. While many of Scott's unorthodox, "outside the box" proposals were rejected by his two older mentors, those that were adopted have made FIRST distinctive in its approach to training.

Ray Moss knows science. Ray Moss is a builder. That combination of talents has enormously benefited Furman University and the Health and Exercise Science department. Ray's science comes from many years of teaching physiology, anatomy, and biomechanics. He is constantly being asked to assist with building—anything from homecoming floats to houses. Fortunately, as his department chair, I have been able to channel his talents into constructing one of the best human performance laboratories in the country for a national liberal arts college. Ray has enabled FIRST to test runners and validate our unique training methods. In addition, Ray spent nearly a decade teaching at and directing an injury rehabilitation center at a medical school before coming to Furman University. He is able to provide FIRST participants with valuable rehabilitation advice.

This book absolutely would not have been possible without Don Pierce, my brother. Don provided all three coauthors with valuable feedback and edited every word of the manuscript multiple times. Since the inception of FIRST, we have relied on Don for developing tables, formulas, and statistical calculations. His input has been invaluable. Of course, for me, he has provided the challenges that come from a big brother, whether in the form of one-on-one backyard basketball as we grew up, present-day Sunday morning tennis matches, racing side by side for 26.2 miles as we have done more than 20 times, or critiquing every word of my drafts.

Mickey McCauley, a member of the FIRST faculty, is a major contributor to the development of our lecture series and is the director of the FIRST Cross Country Running Camp for high school cross-country runners. Mickey brings years of track and field participation, officiating, and coaching to FIRST. He is popular as a coach with local runners and has developed a successful coaching reputation among runners participating in the FIRST e-mail coaching program. His knowledge and ideas about running form have been adopted and promoted by FIRST.

The widespread use of the FIRST marathon training program was the result of national and worldwide exposure from a *Runner's World* feature by Amby Burfoot. After a visit to the Furman University campus to learn about the FIRST program, Amby described our training program in detail sufficient to permit runners to use it for their upcoming marathons. The very day that issue hit the newsstand in August 2005, we began receiving messages with requests for additional information. Months after publication, we began receiving notes of appreciation from runners who had used the training program to run successful marathons—often reporting personal bests. When Amby's article was reprinted in the South Africa, United Kingdom, and Australia/New Zealand editions of *Runner's World*, we were barraged with requests and reports from around the world. We are indebted to Amby Burfoot for believing that FIRST offers a significant contribution to the available training approaches.

Hours after the *Wall Street Journal* published an article about the FIRST marathon training program, Barret Neville, a New York book agent, called to say that he was intrigued by our program and thought that it should be described in a book. Following several phone conversations over less than a month, Barret became our book agent. He guided us through the development of a book proposal that led to an auction with strong publisher participation. We soon had a contract with *Runner's World*'s publisher, Rodale. We appreciate Barret's lending his expertise to lead us through the unfamiliar book-publishing process.

We are grateful to New Balance for its sponsorship of FIRST. Stanford Jennings, former Furman and NFL football standout, has generously provided support from New Balance. We are proud to be associated with New Balance's high-quality shoes and apparel.

Perhaps the most forceful impetus for writing this book came from the more than 1,000 messages that we have received from runners who are using the FIRST training program. Runners wrote us emotional and effusive messages thanking us for helping them reach personal goals they had thought impossible. Those messages goaded us to continue working to make our training programs available in one volume. We have been humbled by the outpouring of support from runners, since assisting runners has always been our primary goal.

We were fortunate to find a talented illustrator among the art majors at Furman University. Katie Blaker clearly depicted the drills and exercises. As a non-runner unfamiliar with the drills and exercises, she provided valuable input for writing the descriptions of how to perform them.

We would be remiss not to thank our colleagues in the Furman University Health and Exercise Science department for their encouragement and support of FIRST. In particular, we wish to thank Lonita Stegall and Martha Vaughan for their administrative and secretarial assistance.

Finally, we wish to thank our families for their understanding of the many weekends and evenings we have been absent from home while giving lectures, conducting laboratory assessments, and doing our homework on the roads. Ray Moss's wife, Laurie, and daughter, Brye, know that the best place to find him is in the Human Performance Laboratory. Scott Murr's wife, Leslie, and children, Cameron and Kirstin, often accompany him to the Physical Activities Center. How else can you get to spend time with an Ironman triathlete? My wife, Marianne, is also a university professor and understands the hours required to produce a lengthy manuscript. She knows that I am a much better companion when I get to train and play.

From the Furman University Administration's approval to establish the Furman Institute of Running and Scientific Training in November 2002, to the publication of this book in May 2007, we have thoroughly enjoyed our involvement with runners. Scott and Ray join me in thanking all who have encouraged and supported our efforts.

Bill Pierce

Index

Boldface page references indicate illustrations and graphs. Underscored references indicate boxed text and tables.

C

D

E

F

G

K

L

M

N

O

P

Q

R

S

Y